YOUTH QUESTIONS

Series Editors: PHILIP COHEN and A[...]

This series sets out to question the w[...] been defined by social scientists and [...] sions and the mass media, as well as in common-sense ideology. It explores some of the new directions in research and practice which are beginning to challenge existing patterns of knowledge and provision. Each book examines a particular aspect of the youth question in depth. All of them seek to connect their concerns to the major political and intellectual debates that are now taking place about the present crisis and future shape of our society. The series will be of interest to those who deal professionally with young people, especially those concerned with the development of socialist, feminist and anti-racist perspectives. But it is also aimed at students and general readers who want a lively and accessible introduction to some of the most awkward but important issues of our time.

Published

Inge Bates, John Clarke, Philip Cohen, Dan Finn, Robert Moore and Paul Willis
SCHOOLING FOR THE DOLE?
The New Vocationalism

Desmond Bell
ACTS OF UNION
Youth Culture and Sectarianism in Northern Ireland

Cynthia Cockburn
TWO-TRACK TRAINING
Sex Inequalities and the YTS

Philip Cohen and Harwant S. Bains (eds)
MULTI-RACIST BRITAIN

Andrew Dewdney and Martin Lister
YOUTH, CULTURE AND PHOTOGRAPHY

Dan Finn
TRAINING WITHOUT JOBS: NEW DEALS AND BROKEN PROMISES
From Raising the School-Leaving Age to the Youth Training Scheme

Robert G. Hollands
THE LONG TRANSITION
Class, Culture and Youth Training

Angela McRobbie
FEMINISM AND YOUTH CULTURE

Angela McRobbie (ed.)
ZOOT SUITS AND SECOND-HAND DRESSES
An Anthology of Fashion and Music

Angela McRobbie and Mica Nava (eds)
GENDER AND GENERATION

Forthcoming

Philip Cohen and Graham Murdock (eds)
MAKING OF THE YOUTH QUESTION

Acts of Union

*Youth Culture and Sectarianism in
Northern Ireland*

Desmond Bell

MACMILLAN

First published 1990

Published by
MACMILLAN EDUCATION LTD
Houndmills, Basingstoke, Hampshire RG21 2XS
and London
Companies and representatives
throughout the world

Typeset by Footnote Graphics, Warminster, Wilts.

Printed in Singapore

British Library Cataloguing in Publication Data
Bell, Desmond
Acts of union: youth culture and sectarianism in Northern
Ireland—(Youth questions).
1. Northern Ireland. Young persons. Subcultures
I. Title   II. Series
305.2′35
ISBN 0–333–45831–1 (hardcover)
ISBN 0–333–45832–X (paperback)

Contents

List of Figures

List of Tables

Acknowledgements

Thanks to the following: Gavin Williams for encouragement during the initial conception of the project: Kevin O'Carroll who gave invaluable help with the school survey; Terry Wright, Conor Doak, Ron Smith, Derek Rowe, Philip Hamilton and the other Derry teachers who generously gave of their time; Fred and Ida Keys and all the kids from the club who made me so welcome; Gabrielle Kelly at the Careers Office for those stats; the Institute of Irish Studies, Queen's University Belfast which provided a much needed stop off point on the train journey from Dublin to Londonderry; Phil Cohen who commented on earlier drafts of the text and provided an invaluable critical input; needless to say not all of the above mentioned will necessarily agree with my conclusions.

Thanks, lastly, to Merlyn for putting up with my absences.

DESMOND BELL

Notes: 1. The research project on which this book is based was funded by the Economic and Social Research Council, London.
2. The personal names used throughout this book are pseudonyms.

Foreword

There should be no need for this foreword. Desmond Bell's book speaks for itself. It is about a whole section of youth whose culture and conditions of existence have for too long been travestied or ignored, simply because they are growing up in Northern Ireland rather than 'mainland' Britain.

Desmond Bell is certainly concerned to challenge the dominant anglocentric accounts of Irish history and youth culture, but he is also critical of attempts to substitute an irredentist 'Irish perspective' which would simply be an alternative form of ethnocentrism. In contrast, if he documents, in such rich ethnographic detail, the particularities of these young people's situation, it is only to show how their cultural forms relate to constructions of masculinity, territoriality and ethnicity to be found in other inner-city areas in Britain. For in many respects what is being enacted on the streets of Belfast and Derry is an all too familiar 'nationalism of the neighbourhood' writ large and encoded in the language of religious sectarianism.

Of course, the rituals of the Protestant Marching Bands have a very different form and function to those of Black Carnival; the purpose of this book is not to assert the claims of some abstracted multi-culturalism which would rob them of their concrete historical individuality, or reduce them to equivalent instances of an exotic anthropology. Nevertheless, Bell's analysis proceeds from a wider concern, which he shares with many black sociologists, to 'deconstruct' unitary notions of Britishness, and put in their place a more complex vision of both national and ethnic identity. His title then is more than a little ironic, given the fundamentalist positions adopted by Protestant Loyalists, not to mention the present leader of the Conservative and Unionist Party!

However this study has a wider implication. I believe that its publication will not simply redress the balance of a specific historical neglect, but push forward our understanding of the kinds of cultural identities which are currently organising a 'return of the repressed' in so many parts of Europe. As we watch the triumphal processions of youth parading behind the banners of nation, religion or race, from the shores of the Baltic to the Black Sea, perhaps we should remember that these acts of union also contain all the elements of what Freud referred to, somewhat ironically, as the 'narcissism of minor differences'.

Today in the context of debates about modernity and post-modernism we are mainly used to recognising the culture of narcissism in the endless bricolage of consumer fashion and style; this has even lead some cultural commentators to announce that we are living in 'New Times' where the politics of difference is creating the conditions for a permanent celebration of changing identities. Bell's book is a timely reminder that the announcement is premature; there is another, rather uglier side to the story, and one which Freud himself would have been the first to stress. . .

For all these reasons this book has a lot to say about the central issues of cultural politics and the youth question at the present time. I can only hope that it will overcome prejudices and that its findings will be widely read and discussed.

PHILIP COHEN

1

Youth Culture and Ethnic Identity

Introduction

In Northern Ireland the sphere of cultural and political identity is a fiercely contested one. Since the late 1960s a series of teenage generations have come to age in this troubled society. Young people develop their sense of ethnic identity – of being Ulster Protestants or Irish Catholics – in the midst of a situation of political crisis and sectarian confrontation. Long-established cultural divisions are reinforced by a segregated educational system. Increasing levels of residential segregation in the wake of sectarian violence have also left their mark. This segregation when combined with the isolating effects of mass unemployment has effectively ghettoized young people within their confessional communities. How has this ongoing process of ghettoization shaped the youth cultural forms and practices to be found in Northern Ireland?

In the 'modern' world youth culture has often been seen as a universal process by which teenagers distance themselves from their parents. The peer-group culture of the young in industrial societies has been viewed as constituting a generational fracture from the parent culture and its values and attitudes. Do youth cultural forms, with their representations of generational differences via music, dress and group style, not provide a symbolic space, beyond the sectarian ghetto, which could allow the young in Northern Ireland to transcend the sectarian culture of their parents?

Understanding youth sub-culture

The idea for a book on youth culture in Northern Ireland first emerged in the late 1970s. At that time I had just returned to Northern Ireland, after seven years' absence, to take up a teaching post at Magee College in Londonderry.

One of my first duties was to teach a course in sociology to a class of students training to be youth and community workers. A body of social theory and set of political sensibilities I had acquired on the radicalized campuses of England was to be immediately subjected to the harsher realities of crisis-torn Northern Ireland.

Some of my new students had already spent years working with young people in some of the most strife-torn areas of the province. A number of them had been involved in the Civil Rights movement and subsequently in the anti-imperialist organizations that emerged after the fragmentation of the Civil Rights movement. Some of them were also life-long socialists deeply perplexed about the increasing levels of sectarian polarization affecting Northern Ireland society in the 1970s and dividing the working class.

As youth workers they had daily experience of how the lives of the young people of Northern Ireland were being shaped by the sectarian conflict. And, by the time they were chosen for secondment to the university for 'professional training', they had developed a healthy scepticism with regards to the tutelary interventions of the British state. Many of them perceived the Northern Ireland Office's youth policy to be a nervous reaction to the threat of increasing levels of youthful disorder in the wake of the civil strife of the early 1970s. The more critically minded students saw the rush to provide purpose-built youth clubs and leisure centres and to train youth workers as a concerted attempt by the government to clear the streets of a generation of combative youth. It was less clear whether youth policy in Northern Ireland was addressing the long-term needs of working class youngsters.

The students' everyday experience in the field tended to make them receptive to the nostrums of radical social-work theory. This perspective identified the primary function of the welfare institutions of capitalist society as being one of social control (Corrigan and Leonard, 1980). My students were, however, somewhat sceptical as regards the radical reformist political strategy espoused by the proponents of critical social-work practice. This strategy sought to unite welfare professionals with the marginalized groups from which they traditionally drew their clients –

welfare claimants, council house tenants, ethnic minorities – in a popular struggle 'in and against the state' (Cockburn, 1979).

However in Northern Ireland many Catholic workers' experiences of discrimination had led them to regard the Northern Ireland state as a 'state beyond reform'. Many had come to support the Republican movement's demands for the removal of the British state in toto from Ireland. Protestant workers, for their part, still clung to Loyalist ideology. They continued to look to the British state to underwrite Unionist hegemony. In this situation, as my students pointed out to me, the space for a politics of radical reformism seemed somewhat limited. They were to prove a most exacting class!

From the outset one thing became clear to me: the sociological literature on youth culture that I had previously used in similar youth studies courses taught in England did not provide for an adequate understanding of the situation facing young people in embattled Ulster. It provided little basis for making sense of how the young in Northern Ireland were responding to the intensifying ethnic conflict in the wake of the disintegration of Stormont rule. In fact it had very little to say about ethnicity at all.

In 1975 Stuart Hall and Tony Jefferson had just edited the by now classic study of youth subculture in post-war Britain, *Resistance Through Rituals*. This collection of essays had quickly established itself as one of the key texts used in courses on Youth Studies. In the book the contributors exploded the myth of the 'generation gap'. Their work represented a stringent attack on the then dominant sociological approach to youth culture. This functionalist paradigm treated 'youth culture' as a universal post-war phenomenon which reflected the new affluence and mass-consumption norms of welfare capitalism.

By contrast, the work of the Centre for Contemporary Cultural Studies (CCCS) in Birmingham indicated that post-war English society (for no ethnographic studies dealing with either Scotland, Wales or Northern Ireland were included in their collection) spawned not a unitary and classless 'youth culture' based on the teenage consumer, but rather a rich tapestry of class-based and regionally flavoured subcultures. Moreover, these subcultures were not merely the product of the marketing ploys of consumer capitalism. They also articulated a series of collective responses by young people to the social changes affecting post-war Britain.

As the CCCS group argued, youth subcultures, as domains of generationally-shared, profane symbols and peer-group practices, emerge within a class riven society. For working class youth, in particular, such subcultures represent an attempt to explore and resolve the material constraints and contradictions confronting *both* young people and their parental class culture. Hall and Jefferson dismissed the then still fashionable idea of the 'generation gap', for, though members of a subculture 'may walk, talk, act, look "different" from their parents and some of their peers . . . they belong to the same families, go to the same schools, work at much the same jobs, live down the same "mean streets" as their peers and parents' (Hall and Jefferson, 1976, p. 14).

Despite the advent of mass consumerism, post-war British society remained a class society characterized by high levels of inequality and concentrations of wealth and power. As Hall and Jefferson argue, within capitalist society cultural relations are also organized hierarchically and involve relations of domination and subordination between classes. Thus:

> just as different groups and classes are unequally ranked in relation to one another in terms of productive relations, wealth and power, so *cultures* are differently ranked and stand in opposition to one another, in relations of domination and subordination, along the scale of cultural power. (Hall and Jefferson, 1976, p. 11).

Youth cultural formations are not immune to class determinations. The lives of the young remain circumscribed by their class location. They have to come to terms with a *parental* class culture. On the other hand, as working class youngsters they have to themselves negotiate their relation with the dominant culture. They confront this culture daily at school, Youth Training Scheme and Welfare office. It is a culture of domination. For the CCCS ethnographers, youth subcultures, whether these be the teddy boys of the 1950s or the new-wave enthusiasts of the 1980s, are seen as not only generationally specific but also *class-located* lifestyles. As such, these subcultures are mapped out around a 'double articulation' to both parental culture and the dominant capitalist culture.

The 'rituals of resistance' practised by working-class youngsters against school authority and against a bourgeois order that promises everything but delivers precious little can in no way resolve the material problems facing the young and their parents. Such a resolution would require organized political action to achieve a radical social transformation of British society. Yet youth subcultures seem to provide a temporary haven from the problems the young working class face – problems such as having to cope with an unequal and disabling educational system and a future of dead-end jobs or the dole queue. They provide free rein for the youthful imagination offering, as Phil Cohen puts it, 'magical solutions' to real world problems with their origins in the economic infrastructure of capitalist society (Cohen, 1972).

For the sociologists of the seventies, the youthful 'revolt of style' involved in most subcultures could be interpreted as *oppositional* in form. The distinctive codes of dress, argot and peer-group rituals was thus worthy of the attention of the radicalised intelligentsia. For, after all, the young were engaging in a form of class politics 'by other means'.[1]

Youth subcultures in Northern Ireland

What, if anything had this materialist reading of subcultural styles to say about the perverse terrain of sectarian identities and youthful ethnic mobilizations to be found in Northern Ireland?

Could it offer any insight into the role of youth sub-cultures in a political milieu characterized by a high degree of ethnic division rather than observable class conflict. For as my students never failed to tell me, the sub-cultural activities of young working-class Protestants and Catholics were more likely to be orchestrated around the age old Loyalist and Nationalist political traditions rather than around any readily identifiable class dynamic or pattern of generational autonomy.

In mid-1970s Northern Ireland male working-class teenagers were playing a significant role in both Loyalist and Republican paramilitary activity. As anyone running a youth club in an urban area knew to their bitter experience 'the lads' were increasingly getting drawn into sectarian trouble. Indeed fairly rapidly after the outbreak of civil conflict in 1968, sectarian territorial demarcations became inscribed in the imagination of the young as a routine and ineluctable part of every day life. Protestant lads were becoming involved in 'Tartan Gangs' – neighbourhood gangs of teenagers clad in denim and sporting tartan scarves. The Tartans engaged in sectarian attacks on Catholic youth and were later to be seen manning barricades in Protestant areas during the Loyalist Workers' strike in 1974. Catholic youth, for their part, continued to play a key role in street confrontations with the security forces and were joining the IRA or Republican youth sections in significant numbers. Catholic support for physical force Republicanism, as suggested for instance in votes for Sinn Fein, remains concentrated in those under thirty.

There were then severe difficulties in applying an interpretative model of youth culture based on an understanding of post-war British youth subculture to the Northern Ireland situation. The CCCS work gave privilege to class determinations over both ethnic and gender factors in its reading of youth life styles. It was politically optimistic with regard to subcultures, assuming that they represented a focal point of youthful class resistance to the assaults of capitalism. In short, the materialist reading of youth subcultural style seemed to talk of a world that none of us could recognise on the 'mean streets' of Belfast or Derry. A yawning gap had opened up for us between sociological theory and our daily experience.

Was this due to the refractory and peculiar character of Irish social reality? Perhaps our society would yet evolve into a 'normal' class-motivated social order? Or, on the other hand, was there a problem with a theoretical model which could not account for the ethnic and gender dynamics of youth formations? This issue is examined in Chapters 2 and 3 of this study in the context of the historical development of sectarian social relations in Ulster.

At one level this concentration by the CCCS on the class dimension of youth subcultures *did* seem to make good sense in the context of Northern Ireland. The Province's secondary-school system remained a selective one within which working-class children remain severely underrepresented in the grammar schools as they are in higher education. This is so despite the imposition of Direct Rule, in 1972, with its explicit promise to introduce 'British standards' of social justice into Northern Ireland for the first time. Northern Ireland's school leavers continued to face high levels of unemployment in tandem with a low-wage economy. Moreover in

Fig. 1.1   Some younger bandsmen out of uniform
(*Photo: Kate Horgan*)

response to youth unemployment and the perceived threat of youthful disorder on the streets of Ulster, the British state was already heavily investing in the sort of training programmes to be introduced by the Manpower Services Commission in Britain years later. The economically marginalized young people of Northern Ireland were some of the first victims of the accelerated decline of British industrial capital. In turn they were finding themselves up against the sharp end of the emerging authoritarian state.

Moreover, the CCCS model with its strong emphasis on the oppositional form of youth sub-culture had other less tangible attractions. Mid-1970s Ulster was traumatised by the ferocity of sectarian violence. It was reassuring to think that the minor explosion of punk culture witnessed in Belfast and Derry, and celebrated in John Davis's documentary film *Shell Shock Rock*, was testament to the power of rock music counter culture to transcend the sectarian divide and provide a sub-cultural refuge for the working class young beyond the ghetto. For a few short months in 1978 the punk movement in Ulster gained momentum attracting adherents from both the Protestant and Catholic communities. It seemed as if rock music had the power to transcend the sectarian divide. The healing had begun.

Belfast's leading punk band Stiff Little Fingers were to capture the tentative optimism of the period:

> What we need is
> An Alternative Ulster
> Ignore the bores and their laws
> Be an anti-security force
> Alter your native Ulster
> Alter your native land.

In retrospect we all recognise the limitations of rock music as a vehicle for politicizing youth. Punk, despite its rituals of protest, became assimilated into a music industry which, although responsive to youthful taste, is primarily powered by commercial imperatives. As the number of gigs declined so did the force of punk as an indigenous counter-culture capable of challenging sectarian ideology. Punk became a subculture of escape rather than revolt.

Most commentators now accept that the street politicization of young working-class people that occurred for Protestants for the first time at the time of the Loyalist Workers' Strike of 1974, and for young Catholics in the street battles of the civil rights period and then most dramatically around the 1981 Hunger Strikes, has been of immeasurably greater significance in defining the parameters of youth culture in Northern Ireland than punk's celebration of generational rupture and stylized assault on 'tradition'. As we shall see, youth cultural practices in Ulster, hinged as they are on ethnic concerns, have more often played a significant role in *sustaining* sectarian 'tradition'.

Perhaps we need to know much more about the role of youth culture in the reproduction as well as subversion of ethnic identity as cultural tradition. Indeed what has been distinctive about the youth cultural activities of working-class adolescents in Northern Ireland has been their apparent continuity rather than discontinuity with parental sectarian traditions and political sensibilities. Young people in Northern Ireland, both Protestant and Catholic, have increasingly become the guardians of 'tradition'.

Take for example the case of Protestant working-class youth with which we are largely concerned in this study. A visit to any Protestant estate in early July will probably reveal the following: red, white and blue kerb markings painted on the perimeter of the confessional ghetto; paramilitary graffiti; recently repainted formal murals depicting the vivid if perennial tableaux of Protestant history – above all William of Orange on white charger crossing the Boyne; bonfires being stacked for 'eleventh night'; the singing of 'party' songs; and of course the shriek of flutes and thundering drums of the 'Kick the Pope' bands.

In Catholic areas the colour of the kerbs will change to the 'green, white and yellah' of the Irish republic; the paramilitary initials change – the Ulster Defence Association (UDA) Ulster Volunteer Force (UVF) and Ulster Freedom Fighters (UFF) markings of the Loyalist ghettoes being replaced by the slogans of the IRA or INLA; the combative murals of the Republican movement replace the Orange iconography; Easter 1916 replaces July 1690 as the hallowed date emblazoned on gable walls and the bonfires are being built for the anniversary of the introduction of Internment. However, on each side of the sectarian divide in contemporary Northern Ireland it is the teenage young who are centrally involved in the celebration of heritage. The form and content of youth subcultures in Ulster are, as we might expect,

Fig. 1.2 Light refreshments
(*Photo: Bryan O'Brien*)

circumscribed by the sectarian dynamics of the imperialized society within which the young are growing up.

Defining the research problem

I was to leave Derry again in 1981 after a summer in which Ireland had been traumatised by the horror of the Hunger Strikes. This was also the year that saw an explosion of inner-city violence in England. On the streets of Liverpool and London marginalized white and black youth fought with the forces of law and order. As black youths took to the streets to resist police harrassment and the growth of a racism underwritten by the British state, Northern Ireland began to look less like an aberrant region of an otherwise 'civilized' and stable United Kingdom and more like the shape of things to come.

In the next two years while teaching at Ruskin College in Oxford, I set about securing the research funds necessary to launch a study into the relationship between youth cultural dynamics and sectarian division in Northern Ireland. At Ruskin, the intellectual heartland of the British labour movement, I became aware of the debate being waged within the Left about how socialists should relate to the political challenge of feminism and black consciousness. The failures of the labour movement to mobilise the working class against the Thatcherite assault seemed in part due to the difficulties the Left experienced in responding to the differentiation of the working class along ethnic and gender lines. Indeed trade unions themselves had been less than success-ful in combating racism and sexism within their own ranks.

Events in England – the growth of racism amongst marginalized white working class youth and the appearance of black youth movements – suggested that youth relations in Northern Ireland were perhaps not quite so 'abnormal'. It was becoming clear to many researchers that a more serious attempt would have to be made to understand the role of young people within ethnic mobilizations.[2] As the situation of Rastafarian West-Indian youth in England and Black Power organizations in the US suggested, youth cultures play a central role in the assertion of ethnic identity by minority groups. After all, ethnic identities emerge and become defined in response to political developments, which confront each generation anew. Youth cultures are one of the key resources through which young people explore, at the level of the symbolic, the life situation and collective experience in which they find themselves as group members. Accordingly youth cultural practices play a central role in the assertion of ethnic identity by minority groups.

And indeed ethnographies of Rastafarian youth in England (Cashmore, 1979, Hebdige, 1976) and of youth involved in Black Power organizations in urban America (Hare, 1973) have explored the ways young black people through their 'cultural work' manufacture and sustain a politically-charged ethnic 'tradition'. This 'tradition' indeed may have only partially existed in those communities prior to its appropriation by, and refurbishment in, youth formations. Youth responding to its own specific generational situation borrows selectively from parental tradition adapting its form and content to forge new repertoires of social expression. In this way 'tradition' is given a new lease of life. In Northern Ireland we were also witnessing the increasing involvement of young people in the reconstruction of traditional identities. What part were youth formations, such as we were witnessing on the streets of Ulster – for instance in Tartan gangs and marching bands of the Loyalist community – playing in the reproduction of ethnic identity and sectarian ideological relations? I became intrigued in particular with the nature of the relation of working-class Protestant youth to a parental culture of Loyalism – a culture subject to acute tensions in the current situation of mass unemployment, with the erosion of traditional working-class community life and given the political crisis around the unresolved national question in Ireland.

Ulster Loyalism often appears to those outside Ireland as a particularly arcane and bewildering politico-cultural phenomenon. The existence of a million Protestants in Northern Ireland who loudly proclaim their loyalty to Queen and country, but who have been most reluctant to accept the sovereignty of Westminster when they perceive this as being exercised against their interests, strikes many as the most perplexing element in the 'Northern Ireland problem'. The national identity of the Ulster Protestants – neither Irish nor apparently fully British – seems particularly complex.

By the end of the 1970s, Ulster Loyalism, despite its continued ability to veto political reform in Northern Ireland, was clearly a formation in decline. The localized culture of the Protestant working class had been subject to particular tensions due to the erosion of Unionist hegemony and the continued economic decline of the province. How were these contradictions within Loyalism manifesting themselves in the up-and-coming younger generation of Protestants?

I for one found it hard to believe that marginalized Protestant youth could any longer in the 1980s take the masonic ritual and constitutional proprieties of official Orangeism seriously – bowler hats, starched collars, arcane regalia and all. On the other hand, there was no indication that Protestant working-class youth was breaking from Loyalist politics. Surveys suggested a hardening of political opinions amongst the young and increased support for militant, irredentist Loyalism (see Chapter 5). Moreover, young Loyalists were taking to the streets – whether in Tartan gangs or marching bands – to parade their ethnic distinctiveness. Their youth-popular Loyalism appeared in some way qualitatively different from traditional Unionism or Orangeism.

But how was it different? Could the subcultural practices of Protestant youth – their bands, parades, bonfires and street paintings – be understood as an attempt to address, at the level of symbolic, the contradictions being experienced by the parental culture? On the other hand, to what extent did this 'cultural work' represent an autonomous generational response to the material problems facing the young themselves? How, in other words, did their subcultural practices express both their own social state of marginalization and, in addition, the focal concerns of their parental culture with group identity and the political future? ·

Understanding ethnicity: Ulster Protestant identity

In Northern Ireland ethnic divisions have had an enduring persistence which has fundamentally shaped social and political life. The development of these divisions is examined in Chapter 3. But Ulster is not unique in this. Indeed it has been generally recognised by sociologists and political scientists that ethnic divisions and mobilizations, and the formations of cultural identity associated with these, are becoming *more* rather than *less* politically significant globally. Despite this the concept of ethnicity remains

14

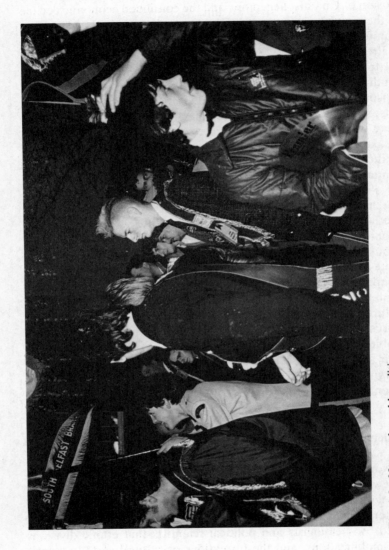

Fig. 1.3 New styles, old traditions
(Photo: Bryan O'Brien)

as obscure as ever. To fully understand Loyalism as a political culture and how the current younger generation of Protestant youth relate to it we shall have to interrogate our notions of 'ethnic identity', 'nation', and 'community'. For in Ulster Loyalism we find a type of ethnicity which is *not* a nationalism and which accordingly must be understood in terms different from nationalism.

Loyalism as a politico-cultural identity has displayed a particularly refractory character to the usual perspectives and concepts of political science. At the heart of this difficulty lies the complex relation of Ulster Protestants as a social group to the ideology of nationalism usually seen as central to understanding the political mobilization and ethnic identities of Catholics in Ireland. We live in a world of nations and rightly regard nationalism as a major mobilizing ideology in the post-colonial era. Yet within the effusive discourse of nation and nationalism the Protestants of Ulster have themselves remained strangely silent.[3]

The nation state may be the most important focal point of ethnic political demands in the modern world. Certainly nationalists clearly represent the nation as the 'natural' expression of the popular will of a primordially-formed ethnic community, or 'race'. However the nation state is not the only, or indeed necessary, object of ethnic political imaginings.

Anthony Smith (1984), reviewing the current debate on ethnic persistence in the contemporary world, identifies two major positions in relation to understanding ethnicity – the *primordialist* and the *instrumentalist*. Primordialists assume that ethnic association is a universal and perennial phenomenon, 'part of the substratum of human association and certainly coeval with recorded history'. The nation in turn is seen as the 'natural' product of primordial ties of blood, race, ancestry, religion and language and homeland. Within the primordialist perspective a somewhat determinist view of the ethnic socialization process tends to be assumed. The young are regarded as passive initiates into a preformed, historically-enduring ethnie.

The 'instrumentalist' approach, on the other hand, argues that 'ethnic ideological relations' are grounded in the material interests of competing elites. These strive to mobilize large numbers of people from subordinate classes, 'for the pursuit of partisan interests of wealth or power'. Ethnic symbols and ideologies play a key role in such populist political strategies. The instrumentalists agree with the primordialists that capitalist modernization, far from eroding the basis of ethnie and nation, has in fact sustained an explosion of new ethnic mobilizations. However, they criticize the latter for naively accepting the claims of nationalists as to the primordial and ontologically privileged status of the 'nation' and 'race', and for paying insufficient attention to the specific historical processes by which ideologies of nation and people are socially constructed and legitimated by certain social strata – often urban intelligentsia.

Ernest Gellner, (1983) an implacable opponent of the primordial approach, warns us against

> oblique acceptance of the nationalist ideologue's most misguided claim: namely that the 'nations' are there, in the very nature of things, only waiting to be 'awakened' [a favourite nationalist expression and image] from their regrettable slumber, by the nationalist 'awakener'.

The difficulty with the instrumentalist view however is that it tends, like the primordialist approach, to confuse and conflate ethnicity and nationalism. Political sociology often seems to assume that the two are synonymous.

A distinguishing feature of Ulster Loyalism is that the Protestants of the north of Ireland have not – despite the traumas of Partition and, in the contemporary period, of Direct Rule, the profound distrust of the British state and its parliament – been prepared to assert its right to self determination *as a nation*.

The Protestant imagined community[4] is not a nation. It remains what it always has been, a beleagured garrison loyal to Crown and Empire, defending an Imperial interest in a hostile and rebellious land. Loyal, that is, not to a British polity and nation, governed by democratic political conventions, but to a sovereign who can guarantee their liberties and ascendancy. As David Millar (1978) has argued in his provocative history of Ulster Loyalist ideology, *Queen's Rebels*:

> Of Ulster Protestant determination to remain part of the British state there can be no doubt. The question is whether they consider their relationship to that state to flow from their membership of a British nation.

He carries on to argue, drawing on Gellner's theory of nationalism, that

> the central peculiarity in Ulster's political culture is that no
> community – not Britain, not the United Kingdom, not 'Ulster'
> and certainly not Ireland – has attained for Protestants all the
> characteristics which a nation commonly possesses in the modern
> world. . .

This position recognises that ethnic political representations may not necessarily invoke the nation as the imagined community of ethnic longings. It locates Protestant political ideology outside the force field of nationalism – any nationalism. As such it represents an advance over previous theorizations of Protestant political mentalities which have operated naively within this discourse.

We can call this essentially instrumentalist perspective the *no-nation* view of Protestant ethnicity in order to distinguish it from traditional *one-nation* and *two-nation* perspectives usually at play in the analysis of Protestant political intransigence vis à vis 'the national question'.

The *one-nation* view is usually associated with traditional Irish nationalism, though it has had its Marxist adherents.[5] Within this perspective, an Irish nation can be unproblematically identified. It is defined by its physical integrity – the island and its ecology – and by the longevity and coherence of its cultural traditions. Within this essentially primordialist perspective only one nation in Ireland can be identified. This nation has a specific history of suffered oppression at the hands of English colonialism. It found its political expression in the last decades of the eighteenth century. This expression took the form of a privileged text – the idea of a secular democratic republic, as envisaged by the United Irishmen. This inclusive, imagined political community incorporates both Protestant, Dissenter and Catholic members. Accordingly the Protestant population of the North are, *whether they recognize it or not*, part of this nation. Their current rejection of an Irish nationality and of Irish nationalism (the two are treated as synonymous) flows from a false consciousness of their 'true' or 'best' interests. Moreover this false consciousness is the product of British political machination, Imperial interests being served in the stirring up of sectarian animosities by 'playing the Orange card'.

Implicit in the one nation view is the primordialist assumption that nations are an ontological given. They are afforded the same existential status as the air we breathe or the stones we stub our toes upon. Nationalism as an ideology and the nation state as a political form, are treated as the consequence of their being nations in the world. The nation state is a political expression of a 'national right' to separate existence and sovereignty. Nations beget states.

Needless to say these assumptions fly in the face of our historical knowledge of the complex process by which national consciousness is formed amongst certain ethnic groups and social classes in specific periods, a consciousness which, in turn, may give rise to political demands for the creation of an independent state. For example, how are we to explain the enthusiasm for the idea of an independent Irish republic amongst certain sections of the Protestant population in the last decades of the eighteenth century, yet determined opposition to the same notion from that ethnic group in the first decades of the twentieth?

The *two-nation* view[6] has the virtue that it does take into account the very real social, economic and cultural differences that materially distinguish the Protestant population in the north of Ireland from the predominantly Catholic population in the twenty-six counties. However, it then proceeds to argue that the material distinctiveness of the north east is sufficient to justify ascribing to the Protestant community residing there the status of a nation. Moreover, in so far as the Protestants of Ulster are a distinct 'people' who actually or potentially comprise a nation, then they have a 'right to self-determination'. In its crasser forms this 'right' is recognised by the apologists of British imperialism in Ireland as finding legitimate political expression in Partition.

The major difficulty with this two-nation perspective on Protestant ethnicity is that it is somewhat unclear precisely what the two nations alluded to are. Are they Ireland and Ulster or Ireland and Britain? As we have argued, the Protestants have no small difficulty in seeing themselves as part of a British nation. On the other hand we have to search very hard to locate anything resembling Ulster nationalism anywhere amongst their political mentalities. Are we to assert, like the primordialist, that they are part of an incipient nation – whether they recognise it or not?

Tacit in the two-nations approach is exactly the same reified and primordial concept of nation that is found in the one-nation view.

Each finds it hard to grasp that nationalism and nationness are, to quote Benedict Anderson, 'cultural artifacts of a particular kind' (Anderson 1983) with quite specific conditions of existence. The virtue of the no-nation position is that it acknowledges that ethnicity is not reducible to nationalism. For it is clear that in Ireland we have two major ethnic groups. One of these, the Catholic Irish, expresses its political aspirations in a national claim. The other, the Protestants of Ulster, do not.

We have, then, to move beyond the conceptual confines of the 'national question' to understand the specific form of ethnie which integrates the Protestants. Have social anthropological conceptions of ethnicity something to contribute here to our comprehension of this perverse identity?

Anthropologists have come to see ethnicity as one of a number of kinds of collective identity, distinctive from, but related to local, national and class identities, through which particular representations of cultural difference function to promote social cohesion within a social group. Fredrik Barth has strenuously argued (1969) that the focus of anthropological research on ethnicity should shift, 'from investigation of the internal constitution and history which separate groups to ethnic boundaries and boundary maintenance.'

If ethnicity is primarily a system of social classification as Barth suggests, 'the critical focus of investigation becomes the ethnic boundary that defines the group, not the cultural stuff it encloses' (1969). The ethnie is then a type of symbolic community in which discriminations are made as regards outsiders. It is in other words a repository of boundary-defining symbols; a socially shared discourse of myths, images and communicative codes through which an imagined community coheres and lives its ideological relations with outsiders.

Seen as such, certain types of contemporary urban ethnicity display a certain 'homology of form' to urban working class youth culture. Both are orchestrated around a focal concern with the policing of territorial and cultural boundaries. Indeed as we shall see, the case of Ulster Loyalist youth is a particularly instructive one in illuminating the role of youth subculture in engendering urban ethnicity.

For the Protestants of Ulster, unlike their Catholic neighbours, their sense of themselves as a distinct ethnic group is not then undergirded by a political ideology of nationalism. In so far as their identity has an ideological base it is one drawn from an antediluvian religious discourse that is schismatic and exclusive. Protestantism in Ulster is fragmented into many different competing sects. Moreover religious observance amongst Protestants is in decline and dramatically so amongst the young.

In reality the Loyalist sense of identity achieves its positive valency (that is, being more than simply *not-Irish*) in being actively paraded. That identity *is* dependent on the rehearsed myths, ritualized practices, and confrontations of the marching season. Indeed these symbolic practices in which the young play such a significant part today – the bonfires, the painting of kerbs, the erection of flags, arches and bunting, the marching bands and the parades themselves – are the specific means by which an exclusive Protestant identity is represented and renewed in the Loyalist mind. Here primarily an embodied ideology is at work. It is the sound of the Lambeg drum rather than the resonance of political ideology which brings tears to the eyes of a Loyalist.

The province of this cultural identity is that of the street confrontation and communal celebration. That in fact gives it a particular attraction to the teenage young. And indeed this is the terrain on which youth subcultures also tend to appear. Absent from Loyalist culture is the political figure of the urban intellectual constructing a consciousness of nation from the bric-a-brac of liberal democratic theory and peasant folkways. We'll find no Hyde or Pearse[7] on the streets of Portadown. But we will find the dispossessed Protestant youth of Ulster.

Protestant ethnicity finds expression then, not in an ideology of nationalism, but in one of 'loyalty'. This ethico-political notion, with its roots in the personalistic bonds of local community, has a particular resonance within the teenage peer group.

Historically the notion of loyalty at play in Unionist ideology has taken two distinct if related forms. Explicitly it has involved a proclaimed loyalty that entails an *external* and *conditional* political obligation to a British sovereign power. Accompanying this however has been a view of loyalty as an *internal* and *unconditional* obligation to the Protestant community itself – a community that experiences itself as a beleaguered frontier group ultimately dependent on its own resources for its security and survival.[8]

Historically there has always been a degree of strain within the

Orange all-class alliance between the aristocratic and bourgeois elite that controlled the Unionist political machine and the working-class and populist ranks of Loyalism. In times of economic malaise or rapid capitalist modernization, class-based ruptures within the fabric of Loyalism have become apparent. Protestant workers have looked to sectarian exclusivism to protect their livelihoods and chastised the Unionist elite about their lack of concern with the social conditions of the Protestant working class.[9] Paramount has been the issue of Loyalists exercising the right to parade in the face of government bans accepted by the conservative Orange hierarchy.

Indeed asserting the right to march and redeeming the obligation of the Unionist elite to rank and file Protestants in terms of privileged access to the labour market, have often been inextricably fused in the minds of working-class Loyalists.

Thus although Loyalism presents itself to the outside world – and indeed to itself – as a united front of Protestants, the unity is deceptive. Class fragmentations operate behind that facade. Loyalism, like other forms of political populism, 'masks the differentiation within itself by using or imposing a common set of symbols' (Cohen, 1985).

The erosion of Protestant community

Loyalism today is however finding it harder to mask the fractures within the Protestant community. Class tensions and generational differences are increasingly manifesting themselves within the Unionist body politic. A specifically Protestant sense of community, which on historically particular occasions is expressed within Loyalist ideology in the form of an asserted ethnic identity – 'the Protestant people' – is under attack on three fronts in the contemporary period.

Firstly, at the economic level the rapid deindustrialization of the Northern Ireland economy has eroded the occupational basis of the Protestant working-class communities which grew up around the shipbuilding/heavy-engineering and linen industries. This has produced levels of unemployment previously only experienced (at least since the late 1950s) in the Catholic population. Job loss has been concentrated in the manufacturing sector where

Protestant males have traditionally been predominant. Accordingly the privileged labour situation of the Protestant manual working class has been eroded in absolute if not in relative terms. Protestant youth is now sharing with Catholic workers in general, a marginalized position within the Northern Ireland economy.

Secondly, at the spatial/residential level, as Ron Wiener has documented (1978), the Greater Belfast urban redevelopments and relocation of the Protestant working-class inner-city population have adversely affected traditional patterns of kinship and neighbourhood solidarity. The extended kinship patterns and local communal networks characteristic of 'traditional' and traditionally militant Loyalist working-class residential districts, like the Shankill in Belfast, or the Fountain in Derry, have given way to a more nucleated and privatized pattern of community life.[10]

It has become harder, given the declining physical and social integrity of Protestant residential space, for Loyalists to identify a physical referent for their imagined Protestant community.

Thirdly, the ongoing political crisis has seen the partial dismantling of the 'Orange system' of political patronage with the replacement of Stormont by Direct Rule. The fragmentation of the Unionist political bloc into a number of competing parties with divergent policies on the appropriate relation between Ulster and the British state (integration, devolution, formal independence) is but one sign of the new political insecurities of the Protestant population. Added to traditional fears of a 'sell-out' by a British government which is recognized by rank and file Loyalists as anxious to wash its hands of the whole 'Ulster problem', is a growing anxiety about the steady increase in the influence of militant Republicanism within the Catholic community. This anxiety concerns not only the military and political strength of Republicanism but also the cultural stridency and ethnic certitude that is perceived as emanating from the Catholic community. In the wake of a resurgence of 'Irish' cultural nationalism, Protestant culture and ethnic identity is often experienced, *by Loyalists themselves*, as lacking coherence and confidence that no amount of political posturing and flag waving can hide.[11]

Sectarian culture is a complex fusion of class, ethnic and religion-based elements. That of the Protestant working class is subject to particular tensions due to the erosion of their privileged market situation and the continued political uncertainties of direct rule.

The cultural practices of Protestant working-class youth are, I would argue, best understood as an attempt to confront and overcome, at a symbolic level, the contradictions experienced in Loyalist parental culture. The resurgence of Loyalist street culture since 1974 – band parades, wall murals, kerb paintings etc., now largely the province of the young – can be seen as a symbolic response to this crisis of community and identity. This mythic representation of the 'Protestant people' and their idealised territory – 'Ulster' – attempt to resolve, at the level of the imaginary, the real material contradictions confronting the Protestant working-class in contemporary Northern Ireland.

Youth subcultural representations of community

But, the young Loyalists of Ulster are today experiencing their own generationally-specific material situation. They have their own problems. This is the generation whose birth coincided with the onset of the 'Troubles'. The ghettoization of residential life since then has affected them perhaps more than any other age group. Their physical mobility is limited by the ever present dangers – real and imagined – of sectarian 'bother'. This sectarian territorialisation of residential space has, as we shall see in Chapters 4 and 5, severely restricted their opportunities for recreation and even employment. Moreover their adolescence is occurring in a period within capitalist society of general marginalization of young workers from paid employment and thus from the modes of consumption enjoyed by a previous generation of waged youth. Contemporary working class youth cultures are being practised with fewer commercial resources. Young people are also experiencing increasing state regulation of their education, training and recreation – particularly with the proliferation of youth employment training schemes introduced by the 'Plan State'.

Militant Loyalism is clearly not capable of providing a *political* solution to the material problems confronting Protestant youth, any more than it is for their parents. It remains however an important *cultural resource* for the 'new dispossessed' Protestant youth of Northern Ireland, as indeed Republicanism is for Catholic youth.

In this respect Loyalist youth subculture shares many of the

Fig. 1.4 Banging the drum: reclaiming territory (*Photo: Kate Horgan*)

characteristics of the territorially-focused subcultures of Britain's marginalized, white, inner-city youth. As Phil Cohen (1972) has argued, these urban working-class youth subcultures are orchestrated around mythic representations of community. These images of community attempt to compensate for the erosion of traditional structures of working-class communality which resulted from urban redevelopment and industrial restructuring. Cohen (1972) has traced this process of erosion of working-class communality in the East End of London – a process that Wiener identified just as clearly in Belfast:

> The first effect of the high density, high rise scheme was to destroy the function of the street, the local pub, the corner shop, as articulations of communal space. Instead there was only the privatised space of the family unit, stacked one on top of another, in total isolation, juxtaposed with the totally public space which surrounds it, and which lacked any of the informal controls generated by the neighbourhood (Wiener, 1978).

As Cohen argues, in this context youth subcultures

> all represent in their different ways, an attempt to retrieve some of the socially cohesive elements destroyed in the parent culture, and to combine them with elements selected from other class fractions, symbolising one or other of the options confronting it (1972).

The mythic retrieval of community with its sharp territorial focus and ethnically exclusivist character can however easily lead to sectarian outcomes. As Cohen (1988) admits, this is particularly the case if the imagined community of youthful representations is a racially inspired one. He warns that as the structures of transmission of working-class culture and 'patrimony' break down in the wake of mass unemployment and changes in family and neighbourhood patterns

> racist discourses do provide a surrogate form of political apprenticeship into an imaginary 'lost' inheritance of kith and kin. The links between origins and destiny is thus restored via a sense of pride in belonging to a 'biological community' of labour whose

territories are then staked out through more or less violent body politics on the streets of the working class city.

In Ireland we have long historical experience of the perverse character of sectarian communality. We are perhaps more circumspect about drawing too close a relation between populist communal associations and class solidarities. Indeed it is now clear that in Britain, also, popular representations of community can easily degenerate, under the current conditions of the marginaliza-tion of sections of white working-class youth, into a blatant racism which serves to fracture rather than consolidate class solidarity. There can be little doubt that Britain's continued economic decline, combined with an upsurge of national chauvinism presided over by the populist Right, has spawned new mythologies of 'nation', 'people' and 'race' amongst sections of lumpenized white youth.

As we found amongst Loyalist youth, the expression of class sentiments, organization of sexual difference and reproduction of sectarian ethnicity go hand and hand. The 'imagined community' of the street-active young in Northern Ireland – as elsewhere – invokes class sensibilities while engaging in exclusivist practices. It embraces collectivist solutions while at the same time naturalizing gender divisions and reifying sectarian segregation.

The analysis of the role of youth-cultural practices in the reproduction of sectarian ideological relations opens up a more general set of issues within contemporary youth studies. At the analytical level these are concerned with relationship between the generational, class, gender and ethnic dynamics of current youth subcultures. At the political level they concern the ways young working-class people accommodate, and in turn reproduce, the ideological differentiation of the working class along gender and ethnic lines through their own cultural practices. Under what conditions could the subcultural preoccupation with ethnic identity and exclusive forms of local communality assume *a progressive political direction* in Ireland and indeed elsewhere?

2

Sons and Daughters of the Gael: Youth in Irish Social Thought

Introduction

In this chapter we examine the treatment of the 'youth question' in post-war Ireland both north and south of the border. Both in the Republic and in Northern Ireland contemporary youth subculture has been seen as a threat to cultural tradition. In the Republic of Ireland representations of 'youth' have been bound up with that society's experience of rapid 'modernization' since the 1950s. Youth is often viewed as a conduit to a baneful modernity. In a real sense Irish youth has yet to be treated sociologically in its own right. Similarly in Northern Ireland the discussion of 'youth' has been dominated by psychological perspectives concerned with assessing the effect of the civil violence on the personal development of the young. There has been a studied neglect of the role of youth subcultural activity and representations in the reproduction of sectarianism. The dominant psychological approach to youth, operating as it does within a 'correctional perspective', has accompanied and legitimized a major expansion of the interventions of the state in the lives of the adolescents of Northern Ireland via the youth service and Youth Training machinery. It has been less successful in actually explaining the persistence of sectarian sentiments and behaviours amongst the young.

Youth in Irish society

From the outset it has to be admitted that social science has rather overlooked the sphere of youth cultural activity in Ireland. Youth culture has yet to become a subject of systematic investigation for Irish social science. The number of serious sociological studies of

27

youth in Ireland could be counted on the fingers of one hand. This is partly due to the very limited resources available for sociological research of any sort in Ireland, particularly in the Irish Republic. As in economic life we have become dependent on foreign expertise and investment. We have to looked to others to provide a sociological account of Irish society. As a result we have figured as an item on other scholars' theoretical agendas. Indigenous social research has remained, like our economy, underdeveloped.

On the other hand, both Church and state in Ireland have maintained a lively interest – both North and South – in the attitudes, values and peer-group behaviour of teenagers in Ireland. In the current situation of mass youth unemployment and ongoing civil disorder in the north of Ireland this has amounted to a sustained 'moral panic' about the vulnerability of youth to careers of deviancy and violence. Indeed, as we shall see, youth policy in Northern Ireland has over the last fifteen years been largely orchestrated around a belief that the ongoing political disorder and violence have led to an inexorable rise in juvenile deviancy.

As Laurie Taylor (1978) has argued, the youth of Northern Ireland has only been 'visible' on the barricades of Belfast and Derry. More recently, we might add it has been spotted in the dole queues, in the drug clinics, at the 'cider party' and boarding the emigrant ship. Taylor and his researchers systematically examined press reports from the leading newspapers in Northern Ireland in 1976 dealing explicitly with youth issues. Their content analysis revealed that over half the newspapers' coverage was devoted to stories concerned with either the involvement of young people in paramilitary activity or vandalism. On the other hand, despite the deteriorating economic climate, less than 5 per cent of the examined articles dealt with the issue of youth and unemployment. As Taylor concluded, 'Clearly the press has already made up its mind about what are the "real" problems of young people' (1978).

The lack of sociological interest in Irish youth is somewhat strange given the demographic features of Irish social structure. Perhaps one of the most striking features of Irish society is the particularly youthful character of its population. As the posters of the Industrial Development Authority, the body vested with the responsibility of attracting foreign investors to the Republic of Ireland, announce over an image of fresh-faced but earnest graduates 'WE ARE THE YOUNG EUROPEANS'. Indeed, of the countries in the EEC, Ireland as a whole (thirty-two counties) has the greatest percentage of its population under twenty-one. The Republic of Ireland has approximately 50 per cent of its population under the age of twenty-five. Northern Ireland, although having a birth rate somewhat lower than that of the twenty-six counties that comprise the Irish Republic, has a birth rate significantly higher than any other area in Britain and a correspondingly more youthful age structure. Thus, for example, of the regions of the UK, Northern Ireland has the highest percentage of its population under fifteen (26.0 per cent of the Northern Ireland total, as compared with e.g. 19.2 per cent in the south west of England in 1984). As elsewhere in Europe the birthrate in Northern Ireland is falling gradually, and average family size shrinking. Yet, by European standards Northern Ireland remains a youthful society.

Table 2.1   *Birthrate per 1000*

	1966	*1971*	*1981*
Republic of Ireland	22.3	22.7	21.6
Northern Ireland	22.5	20.7	17.6
England	18.0	16.0	12.8

However, notwithstanding its demographic strength, Irish youth for its part has kept a low profile in subcultural terms – at least in comparison with its more colourful British counterparts. Ireland has of course seen the influence of each wave of youth-cultural style that swept Britain since the 1950s – teddy boys, mods and rockers, hippies and bikers, punks, new wave and heavy metal. However such 'dissonant' teenage styles, and the forms of collective behaviour and consumption associated with these, have often been seen as primarily the product of commercial and media hard sell. They are seen as 'artificial', as manufactured abroad and imported, and thus as rakishly 'un-Irish'.

Sons and daughters of the Gael

Conservative thought in Ireland has always maintained an implacable opposition to the mass media. It identifies the media as a source of baneful foreign cultural influence polluting the minds of the young. Historically the Catholic church made sustained attempts to censor and control first film, then radio and later television. It has also sought to manage the leisure activities of the young. In the 1930s and 1940s individual clerics thundered against the mass media and the commercial leisure industries with the dire warning:

> present-day youth are growing 'soft' and are more bent on pleasure-seeking. Their natural and national idealism is being undermined by imported decadent literature – books and magazines, by Hollywood neo-paganism, by exploitation in the commercialised dance-halls both in town and country (Devane, 1942).

This praetorian guard of Irish 'tradition' and Catholic mores claim that youth subcultures have no indigenous roots within Ireland. Localized within city life in a country whose cultural centre of gravity is still largely a rural one, youth subculture is seen as a 'foreign import'. Understood as imitative style it is seen as a forthright challenge to tradition.

As one cleric insisted, bemoaning the enthusiasm of Ireland's youth in the 1940s for the cinema and the cosmopolitan style it engenders, 'We cannot be sons of the Gael and citizens of Hollywood at the same time' (Devane, 1942).

In the 1940s the more radical of the clergy, their heads full of biological theories of adolescent crisis and of eugenic notions of racial development, urged a positive response to the newly-discovered problems of 'youth'. Some of these clerical ideologues were greatly impressed by the National Youth Movements of Nazi Germany, Fascist Italy, and Salazar's Portugal.

The Jesuit social theorist Rev. R. S. Devane, who as well as developing a keen interest in Irish youth, was to play a key role in Irish censorship debates[1] perceptively noted that the democratic states did not 'discover' youth until the Great World Slump of 1929–31, when, in his words, 'unemployment raised its ugly head, and workless youth became a social menace' (1942). He commended instead the totalitarian states for the attention they paid to the youth question. In Ireland, he warns:

> Many of the young people ... are dance-drugged and cinema-

crazy. Discipline and organization are obvious necessities, but they cannot be effectively developed unless by a combined effort in which both Church and state will equally and strenuously co-operate (1942).

Devane was to campaign tirelessly throughout the 1940s for the creation of a national youth movement in Ireland capable of engaging the energies of the adolescent and channelling them in more disciplined directions consonant with 'the national interest'. As he argued:

The adolescent requires the support of religious sanctions and the aid of religion in his violent struggle against the world, the flesh and the devil ... It will, therefore, not be necessary to repeat the need for religion in a national organization of youth (1942).

Devane commended, in particular, the example of the Portuguese fascist youth movement, the Mocidade founded by Salazar in 1936. Such a body could, 'arouse patriotic devotion to the Motherland and develop a love of order and discipline in Youth'. Devane concluded his review of fascist youth movements, asking:

What could not an Irish Catholic Youth Movement contribute towards totalitarian Catholicism if we put into it, proportionately, the time, labour, energy and money that the Nazis have put into their various organizations of youth (1942).

The Irish State was in fact slow to rise to the challenge identified by Devane. In 1940 it did establish a Construction Corps to recruit young unemployed males and set them to work in schemes of public works. The scheme, however was modelled on the Civilian Conservation Corps of New Deal America, rather than on the fascist youth movements. In the event it had difficulty in attracting working-class youth. Devane bemoaned this:

The boy is very fastidious and hedonistic, and unless the Corps is made really attractive to him, he will stand aloof and prefer the street corner and its freedom, the dance-hall and the cinema, even though this involves semi starvation and demoralisation (1942).

Fig. 2.1 The construction corps, Eire: voluntary labour corps
(*Photo: Irish Times*)

Church concern with youth came to focus more and more on the regulation of recreational activities. In rural areas up until recently the favoured evening leisure activity of young Irish people 'ballroom dancing' – the only formal setting where the sexes confronted each other in sexual encounter – was organized directly by the parish priest in the local parochial hall. Priests successfully managed to join the roles of impresarios and moral guardians personally vetting bands and displaying a uniform hostility to American and later British rock and roll and beat musical innovations.[2]

The defence of Catholic mores and the preservation of Irish culture and identity – already somewhat conflated in the mind of populist nationalism – became fused in the last-ditch struggle against capitalist modernity made flesh in the form of the teenage rebel.

By the 1960s it was English youth cultural formations rather than American mass culture which were being identified as the major source of influence on the changing attitudes and behaviours of Irish youth. As late as 1967 another Catholic priest and sometime sociologist was alerting us to the fact that:

Youth have always had problems and there have always been problem youths. Now there is a wider problem – the problem of Modern Youth . . . There is at least the danger that in Ireland we may have to face the same problem in the near future (Forde, 1967).

The 'problem' was seen by Forde as being one of the influences on Irish young people of 'English teenage culture':

It is the new way of life, the new attitudes and values, the new entertainment, dress and hair-styles of many English teenagers, the majority of whom are not delinquents. So distinct have they become that one can almost talk of a new culture (1967).

Youth culture became indelibly associated in the popular mind during the late 1950s and early 1960s with the English phenomena of teddy boys and rock and roll riots. Although 'over there' it was undoubtedly the shape of things to come.

Youth culture and modernization

Unfortunately Irish sociology has tended to lend further credence to the view that youth culture is essentially foreign to Irish society and tradition. Social anthropologists and sociologists have frequently argued that such is the level of social and cultural 'integration' of young people into a cross generationally shared, and essentially conservative 'Irish way of life', that no distinctive and indigenous youth cultures exist within Ireland, north or south. This assertion rests on a particular model of Irish social structure and development.

In sociological accounts of Ireland, as in the popular imagination, 'youth culture' – with all its attendant perceptions of deviancy and drift – is seen as an external cultural influence associated with a general process of *modernization* transforming Irish society.

Since the 1930s the study of Irish cultural relations and social structure has tended to be dominated by a 'community studies' model drawn from social anthropology.[3] The pioneering work here was that done by Arensberg and Kimball (1968). Their ethnographic studies of the rural community in the west of Ireland set a research agenda for Irish sociology for the next forty years. It came to be believed that one could arrive at an understanding of the pattern of social change occurring in Ireland at large by examining how specific small-scale local communities cope with changing external economic, social and cultural influences, i.e., 'modernization'.

James Clifford (1987) has labelled this model of ethnography which dominated social anthropology from Franz Boas up until the present, the 'salvage paradigm'. As he writes:

> many ethnographies and travel accounts continue to be written in the style of *après moi le déluge*, with the exotic culture in question inevitably undergoing 'fatal' changes. We still regularly encounter 'the last traditional Indian bead worker' or the last 'stone age people' (though the discovery of the Tasaday, front page news ten years ago, is now revealed to have been a staged media event). The salvage paradigm, reflecting a desire to rescue 'authenticity' out of destructive historical change, is alive and well.

Within the 'salvage paradigm', 'traditional rural communities' such as the groups 'discovered' by Arensberg and Kimball in Clare, are sneakingly afforded a privileged moral status – as indeed they were in official nationalist political mythology. Social change is conceptualised as a unilinear and uninterrupted process of evolution from 'traditional', essentially rural, societies to 'modern', industrial and urban ones.

It is assumed that Ireland, up until recently located towards the 'traditional' end of this rural-urban continuum, is now undergoing a traumatic transition to modernity. (In 1926 only 32 per cent of the Irish population lived in towns of 1,500 people or over. However by 1971 this number had increased to 52 per cent, with one third of the total population of the Republic now living in the Greater Dublin area.)

Whatever the limitations of this typology of social change in explaining the uneven development of capitalist industrialization in Ireland, this sociological approach has certainly supported a particular view of youth culture in Ireland. Youth culture is seen as being in a relation of dissonance and disjunction from 'traditional' values. For example, it is held that it is rural youth's apparent receptiveness to the 'urban values' and material aspirations of industrial society, diffused by means of the mass media and tourism, that spells the 'eclipse' of the traditional communality held to be characteristic of the Irish countryside. This notion is present, for example, in the work of Hugh Brody, an English anthropologist who in the late 1960s revisited the rural area studied by Arensberg and Kimball in the early thirties. He sought in his ethnography to catalogue the changes that had occurred in the intervening thirty years. In particular he was anxious to examine the impact of 'urban industrial capitalist society' on the 'traditional' communities of the west of Ireland. Examining the generational differences now existing in the parish of Inishkillane he notes:

And as the 1950's advanced, the opportunities – social, financial and sexual – with which urban life tends to be identified were forced deeper and deeper into the consciousness of the community: tourists, the new films, television and ever glossier magazines brought their message into every country home (Brody, 1974).

Brody seems to indict the restless youth of Inishkillane with the charge of succumbing to the charms of consumer culture. It is they who are fracturing the continuity of Irish rural tradition, for

> now the young decide their future in relation to factors which lie outside conventional institutions and aspirations. The conceptions of the young have been at least formed by their awareness of other possibilities. They believe in their right to act on the new conceptions, and like urban peoples, suffer considerable stress if their actions and life-styles are too radically out of harmony with these conceptions. The minds of the new generations are no longer the minds of family farmers. Their consciousness of urban forms and their individualistic pursuit of opportunity are profoundly at odds with life on the family land (Brody, 1974).

The late arrival in Ireland of the post-war boom and, more generally, the uneven character of its capitalist industrialization, undoubtedly led to a situation where the conflict between rural cultural traditions and the lifestyle of urban consumer capitalism was posed more starkly than in many other European countries.

In the Irish Republic, large-scale industrialization involving multinational investment did not really get under way until the early 1960s. Economic and social change has been telescoped into an extremely short time span. For example in the seventeen years between 1961 and 1978, GDP expanded tenfold, industrial employment increased by some 24 per cent, while the numbers employed in agriculture dropped by 40 per cent. In 1964, one-quarter of seventeen-year olds remained in full time education, a participation rate that grew to one-half in 1979. The Republic's population which had been in continuous decline since the end of the Famine right up until the early 1960s, grew from 2.8 million in 1961 to 3.4 million in 1981 as the tide of emigration turned and more people married and raised families in Ireland.[4]

Similarly Northern Ireland was to experience in the 1960s a period of rapid economic restructuring and growth after years of economic stagnation. Here again the aberrant character of youth culture was attributed to the stresses of post-war 'affluence'. Thus for example the Northern Ireland authorities in a 1961 review of their fledgling youth service, could claim without any sense of irony that the young people of Northern Ireland have not in general been subjected to the same degree (as the rest of the United Kingdom) to the new strains arising from industrial prosperity and full employment (NIYSC, 1971).

Since the end of the 1950s then, the position of youth in Irish society, north and south, has become inextricably associated in the popular mind with the experience of rapid industrialization and urbanization. The generation gap has been stretched out within the popular imagination along the axis of modernization. Youth subcultures, where they have been accorded recognition at all, have been understood in age-specific terms.

Youth culture, like the era of affluence it betokens in the Irish popular imagination, is represented as a classless cosmopolitan phenomenon essentially *generational* in character. Youth culture is viewed as a formation intimately bound up in a universal modernization process now belatedly affecting Irish society. It makes its most tangible appearance around the emergence of a new consumption norm for working-class youth in post-war European society – the emergence of a teenage market place for cultural commodities, records, fashion, clothes and commercial leisure.

However, such metaphorical uses of the term 'youth' have in fact obscured our understanding of the dynamics of youth subcultures and their complex relation to parental ethnic traditions. As we shall see in our study of Loyalist youth, subcultural practices can just as easily embrace and resuscitate 'traditional' values as undermine or reject them.

Hall and Jefferson have deconstructed the notion of 'youth culture' utilized by the media in 1960s England. As they argue:

The term is premised on the view that what happened to 'youth' in this period is radically and qualitatively different from anything that happened before. It suggests that all the things which youth got into were more significant than the different kinds of youth groups, or the differences in social class composition. It sustains certain kinds of ideological interpretation – e.g. that age and generation mattered most, or that Youth Culture was 'incipiently classless' – even, that 'youth' itself had become a class (1976).

This media-inspired representation of youth culture had the effect of underplaying the significance of class differences in 1960s England. The pop sociology of youth was also imported into the Irish media and reinforced a popular perception of youth culture as a universal harbinger of modernity and affluence. In Ireland, of course, the significance of class differences and conflicts has been further obscured within popular consciousness, by a rhetoric of national identity and community.

Irish society, of course, exhibits levels of social inequality as entrenched as anywhere within capitalist Europe. Moreover, it has a high level of trade union membership both north and south in comparison within the European average. The industrialization of the republic saw a dramatic growth in trade union membership. This expanded from 328,000 members in 1961, representing 51 per cent of all employees, to almost half-a-million by 1979, some 65 per cent of the workforce. Similarly, by the end of the 1970s almost 60 per cent of Northern Ireland employees were unionized. Ireland has also had a long tradition of trade-union combativity around wage struggles. It is in other words, however one defines it, a 'class society'.

However, because of the unresolved national question, populist ethnic ideologies have tended to be the mobilizing basis for political parties rather than articulated class interests. This has taken different forms in the two post-partition states. In Northern Ireland, Unionist hegemony rested on the capacity of the 'Orange System' to build an 'all class alliance' of Protestants – industrial workers, bourgeoisie and landlords – an alliance which faltered only relatively recently.

In what is now the Republic of Ireland the situation has been somewhat different. Here bourgeois interests came to predominate within the nationalist movement after political independence. The revolutionary nationalism of the post-1916 era quickly gave way to the 'official nationalism' of a state anxious to secure itself. This 'official nationalism' became associated in particular with De Valera and his Fianna Fail party which dominated Irish political life from the 1930s to the 1960s. Within this ideology the nation state became idealised within political discourse in the evocative notion of the 'community'. For De Valera the community in question was a projected nation of self-sufficient, rural, small-holders united by faith and adherence to Gaelic tradition. In a now famous radio broadcast in 1943 Eamon de Valera, architect of the Irish constitution, sketched this imagined community with its distinctive gender and generational imagery:

> The Ireland we have dreamed of would be the home of a people who valued material wealth only as a basis of a right living, of a people who were satisfied with a frugal comfort and devoted leisure to things of the spirit. A land whose countryside would be bright with cosy homesteads, whose fields and villages would be joyous with sounds of industry, with the romping of sturdy children, the contests of athletic youth, the laughter of comely maidens.

Within this essentially Narodnik vision the notion of rural Ireland as the only 'true' Ireland gained momentum. In turn conservative nationalists came to view youth culture as a profane threat.

For liberals, on the other hand, intent as they were on a thorough revision of the nationalist canon, youth culture was greeted as a harbinger of a more affluent and permissive era. The hedonistic explosion of youth culture of the 1960s was warmly welcomed. This generational revolt semed to dramatically throw into question the outmoded values and loyalties of traditional Ireland. Moreover it seemed to token the possibility of a more enlightened political future. It seemed the young had at last turned their backs on the shibboleths of traditional religion and irredentist nationalism.

In 1970s Dublin the punk band The Radiators expressed the iconoclastic mood of the moment:

> Look across your shoulder and the
> school bell rings
> Another day of made to measure
> history
> Well I don't mind that your heroes all
> have wings
> But your terrible beauty is torn

For the liberal imagination the world of expressive youth culture, orchestrated around the vibrant rock culture emerging in 1970s Dublin and Belfast, tokened a decisive break with the past. It indicated, as some claimed, 'the new youthfulness of the country'.

The sociologists who contributed to the Sense of Ireland Exhibition mounted in 1981 to announce to the world Ireland's arrival as a modern industrial society, were to comment:

> While changes in youth culture in Ireland have hardly brought down governments, they indicate how the country has become – almost unnoticed from over the water – something very different to either the rural arcadia or traditional tribal battlefield of British fantasy (ICA, 1981).

Despite their political differences these conservative and liberal reactions to post-war youth cultural formations share a common assumption – namely that youth subcultural practices are by their very nature inimical to Irish cultural tradition and identity. The role of youth cultures in the reconstruction of ethnic identity in a period of rapid and traumatic social change was largely ignored.

Youth in Northern Ireland: the spectre of the troubles

In Northern Ireland the situation on the surface seems somewhat different. Here the focus of public interest since the end of the 1960s has centred on the involvement of young people in the civil unrest. More generally it has focused on the effect of the 'Troubles' on the personal and social development of the young.

It is perhaps worth noting that the concern of the Northern Ireland state with the potential uncontrollability of youth in turbulent Irish society long predates the current troubles. Similarly, government resolve to utilize the Youth Service as a machinery of social control has a substantial history.

During the Second World War, a Youth Committee was set up by the Ministry of Education in 1942 to review 'the youth problems affecting youth welfare in Northern Ireland'. This body sketched a scenario of 'problem youth' that would be repeated in subsequent moral panics thirty years later. Commenting on the effect of the war on young people they noted:

> Then the darkened streets afforded to boys and girls a liberty of movement and action bordering upon licence, which, increased by a relaxation of parental control . . . soon made itself apparent

in the large numbers of young people who thronged the streets after dark. At the same time the facilities which had been provided for youthful recreation were reduced by the commandeering of premises and playing fields for war purposes (NIYC, 1942).

The Committee, anxious to make the case for additional funding for the youth service, moved effortlessly from social enquiry to the suggestion of 'preventative measures'.

A Youth Welfare Act in 1944 implemented their recommendations. It established a permanent government Youth Committee to oversee the development of a professional youth service and to buttress the provision of the voluntary, largely uniformed youth organizations. An aetiology of youthful disorder was formulated. This traced the origins of juvenile delinquency to the inadequate policing of the streets and to parental neglect. It prescribed as a cure the professionalization of the youth service and provision of recreational facilities. This diagnosis and 'course of treatment' was to be faithfully repeated with regard to another generation of Ulster 'problem youth' in the 1970s.

The darkened streets of the 1970s were lit up with the flare of the petrol bomb. In the early period of the current conflict, from 1969 until 1972, street rioting was at its peak. Media attention was drawn to the large scale involvement of the young in these street disturbances. The British, US and European television networks whose crews had crowded into the backstreets of Belfast and Derry after the disturbances of August 1969 relayed pictures of masked teenage combatants manning the barricades and locked in fierce struggle with the security forces. Foreign journalists were often poorly briefed about the historical background and political complexity of the Northern Ireland situation. Too often they relied on simple symbols, spurious analogies and striking images in order to represent and 'explain' the tangled web of events and issues to their viewers back home. Arriving hot foot from the streets of Paris or the conflict torn campuses of the US universities, reporters identified the rebellious youth clutching a petrol bomb as an exemplary symbol which could catch the meaning of the exploding civil strife in Ulster.

As with most stereotypes created and relayed by the media this image of youth was not a total misrepresentation of Ulster's youth

– for indeed all the evidence suggests that young working class people *were* involved in a widespread way in the early rioting.[5] It achieved its 'ideological effect' rather by stylization, exaggeration and pseudo-explanation. The complex pattern of involvement of adolescents in the early civil strife, some of it motivated by political idealism, some by concerns with the organization of local defence against the assaults of an unruly police force, and some of it no doubt part of a much older Irish tradition of riot as carnival of misrule, became reduced to the simple narrative of youth in universal revolt.

However, the early 1970s saw the paramilitarization of the civil conflict as the Stormont state moved rapidly towards collapse. The periodic street rioting largely directed against the police and involving large groups of youths in semi-ritualized stone-throwing confrontations, gave way to a more vicious pattern of terrorist violence. The bomb and bullet and the sectarian assassination came to predominate. In the media the image of the juvenile rioter was displaced by the more sinister figure of the hooded and armalite-bearing 'terrorist'. In turn the attention of journalists began to focus on the recruitment of young people into Loyalist and Republican paramilitary groups.

The Chief Constable of the RUC in his annual report for 1975 alerted the public to 'the usage by evil men of young persons in subversive crime', thus giving the official imprimatur to the view that youthful involvement in political crime was the result of the manipulation of adolescents by paramilitary 'Godfathers'.

The media were quick to seize upon and amplify this 'explanation' of youthful deviance. The *Belfast News Letter*'s headline of 2 December 1976 declared, echoing the warning of the then Secretary of State Roy Mason:

> Ulster's Babyfaced Killers, used as 'cannon fodder' by the Godfathers of Crime, will spend the best years of their lives in jail.

Particular newspaper reports of teenage involvement in terrorist-related activity underscored the idea that naive young people were being press-ganged into paramilitary groups by older terrorist figures. This 'Godfather thesis' of juvenile illegalities, as Laurie Taylor calls it, was associated with a sustained attempt by the British government to 'criminalize' the paramilitary groups, and particularly the IRA, after 1975. As Taylor points out:

reports on young people's involvement in paramilitary activities generally stressed the corruption of youth by older members, quite often developed accounts which linked paramilitants with conventional crime and gave much coverage to attempts by politicians and others to discourage young people's paramilitary involvement (1978).

Within this narrative structure the naive innocence of the adolescent delinquent is contrasted to the devious criminality of the terrorist. A crudely determinist cultural-transmission theory of youthful deviancy interacts with a political strategy of criminalization engineered by the British state. An aetiology of juvenile delinquency functions so as to delegitimize political dissent.

Youth research and policy in Northern Ireland: the pursuit of the pathological

The mid-1970s saw a massive expansion of the Youth Service in Northern Ireland. This involved both an extensive building programme to provide new youth centres in deprived and riot torn working class areas and the professionalization of the service. Between 1974 and 1979, funding for the Youth Service increased from £2.25 million to over £6 million per year. Some 60 major building schemes for provision of purpose-built facilities were completed. The number of full-time trained youth workers also doubled during these years. The partial professionalization of youth work clearly involved a recognition by policy makers that the traditional uniformed youth organizations with their confessional basis and middle class ethos were unequal to the challenge posed by the civil conflict. The director of the Northern Ireland Association for Youth Clubs in 1976 issued a dire warning that

> unless there was a positive plan for youth development and a clear understanding of the responsibilties of the state and voluntary movement then the 'scarring' of youth that had taken place in Northern Ireland would erupt in continuing sectarianism and violence in a future generation.[6]

Up to 1975, youth work provision had been largely dependent

upon voluntary effort. Less then one in ten youth clubs were state provided. Sixty-five per cent of all leaders still came from uniformed organizations like the Boy Scouts, Girl Guides, Boys Brigade etc.[7] These uniformed organizations had little purchase on the activities of working-class youth, particularly Catholic teenagers from the most riot-prone areas of Belfast and Derry. It was to be precisely in these 'trouble spots' that the new Youth Centres and staff were to be concentrated. The provision was geared to getting young males off the street, a concern reflected in the limited orientation of the new centres to girls. As elsewhere the form of provision was a response to the 'masculine and delinquent conations of youth' (Niva, 1984). Girls continued to be underrepresented in youth club membership rolls and were poorly catered for in clubs' activities.

This approach to youth policy has been quite explicitly *correctional* in character. That is to say, these programmes and the model of youthful deviance which informs them, concern themselves primarily with the identification and 'treatment' of supposedly 'abnormal' patterns of behaviour amongst the young – particularly the working-class adolescent. British social and educational policy in the middle and late-1970s announced as one of its central aims the combating of sectarianism. This it understood as a structure of *personal prejudice*. And where best to start but with the young?

This correctional stance articulated well with official constructions of sectarianism as a 'social problem' which could be tackled by clearly-delimited, state-sponsored initiatives in the field of education and youth work. The British state, since the imposition of Direct Rule in 1972, has indeed continued to represent the 'Ulster Question' as a social problem rather than an issue of contested sovereignty. From the perspective of Stormont Castle sectarian divisions are invariably seen as the cause rather than the effect of the political conflict. Sectarianism accordingly is approached from a position of high moralism. Ultimately its persistence is attributed to a fundamental defect in Irish character and culture – the irrational preservation of ancient animosities. The early period of Direct Rule, under the Labour administration in office from 1974 to 1978, seemed to offer the promise of transferring British liberal and social-democratic sensibilities to the recalcitrant Irish.

A panoply of psychological and educational expertise was brought to bear on the newly-formulated youth question in Northern Ireland. Institutionally-sponsored research sought to examine and study both the impact of the conflict on the young and on how best to combat sectarianism and promote 'mutual understanding' amongst the school-going population. The initial concern was to try and establish whether a generation 'conditioned to violence' would develop deviant careers that would in future years threaten the entire social order. Frazer (1973), one of the early researchers, gave expression to the widely held belief amongst the authorities that

> the violence that the children learn in the streets spills over into the schools and into the home, toward all authority figures. Once you are patterned to violence it's hard to get unpatterned.

This early research, based largely on psychiatric casework, and behaviourist in orientation, tended to pathologize young people in Northern Ireland. Youth was treated as a 'category at risk'.

The basic questions asked by researchers such as Frazer and Lyons, both of whom were psychiatrists practising in Belfast, was whether the experiences of Ulster's adolescents had left them resistant to the rule of law or indeed any control. As Lyons (1973) was to ask:

> But what will happen when a political settlement is eventually achieved and these young people no longer have licence to commit anti-social acts? It is only to be expected that acts of violence and anti-social behaviour will continue because of the conditioning of previous years. . .

This research sought to make the troubled streets of Belfast a clinical laboratory for the study of adolescent pathology. In turn it sustained a more general moral panic about Ulster's youth already prevalent in official circles. Within the Northern Ireland office at the time, government experts anticipated the likelihood of an 'imminent and dramatic increase in juvenile delinquency'.[8] They predicted that the combination of the deteriorating economic situation and cumulative effect on young people of being exposed to the civil conflict, would lead to such an increase in juvenile deviancy that the existing caring and corrective services would be swamped with young offenders.

The early research became obsessed with the calibration of the long-term effects on children of being 'conditioned to violence'. It both sensationalized the issue and moreover abstracted it from the sectarian character of 'normal' everyday life in Northern Ireland. Its concern with the vulnerability of the province's youth to careers of sectarian violence dovetailed neatly, as we have said, with the British State's rhetoric about sectarianism being a 'social problem' rather than the norm which has to be negotiated by most young people as they grow up in Northern Ireland.

Methodologically this work was highly suspect. It suffered from the frequent attempts by the authors to generalize from the small clinical samples of children referred for specialist psychiatric care with problems thought to have resulted from direct exposure to violence. It was often assumed that the general population of youth, living in a milieu of civil disorder and violence might potentially exhibit similar undetected pathological symptoms. However, attempts even to simply correlate the number of children referred to psychiatric care in any one period with the level of violence obtaining in Northern Ireland at that time proved difficult.[9]

In the 1970s a vast, apparently methodologically sophisticated, yet completely inconclusive, psychological literature on the effects of political violence on young people in Ulster emerged. As Ed Cairns (1987) concludes in a summary of that research:

> To the naive reader it may appear that we now possess a vast amount of information about children's psychiatric reaction to the street associated with exposure to the violence in Northern Ireland. Unfortunately, in this area, as in others, even today we do not really have enough information to reach a clear understanding of such simple facts as how many children have really become psychiatric victims solely because of the violence.

More recently psychological research has retreated from this hot pursuit of the pathological. The majority of the more recent studies have been conducted by social psychologists rather than by psychiatrists. They have been interactionist rather than behaviourist in inspiration and as such have been more cognizant of the general social and political context within which the personal development of young people in Northern Ireland is framed. Indeed the last few years have seen a more sober reassessment of the psyche of the province's youth. [10]

Following the collection of empirical evidence on what might be best called a youth pathology coefficient (incidence of school truancy, vandalism, involvement in petty crime etc.) and comparison of the youth of Northern Ireland with control groups from other areas of Britain, the 'pathology profile' of Ulster's youth was reassessed. It was 'discovered' that compared with many urban areas of Britain, Northern Irish youth in fact exhibited statistically less 'anti-social behaviour'! [11]

This latter corpus of research reported by Cairns (1987) and Heskin and Harbinson (1980) seems to be organized around the central concern of demonstrating to those outside Northern Ireland, the essential *normality* of Ulster's youth. The research addresses itself to the general effects of unemployment, urban deprivation and poverty on the young, rather than to the specific consequences of sectarian division and violence. As Cairns (1987) comments on media preoccupation with images of violence in Northern Ireland:

Perhaps the single most important fact ignored by the media about Northern Ireland is that it has the unenviable reputation of being the least affluent region of the United Kingdom and is officially recognized as one of the least prosperous areas within the European Economic Community. Local social scientists are of course only too aware of this state of affairs and of the fact that poverty can have as great an impact on people's lives as can violence, if not greater. In particular social scientists interested in children in Northern Ireland are very conscious of the fact that violence is not the only form of deprivation that Northern Ireland's children may have been exposed to (Cairns, 1987).

Yet, as we have argued, the sectarian conflict in Northern Ireland which so shapes the lives of young working-class people is not in essence a 'social problem'. It is an illusion to believe that it can be resolved by the caring agencies and committed professionals of the British welfare state. It is, as I have argued, a political problem.

Sectarianism as it is expressed at the level of everyday social relations is the result of an unresolved political problem. The same of course is ultimately true of poverty itself. For, although presented by the media and government as a social problem of managing individual failure, poverty is also in essence the resultant of a particular, politically legitimized, economic order.

Psychological research to date has played down the sectarian character of everyday life in Northern Ireland which confronts the young in so far as they attend segregated schools, live in confessional residential communities and have differential access to the labour market on the basis of their religious backgrounds. Most research ignores the penetration of sectarian modes of experience into the routinized practices of everyday life in Ulster – paradoxically there has been little empirical research and even less theoretical work on sectarianism in Northern Ireland. The issue of sectarianism has been reduced to one of personal prejudice and aberrant cognitions.

The working-class propensity to embrace sectarian attitudes is, in turn, often viewed as the result of a cultural deficit which can be remedied by enlightened schooling. Within this theory of youthful sectarianism the relationship between, on the one hand, youth, their peer-group activities and subcultures and, on the other hand, 'traditional' parental cultures, is posed in a way very similar to how the relation of youth cultures to 'tradition' is understood in the Republic. Youth culture and tradition are regarded as antithetical. The ghettoization of residential life in Northern Ireland and the ongoing civil conflict have been adduced as factors, additional to the 'basic traditionalism of Irish society', to account for the wholesale integration of working class youth into their parental sectarian cultures. Social researchers have claimed (Jenvey, 1972) that

> one of the major effects of living with the Troubles has been to direct the young away from rebellion against the adult world, characteristic of their age group, towards conformity with their parents and the local community.

Again adolescents are either treated as the passive initiates into the 'traditional' or as in full flight from communal identities. Thus, Jenvey can argue that the intensity of the communal conflict and resulting ghettoization of residential life have led to the situation where, 'it is not surprising that the "generation gap" has been cruelly bridged'. We see at work here once again a theory which views youth subcultural formations as constituting a total rupture from a culture of tradition. Where young people are to be seen to be actively embracing and exploring their communal identities it is assumed that they are the passive dupes of adult machination and prejudice or the victims of a deficit working-class culture. Either way a particularly passive conception of the political and ethnic socialization experience of Irish youth is assumed.

In fact during this period groups of Loyalist youth organized in the so called 'Tartan Gangs' were roaming the streets of Belfast and Northern Ireland's other towns assuming responsibility for the 'policing' of Loyalist 'territory'. Young Catholics, in turn, were showing a greater interest in 'traditional' Irish music and culture than had been shown in their community for perhaps three generations. Despite this, researchers continued to ignore the role of youth cultural practices in the reproduction of ethnic identities in Northern Ireland.

To date there has been a general neglect by researchers studying sectarianism in Northern Ireland of the role of youth peer-group activity in the process of *ethnogenesis*, i.e. the social process through which a group's sense of its ethnic identity and difference from other groups is created and reproduced in and through a set of symbolic processes and representations. This omission is somewhat strange given the centrality both in the past and today of youth street activity to sectarian boundary-maintenance practices with a distinct territorial focus.

Indeed, once one accepts that ethnic identity is a *relational* affair, i.e. groups establish and sustain their collective sense of themselves as a distinct group by reference to other 'outsider' groups from whom they wish to be distinguished, then our attention must of necessity focus on the socially-constructed and maintained boundary which embodies this sense of discrimination. And given our knowledge that a distinguishing feature of contemporary urban working-class subcultures is their overriding concern with territory and collective identity, then we are led back to exploring the homology between sectarianism as a situation symbolic practice and youth subcultural form.

Fig. 2.2 Across the generations?
(*Photo: Bryan O'Brien*)

Sociological Approaches

Sadly the only published ethnographic study of youth in Northern Ireland, Richard Jenkins' account (1983) of the working-class Protestant youth of 'Ballyhightown', a fictitious name for a large post-war municipal housing estate on the northern outskirts of Belfast, has little to say about the interaction of working-class youth life styles and sectarian ideology and practice.

Jenkins' study does attempt to address a major deficiency of the psychological literature, namely the tendency to ignore the extra-school setting of the young. In the voluminous research conducted on youth and sectarianism in Northern Ireland the role of peer-group interactions and subcultural activities in the formation of a sectarian *habitus*[12] for youth has not been addressed. Researchers have tended to assume that the segregated character of Northern Ireland's school system itself is sufficient explanation for the emergence of sectarian attitudes amongst the young. The research to date has been largely school-based and of a question-naire-survey character. There has been little sustained collection of data (in particular, informal interviews and ethnographic fieldwork) in 'unattached' street and domestic settings. Within the existing research, youth itself has been largely silent.

Even within the school setting there has been an almost complete neglect of the role of Loyalist and Republican ideology as a discourse sustaining school counter culture. This is surprising because most educational researchers are aware of the extensive literature on working-class school counter culture.

More immediately, most secondary teachers in state (i.e. 'Pro-testant') schools are very much aware of the central role of Loyalist symbolism and sentiment in underwriting 'trouble in the classroom'. The wearing of paramilitary badges, the bearing of Loyalist tattoos, the ostentatious display of football paraphernalia of the Loyalist-supported teams, the mimicry of 'blood and thunder' drumming conducted with pencils at the back of the classroom, the truancy associated with days of outside political activity and the organised skirmishing with neighbouring Catholic schoolkids after school; all are testimony to the ways in which populist Loyalism provides the cultural resources for a vibrant school counter culture for working-class Protestant teenagers.

Jenkins' work does take him beyond the confines of the school.

His ethnographic approach takes him out into the streets. Like Heskin and Harbinson he takes his stand against the ranks of psychological and psychiatric experts who have tended to pathologize Ulster youth. His interviews of a cross-section of the young people of 'Ballyhightown' are assembled to suggest that despite the 'Troubles' the youth of Northern Ireland manage to construct fairly 'normal' lives for themselves. Their lives, like those of their working-class peers in other parts of the UK, are moulded by structures of educational inequality and by a worsening labour market.

Somewhat perversely in the Northern Ireland context, Jenkins focuses on the social-class dimension of their experience in isolation from the ethnic. He declares his major interest to be an analysis of the role of youth lifestyles in reproducing social divisions within the working class in Northern Ireland. Perversely, this does not seem to entail for him an analysis of the sectarian division of the Ulster working class. Nor does it seem to involve a consideration of how youth cultural practices sustain the sectarian segmentation of the working class.

One senses in Jenkins parsimonious treatment of his ethnographic data a systematic playing down of the sectarian and ethnic dimension of Protestant working-class life styles. Like more recent psychological and education research on youth in Northern Ireland, he is motivated by a concern to challenge the received wisdom that young people in Northern Ireland, growing up in the midst of sectarian hostility, fed by political instability and chronic social malaise, experience an *abnormal* childhood and adolescence.

Yet sadly, whether Jenkins wishes to acknowledge it or not, sectarian division remains a fundamental mode of stratification in a region for so long subject to the imprint of British imperialism. Indeed in the current 'raw' political situation such divisions are understandably more decisive in shaping popular consciousness than class sensibilities. Jenkins' neglect of the role of youth subcultural practices in the reproduction of sectarian divisions is remarkable.

We can applaud Jenkins' concern to show how young people in Northern Ireland suffer from the material effects of living in a region which, *like many in Britain* is finding itself economically peripheralized as its traditional industries decline and unemployment accordingly escalates. However, his failure to address in an adequate manner the particular peculiarities of growing up in Northern Ireland – the necessity for teenagers to come to terms with the all-embracing sectarian habitus within which people have had to live their lives through almost a generation of civil and military strife – robs his work of significance. Within it the crucial area of the interaction of class and ethnic practices within Protestant working-class 'life styles' is all but obscured.

Selecting a research strategy

Two years in Oxford gave me ample time to review the existing literature on youth in Northern Ireland and identify the gaps in it – particularly the absence of subcultural studies of sectarianism and ethnogenesis. I returned to Derry in the autumn of 1985 as a full-time researcher to plan the fieldwork for a projected study on Loyalist youth subculture. Theoretical leads and hunches had to be tested on the ground.

The immediate objective of my fieldwork was to examine the particular role of youth cultural practices and peer-group associations in the sustaining of sectarian identities amongst young Protestants in Northern Ireland. The specific focus in my fieldwork was the activities and sensibilities of Protestant working-class young people in the fourteen-to-eighteen age range in the Londonderry urban area. I was anxious to find out how the attitudes and peer-group activities of these young people were shaped by the fact that they were growing up in an area characterized by, not only a high degree of religious and residential segregation, but also by intense ongoing civil and political conflict. Again I was specifically interested in the ways youth cultural practices, particularly territorially-focused peer-group activity on the street – of which the marching bands were to prove an exemplary form – sustain and reproduce sectarian ethnic identities as a set of shared and learned discourses.

Derry was chosen as the centre for the project because of my previous familiarity with the town. This gave me a head start in setting up the project and negotiating access to the field.[13] Derry with a population of around 90,000, some two-thirds Catholic and one-third Protestant – roughly the inverse of the proportion of Catholics to Protestants to be found in Northern Ireland in general

– was also a significant choice for another reason. For here Protestants have lost political power in local politics. They are having to co-exist with a strongly nationalist Catholic population, sections of which have been in almost constant conflict with the British state since the early 1970s.

Because of its size, demography and history Protestants are in much closer interaction with Catholics there than in many other areas of Northern Ireland. In a city which holds a special place in both the affections of the Protestants and Catholics of Ulster, ethnic identities and differences are openly and frequently paraded. Derry, with its sedimentations of history and identity has become a frontier town where the contending claims of Planter and Gael meet in conflict.

Why, you may ask, did I decide to restrict my fieldwork solely to an investigation of Protestant youth? Surely a comparative study would have made more sense? Ethnographic research involving young people is a high-risk business. Access to groups to be studied is often difficult to negotiate, dependent as it is on trust, confidentiality and simple acceptability of the researcher by the group. In Northern Ireland the bitterness of the civil strife has reinforced the natural reserve and suspicion of the subjects of ethnography. To be seen to be talking to the 'other side' could quickly erode the confidence of young Protestants (or young Catholics) and immediately make them suspicious of one's motives. Any meaningful flow of information between researcher and group would soon dry up.[14]

For my own part the fact that I had grown up as a Protestant in Derry opened up various doors. My face fitted.[15] I looked up old school mates now working as teachers and youth workers in the town's Protestant secondary schools. These were able to facilitate access to youth centres and band-practice halls. I badgered school heads into allowing me into their schools to conduct a survey aimed at gauging the peer-group activities and social attitudes of Protestant teenagers and how these had been shaped by the 'Troubles'.[16] We were able to question a representative sample of over 400 pupils between the ages of thirteen and seventeen drawn from Derry's three Protestant secondary schools (one grammar and two non-selective). Our survey, reported in Chapter 4, gave us some sort of reasonably representative picture of how the lives of these young people were being moulded by the 'Troubles'.

At the same time I began to attend on a regular weekly basis two youth clubs used by both current and former pupils from these schools. Over the next four months I recorded interviews with some 30 kids in the relaxed and informal setting of the club, asking them about their involvement in Loyalist organizations and their political beliefs. They shared their experiences of school and Youth Training Schemes with me and we explored their attitudes to young Catholics. I came across many of the young people we had already interviewed in the school-survey sample and was able to follow up and elucidate responses identified in the questionnaire returns.

The initial fieldwork had suggested that the Loyalist marching bands had become the major mobilizing agency for Protestant youth. Protestant Ulster has always had its marching bands but since the mid-1970s these were overwhelmingly youthful, working-class and independent of the Orange Order. The summer's marching seasons of 1988 and 1989 brought to British television screens pictures of the youthful members of Loyalist marching bands in their colourful uniforms locked in violent confrontation with the police over the re-routing of traditional Orange marches away from predominantly Catholic areas. The bands were also to play a key part in the disturbances which accompanied the mass protests of Unionists against the Anglo-Irish Agreement.

These marching bands with their expressive display of Protestant identity via 'party music', and Loyalist iconography and with their focal concern with the symbolic defence of territory (where you can or cannot 'walk') have since the mid-1970s become a central element of popular Loyalism. The bands and their parades seem to provide for the dispossessed Loyalist youth of Ulster a sectarian habitus within which their generational concerns with communal identity and with winning public space become fused with the focal concerns of a parental Loyalist culture with territoriality and ethnic solidarity.

The summer months saw me tramping the streets of Derry and the other small towns of the north west of Ireland observing the sons of Ulster on the march. I followed the progress of two particular bands from the Waterside area of Derry throughout the marching season – the Caw Sons of Ulster and the Maiden City Protestant Boys. From the ritualistic burning of the Traitor Lundy in the dark of midwinter to the annual celebration of the Relief of

Fig. 2.3 The regulars arrive at the youth club
(*Photo: Desmond Bell*)

Derry (from the Jacobite siege of 1689) in August, I followed their activities. I attended band parades and talked with the young bandsmen in their practice halls and on their estates. We documented, with the help of the video camera, their preparations for the big marching days and for the host of other smaller parades and competitions that now make up the marching season. We chronicled the involvement of these young people in the panoply of popular cultural practices – the decorating of the streets, the mural painting and bonfires – which mark the celebration of a Protestant sense of history.

The subculture as sociological sample

As Hall and Jefferson are at pains to remind us in *Rituals*, the great majority of working-class youth never fully participate in a coherent, clearly identifiable subculture at all. Despite this sociologists have been drawn to the most outrageous and expressive, most visible and vocal, youth styles like moths to a night light. Few ethnographers have paused to consider whether these subcultures, to quote Hall and Jefferson,

> may be less significant than what most young people do most of the time. The relation between 'every-day life' and the 'subcultural life' of different sections of youth is an important question in its own right and must not be subsumed under the more limited topic (of subcultural ethnography) (1976).

In Northern Ireland most young people are not involved in Republican or Loyalist political activity. They do not by and large get involved in demonstrations, riots and sectarian confrontations. They do not all spend their summer evenings preparing for Orange or Nationalist parades. [17]

From the outset of our fieldwork I was anxious to address the problem of the *representivity* of the subcultural milieu we were to enter in our ethnography. In much of the recent ethnographic work on youth subcultures, researchers have been somewhat slow to pose the question of whether the engaging subcultural group chosen as the topic for their ethnographies is in fact typical of the young men and women in general from that region, class, and ethnic group. Indeed it has to be admitted that the current tradition of youth-cultural studies approaches this problem with sublime indifference.

In our own research we attempted to combine a programme of survey research and secondary analysis of statistical data on youth with an ethnography of a small and selective group of teenagers involved in bands. We devised a research strategy which identified three settings for fieldwork research – school, youth club and street – each characterized by different levels of institutional formality. We hoped to move progressively during the project from the more quantitative, formalized information-gathering practices in institutional settings to qualitative, open-ended data collection in informal settings with small samples of young people. In this way we hoped to balance the descriptive richness possible in the ethnographic method, which aims to get on the inside of the lived world of the group studied, with some measure of statistical significance.[18]

As I have said, we did manage to pick up individuals in the youth club interviews who had been respondents in the school survey. Also the interview statements and observed behaviour recorded for the ethnographic sample could be placed in the context of our information about a school sample randomly chosen from the total school-attending population of 'Protestant' Derry. In this way some estimate of the representativeness of our ethnographic sample was arrived at. Rough methods indeed, but an advance perhaps on the current tradition of youth cultural studies which approaches the question of the representativeness of its ethnographic samples in a somewhat cavalier spirit.

This is not just an abstract methodological nicety. It is now generally recognized that the ethnographic tradition of youth studies systematically ignored whole sections of youth. Teenage girls in particular have fared badly within this tradition. Not only does the very masculinist form of male youth subculture marginalize young women but the ethnographic practices of researchers, who remain predominantly male, tend to take this gender exclusion for granted rather than treat it as an important focus for investigation in itself.

Millions of 'ordinary kids' play no active part in the dramaturgical world of subcultural display. They are however experiencing the material problems of being adolescents in Britain today. The more recent work of the CCCS has in fact focused on the wider material situation affecting young people in Thatcher's Britain. The earlier semiological interests in subcultural representation have given way to structural concerns with the impact of mass unemployment and Youth Training regimes on marginalized youth. The celebration of youthful resistance has given way to a more sober plotting of what Paul Willis has dubbed the 'new social state of youth' – the exclusion of young people from wage labour and from the cultural relations which have historically conditioned their transition to adulthood as members of the working class (Willis, 1984). The sociology of youth has increasingly focused its attention on the critical analysis of educational and youth policy. This has raised in a sharper way the question of the social and political responsibility of the youth-cultural ethnographer.

The dilemmas of the native ethnographer

This issue of responsibility assumed a more concrete form in the context of my fieldwork in Derry. As the project developed throughout the winter and spring of 1985 and as I got to know the young bandsmen better, I came to be haunted by a number of specific dilemmas.

The chasm that separated me from the young bandsmen was not merely one of age (significant enough in itself) but of politics. Usually an ethnographer, like the professional youth worker, comes to the community he or she intends to study or work with as an outsider. From the start s/he is working hard to bridge the cultural distance that naturally exists between him or her and his or her subjects/clients. Questions of political difference are usually suspended in the midst of the demands of participant observation or of just simply getting on with the young people one is working with. However as a former native of Derry I already had the basic cultural competence to survive in the Protestant community. I could read its cultural codes and was conversant with its central unifying myths.

What my ethnographic work brought home to me was the ideological chasm which time and political experience had opened up between myself and my young interviewees. It brought me face to face with *difference*. Unfortunately I had not the traditional escape of the ethnographer who suffers from moral scruples about how s/he should relate to the host community. I could not 'go native'.

Though born of the Protestant community in Derry I am no longer of it. I have no sympathies with Ulster Loyalism as a political ideology although I have much for the historical predicament the Protestants of Northern Ireland find themselves in. They are after all caught up in a post-colonial situation which, despite their reputation for intransigence, is neither of their making nor of their choice.

The paradoxical feature of all ethnographic work is that in the process of identification with one's subjects one experiences difference. In seeing the world through the eyes of one's subjects one realises the separateness of that vision from that provided by one's own culture of origin. For the native researcher however, the ethnographic enterprise surveys not the field of the exotic but that of the *taken for granted*. As in phenomenological analysis the native ethnographer must place his/her culture of origin and its lived world in brackets, rendering it problematic. He or she must assume an objective stance to it – the viewpoint of the outsider. In turn such objective distance is rarely achieved without in turn opening up a fissure in the socially-received self.

Indeed the longer the field work went on the more I became aware that all ethnography of necessity entails self-exploration. In interrogating the young bandsmen about their political attitudes – mentalities that I had once partly shared – I was also asking questions of my own biography. In addition I was coming face to face with issues of political responsibility.

Youth ethnographers have traditionally defended their right to take a naturalistic stance with regard to their subject matter. They have attempted to be non-judgemental when dealing with deviant subcultures and to resist corrective impulses which might obtrude into the fieldwork situation. Subcultural theory has been considerably influenced by a critical tradition within deviancy theory which has tried to uncouple criminological research from the corrective and coercive activities of the state.

'Whose side are we on?' critical sociologists have asked. By and large youth ethnographers have responded to this invocation by identifying with the marginalized and deviant at the receiving end of the state's exercise of disciplinary power. Subcultural theory has rather tended to regard youthful deviance as intrinsically a good thing in so far as is held to be implicitly *oppositional*. But not all youth subcultures are oppositional in any real sense. Indeed some are repositories of chauvinism, racism and sectarianism. Most of us, whatever our belief in the merits of the appreciational stance as a methodological principle, don't wish to be neutral as regards these prejudices.

Have we as researchers – particularly as native ethnographers – a responsibility to challenge the entrenched sexist or racist views of the young people we work with? Most progressive youth workers would unhesitatingly say yes! Many of them have risen to the challenge of providing a forum within which young people can confront their own beliefs. Most progressive youth workers believe that young people should be given the opportunity to transcend the disabling ideologies of sect and race. Should sociologists be absolved of this social responsibility?

Sadly, the Youth Service in Northern Ireland has often found the problem of sectarianism and how to respond to it too hot to handle. It has been unwilling to provide any programme to facilitate political discussion amongst young people or to allow young working-class Protestants and Catholics to explore, on the one hand their own culture and its limits and, on the other, the culture of the other 'side' and its possibilities. The tragedy is that young people are already engaged in exploring their own cultures in more dangerous ways – on the streets.

As our research project developed I came to be haunted by the question of how much of my own political viewpoint should be communicated to the young people who I was spending so much time among? On the one hand, to say nothing to these young people of my own political views while I interrogated them intensely about theirs seemed disingenuous and smacked of the worst colonial anthropology. Additionally, my appreciative openness to their expressed views might suggest to them my concurrence with their sectarian world view. This seemed unwarranted and dishonest. On the other hand, to be seen to demur too vocally at their political assertions and to be completely open about my own political views might at the least close off my access to the group and their lived world. At worst it might put me at physical risk from those – perhaps outside the immediate youth club situation – who were unimpressed by my claims to 'scientific objectivity'!

As it turned out this wasn't a great problem when dealing with the young people themselves. Like young people elsewhere my subjects were amazingly open and willing, indeed eager, to talk about their activities. They were prepared to examine their own attitudes and prejudices – even if they did often proceed to rationalize these. In one of the youth clubs I attended I ran a discussion group which met regularly over a six week period and provided a highly successful forum for an exchange of ideas between researcher and subjects. As they got to know me they became quite prepared to openly debate political questions with me. They, I think, learnt, as I did, to accept the significant political differences that existed between us. They came to value, I believe, the opportunity to explore the interiority of their own normally, sullen, unreflective political culture. Oh that such openness were as common in adult political circles in Northern Ireland!

3

Situating Sectarianism: Territory, Identity and Empire in Ulster

Introduction

In this chapter I propose to examine the historical and political background to the entrenched sectarian divisions which characterize Northern Ireland society. In Ulster the ongoing conflict of national aspiration remains one of the rawest in the advanced capitalist world. In twentieth-century Northern Ireland, as indeed in many other colonized regions, class relations and ethnic mobilizations relate in the most complex of ways. And as we might expect, youth cultural formations reflect that matrix of relations. Our theories of youth subculture have been dominated by a metropolitan 'pure class model'. This has tended to overlook the role of both the gender and ethnic dynamics involved in youth formations. In an imperialised region, or 'ethnic frontier' like Ulster, one has to examine how youth-cultural practices crystallize around not only the *class* but also the *ethnic* dimension of their parental cultures.

Theorizing Sectarianism in Northern Ireland

In many ways it seems particularly perverse that those researching youth-related issues in Northern Ireland have been slow to examine the active role of the young in the genesis and reproduction of ethnic identity. How are we to explain this in the context of Northern Ireland's ongoing political conflict which clearly involves a clash of national aspirations and a form of political mobilization based on ethnic solidarities?

The answer would seem to lie partly in the tendency to reduce the analysis of ethnicity in Ireland to the question of sectarianism.

63

Sectarianism in turn is treated as an aberrant mentality based on outmoded religious prejudices. Yet the reality in Northern Ireland is that the civil conflict is *not* in essence a religious one. Certainly the two communities in Ireland identify each other and themselves by reference to religious affiliation. And Loyalism in particular certainly utilizes religious representations in its political discourse – as witnessed in its traditional dedication 'For God and Ulster'. However, in Northern Ireland religious identifications serve fundamentally as ethnic markers for communities with conflicting *political* aspirations. These aspirations are the product of a specific colonial situation.

In general we rightly tend to regard sectarianism, like racism, as a pernicious evil. On the other hand the expression of ethnic identity, particularly that of minorities subject to political oppression or economic exploitation, is often viewed as an intrinsically 'good thing'. In other words we tend to use the term sectarianism for negatively-evaluated ethnic modes of differentiation such as are found in contemporary Ulster.

Whatever the normative value of this term, its use often precludes an adequate explanation of how such divisions within the working class in fact appear and how they are reproduced across the generations. As Phil Cohen has argued (1988), those concerned with combating racism in the school or youth club often fall back on a deficit model of working-class culture to 'explain' the persistence of racism or sectarianism amongst the working-class young. In this model, ' "teaching against racism" becomes too easily incorporated within the (traditional) remit of the civilizing mission *vis-à-vis* the working class. Reason and tolerance are made the prerogative of the "educated classes" while "unreason" and racism become inherent traits of the rest' (1988). Such an approach fails to address the historical conditions under which patterns of working-class ethnicity express themselves.

During the 1970s many British-trained social scientists were perhaps too inclined to assess the 'Northern Ireland problem' in terms of a somewhat mechanical model of British 'class politics'. In addition, for many Irish socialists who have to deal with the destructive disunity of the working class it seemed imperative to stress the common economic interests of working-class people in Northern Ireland. To do so and to reveal the 'false consciousness' of sectarianism would, it was hoped, dispel this phantasm.

Within this perspective sectarianism was often seen as the product of some form of ideological manipulation. Young people tended to be viewed as the passive victims of sectarianism – initiated into sectarian attitudes and political behaviour by either the operation of the segregated education system or by their immersion into the 'traditional prejudices' of their local communities.

An emotive commitment to class loyalty is fused with a formalistic approach to politics in this reductionist interpretation of sectarianism. Seen from the perspective of the 'pure class model' of British society, Northern Ireland, with its enduring sectarian divisions, seemed an aberrant social formation. 'Normal politics' seemed an impossibility.

British labourism when confronted with the political reality of sectarian division in the Irish working class has too often retreated to positions of moralism and indeed chauvinism. Sectarianism is treated as a type of *false consciousness*. It is seen as the result of ideological manipulation by bourgeois interests. By playing the Orange card, division within the working class is fomented in order to secure the interests of capital. It is believed that a good dose of syndicalist spirit and British social-democratic reform will create the conditions in which Protestant and Catholic workers will bury their differences and 'recognise' their true interests.

Of course when this didn't happen in the years after 1972 and during the introduction of Direct Rule (under a Labour administration from 1974 to 1978) cruder explanations were turned to. Sectarianism came to be viewed as a form of irredentist 'tribalism'. Within this perspective the structural relation between class and sectarian division and the mediating role of British imperialism in the north of Ireland cannot even be posed, let alone explained. Sectarian movements and divisions can only be treated moralistically as unfortunate aberrations from economically-rooted class solidarities, as 'unreason'.

In turn, the question of young people and sectarianism, as we have seen, is reduced to the problem of how individual prejudice is acquired and how it might be abandoned by the introduction of some correctional practice. The attention of the liberal conscience fixes on the education system which is identified as both the cause of sectarian persistence and, if reformed, as a potential antidote to it.

The parallels with the incapacity of the 'race-relations industry' in Britain to understand the political significance of racism, and the historic role of British imperialism in creating and sustaining the ethnic divisions within the British working class, is striking. As Paul Gilroy has argued:

> Racism as it exists today cannot be treated simply from a sociological perspective, it has to be located historically and in terms of the wider structures and relations of British society. The historical roots of racist practices within the British state, the British dominant classes, and the 'British' working class, go deep and cannot be reduced to simple ideological phenomena. They have been conditioned, if not determined, by the historical development of colonial societies which was central to the reproduction of British imperialism. This process generated a specific type of 'nationalism' pertinent in the formation of British classes long before the 'immigration' issue became a central aspect of political discourse (1982).

If we are to understand the complex relation between class and sectarianism in Northern Ireland, we must recognize from the outset the difficulties Marxism as a form of critical social analysis has had in theorizing non-class divisions.

Gilroy (1982) argues with regard to the ethnic differentiation of the contemporary British working class:

> Though for the social analyst 'race' and class are necessarily abstractions at different levels, black consciousness of race and class cannot be empirically separated. The class character of black struggles is not the result of the fact that blacks are predominantly proletarian, though this is true. It is established in the fact that their struggles for civil rights, freedom from state harassment, or as waged workers, are instances of the process by which the working class is constituted politically. . .

Marxist political economy roots its analysis of social class in an abstract understanding of the social organization of economic production. This formal level of analysis does not specifically address the concrete historical formation of the working class within the mode of production. Gender and ethnic social relations receive no theoretical treatment in Marx's most developed work, as represented in *Capital*.[1] Yet quite clearly these social divisions have significant import for modalities of political mobilization.

As Liam O'Dowd (1980) has argued, an adequate materialist analysis of the Northern Ireland question must

> confirm the importance of social divisions other than class in all historical capitalist societies. Sectarianism is not a superstructural phenomena floating free of an abstracted economic base which in turn is divided into classes. In NI sectarian division is a *material* reality which has been constituted and re-constituted throughout the history of capital accumulation and class struggle in Ireland as a whole. It is not merely an overlay on class divisions to be seen as something which is either more or less important than class. As a material reality it has a history embedded in colonisation, industrial revolution and the emergence of new class forms under capitalism. Class in NI, as elsewhere, is not simply a matter of an 'economic relation' – it cross-cuts politics, ideology and culture (O'Dowd, 1980).

Sectarianism must be understood as a historical phenomenon. The British solution to the historic 'Irish Question' was to partition the island in 1920. This political step was justified by the metropolitan state as the only way to reconcile the conflicting aspiration of Unionists and Nationalists and to avert civil war. Partition also of course served to further British strategic and economic interests. By effectively securing Unionist hegemony in Ulster, British imperial interests were secured throughout Ireland.[2]

The Partition settlement bequeathed to Ireland two reactionary confessional states. In turn each of these sponsored states came to be dependent for its political support on cross-class alliances mobilised around forms of populist ideology. A 'pure model' of a class society did not develop.

Today of course, it is being increasingly argued by sociologists that not only is the pure class model of political mobilisation inappropriate to understanding political life in Northern Ireland, but that it also faces severe difficulties in explaining cultural and political developments – including youth subcultural formations – in Britain itself.[3]

The post-war immigration from the West Indies and from the

Indian subcontinent was accompanied by the growth of popular racism amongst the white population. This was sustained by the discriminatory legislation of the British state. However this ideological code had its origins, Gilroy argues (1982), in the sedimented racial mythologies of the high imperialist era. The growth of racism together with the radical restructuring of the British economy since 1980 which has found blacks increasingly economically marginalized, has significantly affected the character of class relations within contemporary Britain. As Stuart Hall (1978) concludes:

> The class relations which inscribe the black fractions of the working class function as race relations. The two are inseparable. Race is the modality in which class relations are experienced. . .

From the late 1970s British researchers began to argue that black youth sub-cultures in post-war Britain had to be understood as constituting a *political* response to a racism bequeathed by British imperialism. These reflections in turn led the CCCS theorists to reflect more generally on the constitution of ethnicity within youth cultures.[4]

A characteristic feature of the work of the CCCS group has been that their work as far back as *Rituals* (Hall and Jefferson, 1976) did involve a conception of class culture which went beyond the narrow sociological fetishing of the working-class 'community'.[5] It also represented a serious attempt to develop the narrowly-economic model of class which at the time informed much of Marxist political science.[6] By considering the sphere of cultural relations as a domain of class contestation, they had undoubtedly committed themselves to a dialogue with feminism and black power.

Indeed the CCCS ethnographic work on the sub-cultural worlds of skinheads and Rastas had already raised questions about the interaction between class and ethnicity within youth subculture.[7] The critical ethnography of both black youth formations and marginalised white youth did hint that a category of social analysis was missing from the Gramscian problematic embraced by the CCCS theorists – namely an understanding of imperialism. This was, after all, a central historical dimension in the formation of the dominant culture in Britain. Social historians had in fact long drawn our attention to the direct association between the growth of social-imperialist ideology in Britain and the emergence of the 'youth question' (Springhall, 1977, Pearson, 1983). As we all know, the development of youth movements in Britain from the Church Lads Brigade to Baden Powell's Scouting movement was conditioned by eugenic and racist concerns with the health and discipline of the children of the imperial power. Significantly up until recently, uniformed youth movements of a confessional character have been particularly strong in Northern Ireland. Their imperialist ethos articulated particularly well with the local political sensibilities of Unionism.[8]

Historical origins of sectarian division in Ulster

To adequately understand the material character of sectarianism and how this conditions the social development of young people in Northern Ireland today we must now examine the historical origins of Ulster society. Frank Wright (1987) has characterised post-plantation Ulster as being 'an ethnic frontier'. He defines this term for us:

> The places I call ethnic frontiers are places where the populations of citizen and native were fairly evenly balanced numerically ... the citizen population was not only the overwhelming element in landed, urban propertied or office-holding strata, but also comprised a great part of the lower strata of peasants and artisans.

What was distinctive about the seventeenth-century colonisation of Ulster, and distinguished it from areas subject to nineteenth-century British imperialist rule was the scale of the settlements. The plantation established a land-owning Protestant ascendancy in Ulster. However it also settled a mass colon population drawn from all social classes. This created the conditions within which ethnic differentiation would remain as important a historical dynamic as class division in Ireland.

The original plans for the plantation envisaged that the old Gaelic order would be replaced in toto by a new social order, of armed British merchant capital. A planted population of

Protestant settlers drawn from England and the lowlands of Scotland would displace the native Catholic population. The intention of the English state was to establish, within the north and west of Ulster, areas from which the native Irish would be totally expelled. These areas would be inhabited solely by Anglo-Scottish colonists and would serve as effective bridgeheads of English rule in this most Gaelic and intransigent area of Ireland.

As it turned out, there were early difficulties in attracting sufficient planters to settle and hold the lands confiscated from the Gaelic earls. This necessitated an accommodation with the native population. Workers were needed for the new forms of agricultural commodity production. Paying tenants were needed to maintain the value of rents and land holdings. It proved impossible to find enough of each amongst the Protestant planters. Accordingly land was granted, admittedly under restricted-tenure conditions, to Catholics. English plans to displace the Irish population were effectively abandoned. Planter and Gael would have to live together on the same 'narrow ground'.

The native population was neither totally assimilated into the new order nor – despite the existence of legal restrictions imposed upon them in the form of the Penal Laws – excluded from it. Planter society and native society continued to co-exist together. Each developed its distinctive ethnic identity in relation to the other. Political relations between the two communities were, as they remain today, mediated by a metropolitan state actively pursuing its own ends. *From the outset sectarian relations were politically constituted within the framework of British colonial interests.*

Derry developed as the border garrison of this ethnic frontier. The plantation of the county of Derry had been trusted by the English state to a number of London merchant companies, who already had invested funds for a plantation in Virginia USA. These companies renamed the town Londonderry to signal the link with the colonizing metropolis. In the first decades of the seventeenth century they fortified the town which was strategically located at the mouth of the river Foyle.

The settlement of Protestant merchants, ex-soldiers, tradesmen and farmers became a bulwark of British mercantalist domination within a hinterland still overwhelmingly Gaelic and resistant to English rule. Derry became, as it has remained, a microcosm of political life in Ireland.

The city was to endure a number of sieges throughout the seventeenth century as, in the context of greater British political conflicts, the native Irish seized the opportunity to rise and attack the Planters. It is however the siege of 1688–89 which has become lodged in the Loyalist popular memory and is still celebrated annually by the Apprentice Boys organization. In that year the Protestants of Ulster declared for William of Orange in his struggle against the Catholic James II for the English throne. They held out for over four months against a combined Irish and French army sent by James to occupy the garrison for the Jacobite cause, enduring great hardship and starvation as a result of the blockade imposed by James's troops.

Historians argue about the strategic significance of the Siege of Derry within the Jacobite wars. However, what is not in dispute is the emergence of the story of the siege as a key *political myth* within Ulster Loyalism. Leonard Thompson (1985) has defined this term for us:

> By a political myth I mean a tale told about the past to legitimise or discredit a regime; and by a political mythology, a cluster of such myths that reinforce one another and jointly constitute the historical element in the ideology of the regime or its rival.

Thompson has examined the construction and transformations of Afrikaner political myths in South Africa. For the Afrikaners of the Broederbond the Voortrekker Covenant of 1838 associated with the victory of the Boers over the Zulu is a key myth still informing political sensibilities in white South Africa today. For the Loyalists of Ulster the Siege of Derry performs similar functions. Such narratives with their motifs of encirclement, collective endurance and heroism appropriate the past – as myth. They do so in order to make sense of the present experience of the laager.

In Derry a political myth was to become embodied in the very topography of the city. Almost 300 years after the ending of the siege, Protestant youths paint on the gable of a wall in the strongly Loyalist Fountain area and now the only remaining Protestant-dominated estate on the west bank of Derry, the slogan: LONDONDERRY STILL UNDER SIEGE – NO SURRENDER! Young Loyalists in common parlance refer to Catholics as *rebels*.

Young Republicans with not a little sense of historical irony, inscribed in painted letters six-foot high the slogan – THEY HUNGER FOR JUSTICE on the exterior of the city's ancient walls during the Hunger-Strike campaign of 1981.

Sectarianism and capitalist development in Ulster

The development of capitalist relations in eighteenth and early-nineteenth century Ireland in no way undermined the ethnic differentiation which had developed as a result of the plantation. Certainly capitalism tended to erode the preferential economic basis enjoyed by Protestant labour and small tenant farmers. By the end of the eighteenth century all labour became increasingly subject to the wage form and Protestant and Catholic labourers became competitors in a common labour market, as they were already for rented land.

Protestants from the lower orders began to utilize the tactic of sectarian exclusivism – the Orange Order emerged in the early 1790s – in an attempt to prevent the erosion of their marginal economic privileges vis-à-vis the native labouring classes. In the context of capitalist modernization and political reaction after 1795 ethnic solidarities became entrenched (Gibbon, 1975).

Capitalist development had advanced further and faster in the north east of Ireland than in any other part of the island. In so far as it was accompanied by the extension of both state administrative power and limited bourgeois democracy it created opportunities for the political advancement of Catholic interests. As Wright explains:

> The onset of capitalism tended to create space in which the native societies of the ethnic frontier could undermine established patterns of citizen dominance. But the process involved self-assertion that also sharpened the distinctions between 'citizen' and 'native' and increased possibilities for open antagonism (1987).

The Catholic population became politically mobilised, first in the struggle for Catholic emancipation and later in the movement for Home Rule. As they did the internecine struggle over scarce resources between the Protestant and Catholic masses became overlaid by the political struggle between the enfranchised Catholic middle class and the Protestant landed interest that began to crystallize around the national question. With the extension of the franchise and the rapid urbanization of the north east of Ulster in the second half of the nineteenth century, these two axes of conflict fused in the most explosive of ways.

Throughout the century and into the next, both Belfast and Londonderry were to experience recurrent rioting occasioned by election activity, by parliamentary developments concerning the Irish question and, of course, by clashes between rival groups of marchers asserting traditional rights to parade. In the eighteenth century these conflicts had been largely local confrontations between Protestant and Catholic groups. Now in the age of mass democracy they became generalized into a pattern of sectarian confrontation between two confessional communities with conflicting national aspirations.

In Derry, for instance, the perennial rioting which surrounded the Loyalists' annual Siege of Derry celebrations developed significantly in scale as the advent of the railways enabled hundreds of Orange supporters from all over Ulster to converge on the town. Even before the opening of the rail link to Belfast and the other small towns of the north west of Ireland, government commissioners were noting the growth in the size and the changing complexion of the siege celebrations. In the climate of political tension which accompanied the passing of Catholic emancipation, loyalists from all over the north west flocked to Derry for the Orange parades. As a local commentator noted:

One circumstance stated to us in evidence as tending to aggravate the sense of annoyance and irritation on the part of the Roman Catholics towards the Shutting the Gates of Derry, is, that the persons who take part in it are not the citizens of Derry alone, (who might be supposed naturally to feel a local pride in the recollection of the achievements thus celebrated) but persons supposed to belong to the party, usually called the Orange party, who on these days crowd to the city of Londonderry, not from the county of Derry only, but also from the counties of Donegal and Tyrone. This circumstance is felt as depriving the ceremony of the character of being connected with merely local associations, and of giving it the complexion of being an occasion for general rallying of an affiliated party, to make public demonstrations of physical strength and of sentiments and sympathies which its members hold in common.[9]

As the century proceeded it became clear that the metropolitan British state was unsure of its governmental role on its ethnic frontier. It was unable or unwilling to bring the full force of the law against plebeian Orangeism – witnessed in its inability to properly police the various Procession Acts passed throughout the nineteenth century in an attempt to curb sectarian parades and preserve public order. The government officers who conducted the various commissions of enquiry into the periodic rioting which traumatised Belfast and Derry, might fulminate against Orangeism declaring that:

> The Orange system seems to have no other practical result than as a means of keeping up the Orange festivals and celebrating them, leading as they do to violence, outrage, religious animosities, hatred between the classes and too often bloodshed and loss of life (Hepburn, 1978).

However, the authorities were reluctant to tackle Orangeism head on. Indeed on occasions they were to turn to Loyalist militancy to counteract Catholic dissidence and secure British imperial interests. In the absence of consistent governmentality, or indeed a state monopoly of physical force, political life inevitably took the form of a war of position and deterrence between the two communities.

The sectarian spatialization of Ulster had been established in the original pattern of plantation settlement. It was maintained throughout the late eighteenth century and early nineteenth century in the context of agrarian conflict. However it was reproduced in new and virulent forms in the mass urban society of the late nineteenth century.

Belfast experienced in the second half of the nineteenth century a series of explosive demographic changes. In 1821 Belfast was still a small town of some 19,000 souls. By 1871 its population had soared to 174,412 and by 1891 stood at over 350,000. Belfast at the end of the eighteenth century was a Presbyterian stronghold with a small Catholic minority. However, by the middle of the nineteenth century the Catholic population had expanded dramatically and was now a third of the city's total population.[10]

Derry, too, was to experience significant if less dramatic social changes. The population of the town expanded from around 5,000 in 1800 to 25,000 in 1871 and by 1891 was over 33,000 (Murphy, 1981). By the later decades of the century the city had a thriving shirt industry as domestic forms of production were transformed with the introduction of machinofacture by Scottish entrepreneurs. No lesser an authority than Karl Marx was to quote the case of the developing Derry shirt and collar industry to illustrate the changing relation between the factory system and domestic industry. As he notes in volume one of *Capital*:

> Besides the factory operatives, the manufacturing workmen and the handicraftsmen, whom it concentrates in large masses at one spot, and directly commands, capital also sets in motion, by means of invisible threads, another army; that of the workers in the domestic industries, who dwell in the large towns and are also scattered over the face of the country. An example – the shirt factory of Messrs. Tillie at Londonderry, which employs 1,000 operatives in the factory itself, and 9,000 people spread up and down the country and working in their own houses.

At the turn of the century there were over 30 shirt factories established in Derry, directly employing some 7,000 persons, with as many again hired as outworkers in the surrounding districts (Mullin, 1986).

The port was also expanding, in part due to a developing North American trade – much of it concerned with the transporting of the famine-stricken emigrants from the western sea board counties to America. The expansion of this trade, in turn, encouraged the development of ship building and from 1814 to 1924 ships were built in yards on the Foyle. At the peak of the yards' expansion during the First World War there were some 2,000 men and youths involved in the industry which was now controlled by the Tyneside consortium of Swan and Hunter. In the post-war recession however the Clarke yard quickly went to the wall with a disastrous impact on the level of male unemployment in the city.

By 1891 the population of the city was over 33,000 and had

spread well beyond the confines of the walled city. As significant as the steady expansion of the population was the changing religious composition of the town. In 1834 the number of Protestants and Catholics in the area had been roughly equal. However by 1891 Catholics were in a clear majority comprising some 56 per cent of the population. As the surrounding rural area suffered a dramatic population loss due to the ravages of the potato famine, displaced Catholic cottiers flocked to the town in search of employment, leading one of the local Protestant papers to note that:

> The character of the population has undergone a material change in late years, large numbers of the Celtic race having immigrated into the city and found employment as labourers and in other capacities (Doak, 1978).

This Catholic population settled in the south and west of the town outside the walls in the area known as the Bogside. Widespread overcrowding occurred in the cheap insanitary buildings thrown up to house the influx of rural workers. This resulted in a severe public-health problem and a high mortality rate considerably above the UK rate (Duffy, 1985). A Protestant artisan area developed on the eastern flank of the walled city which eventually became known as the Fountain.

Despite its relatively small size the city became territorially stratified on both sectarian and class lines. The Fountain and the Bogside emerged as both exclusively working class *and* religiously segregated. By the 1830s the residential class segregation of the town between bourgeois and Protestant dwellings within the walls, and working class and largely Catholic multi-occupancy houses outside, was well advanced and was reflected in the recorded preponderance of epidemic and poverty in the working-class suburbs.

As historians have noted, this rapid urban development imposed severe tensions on the existing exclusively Protestant order:

> The city walls about one mile in length enclosed an area at the top of a hill where the residents and owners of businesses were Protestant and comparatively wealthy; outside the walls to the south and west lay an area where the majority of the people were poor and Catholic. To the Catholics the siege celebrations

were not in memory of past glories but the defiant voice of Protestantism announcing stridently that 'what we have we hold' (Doak, 1978).

Indeed from the 1840s right up to the 1960s the distinctive topography of Derry was to exert a particular influence on the form of riots in the city. These habitually occurred when Loyalists twice-yearly celebrated the siege of 1688–89, in December in the Shutting of the Gates ceremony when an effigy of the traitor Lundy was ritualistically burned, and in August when the Apprentice Boys marched to celebrate the relief of the city from the besieging Jacobite armies. On these occasions Catholics counter-demonstrated. They tried to gain access to the walled part of the city through the gates leading from the Bogside in order to confront the Loyalists marching inside the walls. The Loyalists for their part attempted to repel the invaders often with the direct help of the police and military. The psychological effect of the city's walls as a fortified pale excluding Catholics was further reinforced when the Apprentice Boys erected a substantial memorial pillar to the Governor of the Protestant garrison during the siege on the western walls in 1828.[11] This towered over the Catholic Bogside until it was unceremoniously blown up by an IRA bomb in 1972. Significantly it was the clashes surrounding the relief celebrations in 1969 which initiated the current period of civil strife in Northern Ireland.

The primacy of territory in the emerging popular politics of mid-nineteenth century Ulster was not only a question of residential boundaries, although this was its most concrete expression. It became also linked on the one hand to questions of access to scarce economic resources – jobs and housing. On the other hand, it became associated with wider political questions concerning the integrity of the national territory in the historical context of the rise of the Home Rule movement. In the minds of popular Loyalism these representations of territory – the residential, occupational and national – became intertwined.

Loyalist sentiments were given their sharpest focus in the traditional Orange marches. These gained their largest followings amongst the Protestant population when the threat of Catholic political advances – emancipation, Fenianism and Home Rule – were in the air. The Orange organizations provided the institutional framework to cement together the different Protestant sects and to sustain networks of sectarian nepotism. The marches often involved parades through either mixed or predominantly-Catholic areas where they were likely to cause offence with their Loyalist triumphalism. These confrontations concretized the aggressive territorial assertion at the heart of political life in the ethnic frontier.

As the historian of populist Orangeism, Henry Patterson (1980) has argued:

> The basic principle of sectarian exclusivism upon which Orangeism was organized, achieved its most significant embodiment in marches and the frequent violent confrontations they produced. In the practices of the march and confrontation Orange identity was forged.

This identity was, somewhat paradoxically, both an ethnic *and* a class identity. The division of residential territory in the context of industrial Belfast and Derry took its clearest form in not only the confessional purity but also the class homogeneity of the Loyalist strongholds. In turn, residential sectarian exclusivism sustained Protestant workers' demands for privileged right of access to skilled employment. Urban rioting was often directed, not only at securing the exclusively Protestant character of Loyalist-dominated neighbourhoods, but also at achieving the expulsion of Catholic workers from certain firms and occupations. In the riots in Belfast in 1856, 1872 and 1920, Catholic workers were expelled from the shipyards as they were from certain residential districts. As Wright (1987) says:

> everything a community had which helped it to sustain its position – control of economic, residential and occupational space – would become a resource in battle. Privileges of Protestants would be defended, not because they were privileges, but because the defence of every privilege was locked into the defence of everything.

Belfast was to endure serious rioting with loss of life and sectarian expulsions in 1857, 1864, 1886, 1898, and 1920. Derry was to experience similar if smaller disturbances in 1841, 1868, 1870,

1885, 1899[12] and indeed on a host of other occasions associated with the siege celebrations. On these occasions, when direct sectarian violence and expulsions amplified the polarization of the two communities, rigid territorial boundaries between them became established. Every generation in Ulster since the mid-nineteenth century has either directly experienced serious sectarian conflict or inherited stories concerning such strife from its parents. A vivid popular memory of past clashes – their form, location and outcome – has been transmitted from generation to generation, and given renewed saliency in every fresh outbreak of violence. The sectarian territorialization of urban space established as a result of these confrontations continues to provide the spatial framework within which sectarian youth cultures flourish.

Ethnicity, territory and youth

To many, both inside and outside Northern Ireland, this cyclical pattern of sectarian violence begetting ethnic segregation seems a uniquely Irish situation. Yet, as historians of the Irish diaspora remind us, the backlash against Famine migrants, 'produced anti-Irish riots as far apart as Boston and Liverpool, New York and London' (Hepburn, 1983).

Moreover, as English social historians have shown, urban youths were centrally involved in ethnically-motivated gang conflict in late nineteenth century and early twentieth century British cities. Stephen Humphries (1981) has noted in his oral history of working-class youth in England, how perennial youthful neighbourhood conflicts were most likely to escalate into serious violence when they involved conflicts between ethnic groups, particularly newly-arrived immigrant groups. These newcomers to the inner city found themselves in competition with the indigenous working class for housing and jobs. In these circumstances as he notes, 'territorial divisions were deepened and reinforced by racial division'.

In London, Liverpool, Glasgow and Cardiff competition between the indigenous, unskilled working class and the new influx of Irish and Jewish immigrants for scarce resources, such as jobs and housing, led to tensions and physical confrontations. As Humphries documents, in these cities gangs of teenage males often played a key role in instigating ethnic conflict as territorially-focused popular street activity.

In these cities of high Irish immigration where Irish political questions had significant resonance in local politics, gang subcultures have continued to crystallize around residual sectarian hostilities now often transposed to the rivalry of football teams.

Phil Cohen (1988) has probed in some depth the historical construction and social reproduction of territorially-focused, popular racism – a phenomenon he has labelled a 'nationalism of the neighbourhood'. As he argues, the English working class at the turn of the century developed a fiercely localistic culture. This generated its own modes of ethnic exclusivism, autonomous from but related to the 'official racism' of social imperialism. These practices of ethnicity

> were bound up with rules and rituals of territory, which staked out magical forms of ownership and control over key sites of proletarian combination outside the labour process itself. These rough and ready rituals were largely enacted through street cultures, and by young men putting their aggression to work in defining and defending 'their' areas, against real or imaginary attack (1988).

In Ireland, historians have also noted the widespread involvement of youth in sectarian street conflict. They have recorded their role in sectarian boundary-maintenance practices involving the expressive display of Loyalist and Nationalist symbols with a distinct territorial focus. For example, historians of Orangeism – centrally concerned with the relation between plebeian Loyalism and the hegemonic politics of Unionism – have noted the prominent role played by youth in initiating sectarian trouble as popular street activity from the second half of the nineteenth century. Peter Gibbon (1975) discussing the sectarian riots of the 1850s and 1860s in Belfast, reports an eye witness account of such a riot made to the Riot Commission set up to investigate the causes of the regular civil disturbances of the period. In Sandy Row, a neighbourhood comprised largely of unskilled Protestant workers in west Belfast, a local landlord reported the ritualized process of confrontation between rival groups at the interface of Protestant and Catholic residential areas:

The riot begins as boys and girls of each party collect, party feeling [becomes] so excitable that older people come out and the mêlée begins.

This witness was able to identify particular locations (such as an open area between the Protestant Sandy Row and the Catholic Pound area) which had become established sites of sectarian confrontation. Here in the riotous summer of 1857, he reports that

the two parties had met: they were lumps of little boys from fourteen to sixteen and from that to ten . . . they fought there for eight weeks after the 'Twelfth' [of July] (Gibbon, 1975).

As Gibbon notes, these 'shatter zones' at the interstices of rival sectarian ghettoes became the site of habitual confrontations, 'only through a process by which they acquire a tradition of conflict between rival gangs of youths.'

Similarly in Derry, rioting had a distinctively ritualistic character involving set-piece confrontations at long-established flash points located at the interface of Protestant and Catholic areas. In Derry, as we have seen, the riots were often associated with Loyalist celebration of the siege and rival Catholic counterdemonstrations. Marching bands and their youthful supporters played a key role in this faction fighting. As a police witness who appeared before the 1869 Londonderry Riots Inquiry Commission reported:

The flute band of the Bogside is out oftener. They do not appear in the city or within the walls; they parade more within their own boundaries, along Foyle Street and the Quay [Catholic areas]; sometime they visit us at the Waterside [mixed area containing Protestant strongholds] and when they come there a large crowd gathers. I mean one party would lie in wait for the other and throw stones (Doak, 1978).

Conor Doak describes the clashes of 1913:

In Fountain Street . . . bonfires were lit and the crowd sang 'Derry's Walls' and 'Rule Britannia'. An opposing crowd gathered opposite the lower end of Fountain Street, that is at the top of Bridge Street. At that point an arch had been erected with the words 'Home Rule and a Fenian King' clearly displayed. When the opposing factions clashed the police tried to separate them but their efforts were frustrated because every time they charged up Fountain Street the nationalist mob followed on their heels; when they pushed the Catholics down Bridge Street the Protestants adopted the same tactic. Each side cheered in turn when they felt that their opponents were being punished.

As he notes, these riots were highly stylized. Each side, by and large, respected the other's territorial rights. Wholesale invasion of the other's area was in fact rare. Each party was usually satisfied with the symbolic gesture of a brief incursion into the outer periphery of 'enemy territory'.

How 'political' were these confrontations in reality? Cohen (1984) has in fact argued that the street battles of turn of the century urban Britain between rival gangs

were only a more overt and violent expression of the kind of local feelings which were expressed more decorously though no less competitively, organised in displays of municipal (socialist) pride. Territoriality and public propriety worked together to produce a framework of intensely insular loyalties, a sectional class consciousness based on a 'nationalism of the neighbour-hood' and popular sovereignties of place.

Similarly Peter Gibbon (1975) has argued that the form of rioting in Protestant working class Belfast has much to do with 'living out the obligations attached to the personalistic bonds within the community'. Indeed Loyalist cultural practices such as traditional parades and street activities and decorations as well as perennial concerns with 'telling the difference' between Protestants and Catholics, might be best understood as being more concerned with sustaining a Protestant sense of a 'loyal and true' community than with identifying and repelling 'the other'. In other words these boundary-maintenance practices function primarily to sustain localistic loyalties rather than to generate mere hostility to recognized outsiders.

Gibbon's perspective, like Cohen's, seeks to interpret working class sectarianism as a form of regressive ethnicity which is only intelligible in relation to, on the one hand, the hegemonizing influence of social imperialism – in the guise of Unionism in Ireland – and, on the other, plebeian resistance to bourgeois values and leadership expressed through a combative localism.

These managed rituals of violence and the forms of common-sense knowledge about riot – how to do it and how to minimize the risk to oneself and one's peers – have been inherited by a contemporary generation of Ulster teenagers. Riot remains a favoured mode for the militant assertion of territorial claims. It retains a role in the politics of communal deterrence. This patrimony has been eagerly appropriated today by a new generation of Ulster's youth.

Although adolescents often participated in the faction fights of the nineteenth century, sectarian riots were, up to the 1930s, still dominated by adult males. Firearms usually played a small part in these clashes. And, considering the frequency and scale of the intercommunal conflict, the actual fatalities on each side throughout the nineteenth century were relatively low. The majority of those who died were killed by gun shot from the police and militia who throughout the second half of the century proved particularly inept in controlling riotous situations. All of this changed in the era of industrialized war and with the intensification of the national struggle.

The early twentieth century saw the introduction of more powerful and accurate firearms into the sectarian struggle. And with the appearance of trained gunmen on both sides, many of whom had gained their military experience in the trenches of Flanders, the character of sectarian violence changed dramatically. Derry experienced bloody clashes in June 1920 which left fifteen dead in a week's fighting between the IRA and the UVF, and the town was occupied by an enormous force of British military (Farrell, 1983). In Belfast, between July and September of that year, 64 people lost their lives (Boyd, 1987).

As Doak (1978) has noted with regard to Derry:

> The riot of 1920 marked a distinctive turning-point in the pattern of sectarian strife. The ritual of conflict at processions and elections disappears in the violent years between 1920–22 when more sophisticated weaponry, the psychological impact of the Great War and a complex series of political developments, both at national and local level, produced unprecedented

violence. Between 1868 and 1920 – the period of the most serious rioting – four people had died as a result of the disturbances; in one week in June 1920 five times as many perished.

The paramilitarization of intercommunal violence first witnessed in the 1913–22 period was seen again after 1970. Highly trained loyalist and republican gunmen once again clashed on the streets. This led to what could be termed a 'professionalization' of the sectarian conflict. Small numbers of adult males from paramilitary groups engaged in sniping exchanges with each other or the security forces. Premeditated sectarian assassination attempts also became common.

On the other hand, from the 1970s mass street rioting seemed to inherit the ritualized forms of disorder established in the previous century. This relatively less dangerous, territorially-focused activity became the province of the young. Adolescent gangs are now playing the leading role in the policing of sectarian territorial boundaries in the Derry and Belfast of the 1980s – often along the geographical divides etched into the sectarian urban landscape in the last century. This sectarian territoriality of the young in Northern Ireland has its roots not only in the political conflict but also in the more 'universal' working-class codes of community, territory and race.

British imperialism and Ireland

By the later decades of the nineteenth century, with the emergence of mass democratic politics and the expansion of the British Empire, the British state was becoming increasingly implicated in the 'Irish Question'. Social imperialism became an important mobilizing ideology in Conservative attempts to secure the support of the newly-enfranchised lower-middle classes and skilled workers (Semmel, 1960).

In this context the Right in England began to more systematically champion the Unionist cause. The Conservatives were to accuse Gladstone and his Home Rule supporters of 'plunging the knife into the heart of the British Empire'. Conservatives pledged their support for the Unionist cause. For if one's 'kith and kin', as

Fig. 3.1 Home Territory: real and imagined
(*Photo: Desmond Bell*)

Bonar Law the Conservative leader designated the Unionists of Ulster, were not to be supported in their demand to remain part of the Empire in what was after all the oldest and nearest British possession, then what hope was there for imperial rule elsewhere? For the Conservatives it was a case of 'the higher interests of the Empire precluding . . . any licence to the majority in Ireland to govern the rest as they please'. As Frank Wright (1987) argues:

> The flag flew over more precarious peripheries and its maintenance in Ireland was part of the new sacred principle of Imperialism.

Nor was the British labour movement immune from this current. As is well known, sections of British labourism flirted with social imperialism. Indeed that peculiar alliance of social progressivism and national chauvinism remained a major current in the British socialist movement up to and beyond the First World War. Fabianism was the most coherent articulation of this social-imperialist current, which sought to justify collectivist and welfare policies in terms of arguments concerning the promotion of 'National Efficiency' and the combative strength of the Empire (Semmel, 1960).

Little wonder that the Labour politics that emerged in Belfast after 1895 failed to take an anti-imperialist stance on the Union. Little wonder that the Protestant workers of Belfast found it hard to distance themselves from Unionist hegemony at a time when the Webbs were entertaining to dinner prominent Conservatives, alongside Liberal-imperialists, in an attempt to cobble together a party of 'National Efficiency' in order to safeguard the integrity of the British Empire. There can be little doubt that the stolidly Unionist stance of the Protestant aristocracy of labour was partly conditioned by the prevailing climate of social imperialism emanating from the metropolitan core of the United Kingdom. Given the uneven character of capitalist development in Ireland and the relative backwardness, economically and socially, of the south, Unionist ideology was able, as Patterson (1980) reminds us, to link, 'opposition to Home Rule with a series of identifications of the Union with "progress" and "civilisation".'

Indeed, as we know, Sidney Webb's enthusiasm for empire

loyalty led him not only into a position of chauvinism, but, under the impact of Karl Pearson's eugenic theories, also into a rampant racism. In 1907 he could declare that

> twenty five per cent of our parents, as Professor Karl Pearson keeps warning us, are producing fifty per cent of the next generation. This can hardly result in anything but national deterioration; or, as an alternative, in this country gradually falling to the Irish and the Jews (quoted in Semmel, 1960).

Within the Social-Darwinist discourse embraced by social imperialism, images of racial degeneration and panics about youthful disorder mixed and merged. This fusion took its most concrete form in the figure of the 'hooligan'. This term was explicitly employed to sound the alarm about working-class juvenile delinquency in the first years of the twentieth century. However, the imagery used to portray this 'frightening new race of people' drew on existing racist representations of the Irish already in common in the British press. As Geoff Pearson (1983) has noted:

> once they were christened, as we might expect, the 'Hooligans' were understood as an entirely unprecedented and 'un-British' phenomenon: indeed, we must allow that it was most ingenuous of late Victorian England to disown the British Hooligan by giving him an 'Irish' name.

The 'hooligan' was christened not only with an Irish name. He also inherited 'Milesian habits' and a Gaelic temperament with its supposed love of anarchy and violence. It was a short step from Tenniel's virulently racist cartoons of the 'Irish Yahoo' to the alien degenerate of the Edwardian era, the 'hooligan'. An ideological code conceptualized in terms of a pseudo-scientific theory of racial evolution and degeneration which functioned to discredit Irish nationalism (Curtis, 1984), became embedded in the collective unconscious of imperial Britain. It was later to surface in free association with respectable fears of youthful anarchy and working-class disorder.

Its important to remember that explicitly racist ideological codes which represent the Catholic Irish as a biologically inferior species to the 'free-born Briton' are largely an import into Ireland *from*

5. *English Child:* "Will you help us to build the pretty castle?" *Irish Child:* "No. Shure and I'll be the one wid the dynamite what blows it up."

(*Funny Folks, 3 June 1882: courtesy of Marcus Free*)

England. Such codes play a small part in the sectarian conflict within the working class in Northern Ireland. Even Ulster Loyalism has, by and large, not expressed its considerable political hostility to the native population in racial terms. Loyalism, apart from a few folk nostrums about 'the Protestant way of life', has not developed any theory about the racial distinctiveness of the Ulster Protestant or inferiority of the native.[13] In the nineteenth and twentieth centuries, Irish nationalism, partly because it attracted some degree of cross-sectarian support in the South of Ireland, could never be treated as just a perfidious Catholic conspiracy.

However, the partition of Ireland, whatever its explicit objectives, had the unintended effect of politically institutionalizing long-established, cultural and economic differences between Protestants and Catholics in Ulster. The cultural roots of sectarian division may lie in the sevententh century colonial plantation of

Ulster; its economic foundation may lie in the uneven development of capitalism in Ireland which saw large scale industrialization confined to the north east with Protestants dominant in the labour market; yet there can be little doubt that the British state, in supporting the Unionist veto against Home Rule and in imposing the Partition settlement, fostered the political and ideological conditions for the growth of sectarianism in twentieth-century Northern Ireland.

The state in Northern Ireland and the institutionalization of sectarianism

As the Home Rule movement grew in strength and made converts within the English liberal establishment, the British claim to Ireland changed in character. Partition became a new strategy for maximizing a continued imperialist presence in a post-colonial era. As Frank Wright (1987) argues, comparing the role of the British state in Ireland with that of the German in West Prussia, the claim of the metropolitan state to its estranged colony

> could not rest on democratic headcounts in respect of the entire territory in question. Democratic principles could only be invoked for the ethnic frontiers where there were citizen majorities. Territorialism was a way of turning democratic values upside down (if we have to have a majority, then we will make one wherever we can) but in turning them upside down they were deprived of their sacred quality. . .

The NI state that was set up as a result of the partition settlement developed as a political apparatus to secure continuing Unionist hegemony. As such, both in its form and function, it sustained sectarian division within Northern Ireland. While preserving the surface features of a liberal democratic state it in effect emptied Northern Ireland politics of any democratic content. From the outset the nationalist minority unwillingly trapped within the new political arrangement denied the Belfast state any legitimacy. The British state, anxious to secure its own interests in post-colonial Ireland, presided over this 'solution' to the Irish Question.

From the outset the Orange state responded to nationalist

intransigence with extensive repression. An armed, and mainly Protestant police force, and an exclusively Protestant special constabulary, were used to curb Catholic dissent (Farrell, 1983). The development of draconian, governmental security measures in the form of the Special Powers Act eroded citizens' legal rights. In so far as these powers were directed almost entirely against the nationalist population, this further alienated Catholics from the new administration.

In Derry, where the Nationalist council refused to recognize the Belfast administration and declared its allegiance to Dail Eireann, 2,000 British troops were sent to the town to police a population of less than 50,000.

In the context of benign neglect from the sovereign parliament in London, the devolved government in Belfast sought to systematically minimize Catholic political representation by tinkering with the franchise and redrawing political boundaries to the advantage of Unionists. This had particularly devastating effects in Derry. By this process of 'gerrymandering' Unionists gained control of the council chamber in a town that was by now three-quarters Catholic. Here, as elsewhere in Northern Ireland, housing policy became subsumed under the demands of Unionist political strategy. Houses were allocated not on the basis of need, but preferentially to Protestant families. Where housing was specifically built for Catholic habitation, it was located in the existing Catholic ghetto areas so as not to upset the delicate political demography of the city. Sectarian residential segregation spread beyond the older inner-city working-class areas to the green field public housing estates built in the 1950s and 1960s. Sectarian spatialization proliferated and indeed became institutionalized and legitimized in public housing administration. As Mike Tomlinson has shown (O'Dowd, 1980), British housing policy in Northern Ireland, even in the Direct Rule era, has done little to tackle this sectarian legacy. Public housing planning has continued to reproduce sectarian division.

Education, the traditional instrument employed by new states to secure social cohesion, remained segregated. The Catholic Church was encouraged by state subsidy to provide voluntary provision for Catholic children. State schools, in turn, became exclusively Protestant (Akenson, 1973). The religious segregation of education has remained unchallenged despite over fifteen years of Direct Rule from London.

Catholics found themselves excluded from state employment, and government ministers openly advocated the awarding of jobs in the private sector on the basis of religion and 'demonstrable loyalty' to the new state. Sixteen years after the introduction of Direct Rule, the British state is still to introduce meaningful legislation to tackle the problem of sectarian discrimination in the workplace.

However it was the belated attempt, by the Stormont state in the 1960s, to manage the transition to the post-war world which led to its demise. Somewhat paradoxically, the collapse of Stormont which occurred so rapidly after the outbreak of serious Catholic dissent in 1968, was due in part to the Unionist government's attempts to restructure the state apparatus and the local economy in an era of multi-national capital penetration and rapid expansion of largely Westminster-funded public expenditure (Farrell, 1976). As the sphere of state intervention in society increased in the social democratic era, so did the scope for nationalist political opposition to the Unionist administration. A new terrain for political struggle opened up in Northern Ireland. A new generation of educated young Catholics found the space to prosecute a broadly-based struggle against Unionist discrimination in housing, the economy and electoral affairs. Derry – a citadel of Unionist power where Catholic grievances were particularly acute – became a focal point for the Civil Rights struggle which gained momentum from the mid-1960s (McCann, 1974).

The period after 1967 saw the rapid distintegration of Unionist social and political order. Premier O'Neill's strategy of managed change came to grief. A combination of intensifying Catholic demands for reform and a militant Loyalist backlash led to his downfall. As the civil and military conflict intensified after 1969, it soon became clear that no class or faction was capable of securing the Protestant state. Westminster was forced to intervene directly in Northern Ireland. The 'Troubles' rapidly became a British problem – the return of the repressed. The role of political and social regulation of an increasingly polarised society passed directly into British hands. In 1972, three years after British troops had marched onto the streets in Derry and Belfast, Westminster assumed direct political responsibility for the government of Northern Ireland.

It did so in the context of a traumatic escalation of intercommunal violence after 1969. Between 1969 and 1974, in perhaps the worst period of sectarian violence and intimidation in the troubled history of Northern Ireland, an estimated 60,000 people, representing nearly a quarter of all households in Belfast, moved house (Darby and Morris, 1974). The Catholic population in Belfast was particularly vulnerable to sectarian intimidation and displaced Catholic families crowded into the Greater Falls area of west Belfast.

Similarly in Derry it is reckoned that between 1968 and 1985 some 6,000 Protestants moved from the Catholic-dominated city side of the town across the river to the predominantly-Protestant Waterside area.[14] Most families in both Belfast and Derry were moving as a result of the real or perceived threat of sectarian violence. Most moved, seeking the security of the confessional ghetto. In working-class areas of Belfast and Derry religious residential segregation is now virtually total. In Derry the river Foyle now effectively divides the town into two areas of confessional influence.

The limits of direct rule

The arrival of the British troops onto the streets of Belfast and Derry in 1969 did curb the possibility of a Loyalist pogrom in Belfast. Moreover, Direct Rule removed the major instrument of Orange political domination – the Stormont statelet. It curtailed the worst excesses of Unionist local government discrimination by transferring administrative responsibility for major public services (housing, education, health and social services) to non-elected quasi-professional bureaucracies. It transferred responsibility for security and policing from Stormont to Westminster and disbanded the partisan paramilitary police auxiliaries, the 'B specials'.

Indeed, with the imposition of Direct Rule, the 'Northern Ireland Problem', as it was becoming called, seemed amenable to solution by an internal settlement involving patient and sustained social and economic reform. The source of the malaise in Ulster came to be identified in British eyes with Stormont's 'maladministration' and indigenous 'outmoded prejudice'. The introduction of 'British standards of justice and fairplay' would, many in England believed, both address Catholic grievances and reassure the Protestants that no change in the constitutional status of the province was being contemplated. Sectarianism would simply wither away.

However, sectarian division rests on deeper material foundations than Unionist 'gerrymandering' and clientelism. It cannot be swept away with a few cosmetic reforms. It is not simply a matter of 'forgetting the past' and promoting 'mutual understanding' between the two communities. Sectarian divisions are structurally interlaced with a pattern of social inequalities separating Protestants and Catholics. The historical basis of this pervasive pattern of class segmentation has been the uneven development of capitalist industrialization in Ireland and the persistence of residual patterns of cultural and residential segregation originating in the plantation of Ulster. In addition, as we have seen, the ideological reproduction of sectarianism – in intransigent Unionism – was effected in and through the dominant ideology of social imperialism and was later institutionalized in the Stormont state.

The division of the working class along sectarian lines was, then, built into the very social fabric of Northern Ireland society and nowhere more so than in its occupational structure. Catholics have been under-represented in manufacturing employment and in the skilled jobs associated with it. They were correspondingly over-represented in construction and the clothing industries where unskilled employment prevailed. In the historically key sectors of shipbuilding and engineering they have been systematically excluded. In addition, the higher professional and managerial occupational category remained, throughout the post-war period of growth in state employment, largely dominated by Protestants. Throughout this period Catholic unemployment was over twice that of Protestants – a differential which continues to this day (FEA, 1987).

Thus, for the British state after 1972 to seriously address even the occupational dimension of sectarian division and to attempt to remove the structural inequalities facing Catholics in the labour market, it would have required a high level of state economic planning combined with a concerted programme of legislative reform aimed at achieving 'affirmative action'. Such an initiative was quite incompatible with the actual industrial policy followed which involved attracting multi-national investment to promote export-led growth (Rowthorn, 1981).

Despite a barrage of government incentives, as the pace of world economic growth slowed down after 1974, foreign investment in Northern Ireland was reduced to a trickle. After 1975 the number of closures of government-assisted, manufacturing projects started to significantly exceed the number of openings of firms attracted to Northern Ireland by the government systems of grant aid. The dependent character of the North's economy became starkly apparent as the world capitalist system was plunged into crisis. The structural weakness of British capital, which became highlighted in the context of an intensification of industrial competition on a world scale in the 1970s, had severe consequences for levels of manufacturing investment in Northern Ireland, and ultimately for employment growth.

Between 1973 and 1981, Northern Ireland lost a third of its manufacturing jobs as traditional industries continued to decline and the artificial textile and chemical sector, established in the 1960s, entered an acute decline. The economy had become a service-based one. By 1981 censuses of employment revealed that two-thirds of the Northern Ireland workforce was now working in the service sector, with less than a quarter of those employed now working in manufacturing industry. In so far as the largest part of service employment has been in the public-service sector (it is reckoned that today over a half of Northern Ireland's jobs are either in the public service or directly dependent on government expenditures), employment levels have become critically dependent on British exchequer expenditure.

As elsewhere in Britain, deindustrialization has led to a pattern of job-loss that has disproportionately affected the manual working class, particularly unskilled workers. Although Protestant workers are now experiencing mass unemployment for the first time since the 1930s, the differential rates between Protestant and Catholic levels of unemployment have been maintained.

Immiseration remains, then, a relative process and has not led, as some commentators predicted (Byrne, 1978), to any lessening of sectarian division between Protestant and Catholic working class households. Mass unemployment has not led to an emergence of class solidarities in Northern Ireland any more than it has elsewhere. By 1984, over half of unemployed men had been out of a job for over a year, and even with the development of the various 'Youth Training Schemes', over half of unemployed sixteen to nineteen year-olds had been on the register for more than six months (Morrisey, 1984). Unemployed workers become ghettoized, residentially-segregated on sectarian lines. The narrowed horizons of family life and confessional community reinforce a culture of sectarian segmentation and provide, as they historically have done, a social basis for a politics of 'communal deterrence'.

In effect, the fiscal crisis of the British state from the mid-1970s, which facilitated the rise of the New Right and the subsequent collapse of the post-war social democratic consensus in the UK, sounded the death knell of 'reform' in Northern Ireland. The new reluctance of Westminster to provide sufficient resources to tackle the economic and social problems of Northern Ireland was accompanied by a painful recognition in political circles in Britain that the problems of Ulster were more profound than the early reformers in the Northern Ireland Office had anticipated. Inevitably, British resolve to tackle the material dimensions of sectarian inequality in Northern Ireland weakened.

Indeed it could be argued (Bell, 1984) that just as the failure of Liberal attempts in the nineteenth century to 'kill Home Rule with kindness' had spelt the strange death of liberal England, so too the British state's inability to 'reform' Northern Ireland and dismantle the structures of sectarianism became a telling sign of a more general crisis in British democracy in the 1970s. The failure of British policy in Ireland had once again revealed the limits of British liberalism and the reforming capitalist state. The crisis in British capital imposed stark limits on the capacity of the British state to implement a social and political programme for the reform of Northern Ireland within the Union. Direct Rule in Northern Ireland has proved the graveyard of British social-democratic illusions about the reforming capacities of the state in capitalist society.

Increasingly the British state has come to reduce the 'Northern Ireland problem', previously an exemplar of the 'social question', to one of 'containing terrorism'. The reactionary kernel of British intervention asserted itself. The legitimacy of British rule could no longer be achieved by means of a welfare-backed political consensus, but now only via its claim to be a guardian of a universal law and order. Its legitimacy became constructed as an inverted representation of the generalised illegality of the 'terrorist'.

Conclusion

Young people in Northern Ireland are heir to a historical legacy of sectarian social division. On the ethnic frontier these divisions manifest themselves materially in the territorialization of economic, residential and cultural life.

In attempting to grasp the character of youth cultures in Ulster, it is important to grasp that class relations have been largely experienced by working people as 'sectarian class relations'. Young people relate to their sectarian parental cultures as sectarian class cultures. That is, Catholic workers have experienced their social position precisely as that – as *Catholic* workers. Young Catholics develop their social identity as a segment of the workforce marginalized from skilled employment and disproportionately suffering from unemployment. They are born into an ethnic group still subject, in the era of Direct Rule, to state repression. They are heir to a tradition of nationalist political struggle. Conversely, Protestant workers have sought to defend their marginal privileges through their participation in a Protestant all-class alliance ideologically and politically underwritten by British imperialism. Protestant youth relate to a parental culture of Loyalism now stripped of its institutional hegemony since Direct Rule and now facing the indignity of the Anglo-Irish Agreement. They give expression in their youth-cultural formations to their community's experience of seeing its historic privileges being eroded. Youth cultures in Northern Ireland are in part – as in Britain – a response by the young to a post-colonial situation as yet awaiting political resolution.

4

Sketches of the Marching Season

Early days

It had been a cold spring in Ulster. Yet by early April throughout the Protestant working-class housing estates of the province the sounds of marching feet, of fife and drum could once again be heard. New skins were being stretched taut across drum heads, snares tightened and tuned for outside performance. Flags were unfurled once again after the long winter, uniforms cleaned and badges and belts polished ready for the first parades of a new marching season. A hundred practice halls across the North resonated with sharp volleys of triplets and paradiddles from a colourful army of aspiring drummers.

Out on the Streets of Irish Street, one of the staunchest Loyalist estates in the Waterside area of Derry, the Maiden City Protestant Boys prepare themselves for the first parade of the new season. It's seven o'clock on a bright April evening and knots of young people are already gathering on the open ground at the centre of the state awaiting the start of the parade. As I enter Irish Street I notice that already a cordon of police land rovers has been placed at the entry to the estate where it borders with the Catholic, and fiercely Republican, Gobnascale estate.

The marching season is generally regarded as beginning on Easter Monday when the Apprentice Boys of Derry hold marches throughout Northern Ireland, ostensibly to celebrate the siege of 1689. The bands have been meeting regularly, however, on a weekly basis throughout the winter months practising for the forthcoming season. New members have to be instructed in the rudiments of flute playing and drumming. Tunes from the repertoire of 'old faithfuls' – 'Orange Lily O', 'Derry's Walls' and, of course, the 'Sash' – have to be polished up. New tunes, para-

97

military airs[1] and simple pop marches, have to be tackled and mastered. Colour parties go through their steps bearing the chosen flags of Loyalist Ulster – the Union Jack, the blue Scottish flag of St Andrew, the crimson ensign of Derry and, of course, the Ulster flag, a St George's cross on a white background and, at its centre, the bloody red hand of the O'Neills mounted by a crown.

Resplendent in their newly acquired orange and blue uniforms with matching cockades, the lads from the Maiden City Protestant Boys (the 'Boys') congregate with their highly polished instruments beside the boarded-up shops and health clinic at the centre of their estate. The walls of these buildings are festooned with paramilitary graffiti: WE WILL NEVER FORESAKE THE BLUE SKIES OF ULSTER FOR THE GREY MISTS OF AN IRISH REPUBLIC proclaims a carefully painted slogan on the gable of the community centre. GOD SAVE ULSTER – CAUSE THE UDA WON'T declares another, testifying to paramilitary rivalries on the estate. These slogans, like the painstakingly produced traditional mural of William of Orange on white charger, were the work of lads from the band.[2] By the shops which, in the absence of any other focal point on the estate, have come to serve as the major gathering point for the youth of the area, leather-jacketed teenagers gather. It is here at the centre of the estate that the young men muster when there is political tension in the area and the likelihood of a more sustained confrontation with the Republican youths from Gobnascale down the road. As Ally Hetherington who lived on the estate had told me:

> If there's goin' te be a bit of fightin' they gather from all around down at the shops ... come running from miles and anybody's who's about just piles in. But usually the police stops us.

Other bands from the town and the surrounding, mainly Protestant, rural hinterland are also arriving on foot and by hired bus, bearing their instruments and furled flags. The young bandsmen engage in good-natured banter. A natural rivalry exists between these bands, in part a reflection of the fact that each is a representative of its local area and a focal point of local solidarities. Each of the Protestant estates in the Derry area has thrown up a marching band over the last decade or so. The wayward Caw Sons of Ulster from Nelson Drive; the unruly Pride of the Valley from Tullyally with their crimson uniforms, paramilitary style dark glasses and three teenage girl flag-carriers; the Orange and Blue from Newbuildings; the immaculately turned out William King from the embattled Fountain estate (named after a resident of the area who had died in hospital after a sectarian assault in the early seventies); the Lyndsey Mooney from Clooney, named after a UDA member who blew himself to pieces planting a bomb. These titles commemorating recent victims and martyrs of the current violence sustain a popular memory of contemporary history as seen through youthful Loyalist eyes. The names of the bands inscribed on their colourfully decorated bass drums, beaten to such effect to stir the marchers, proclaim a loyalty to local community and Ulster Protestant identity rather than to any distant polity.

But this is no traditional Orange march. Absent are the dour faced and dowdily-dressed patriarchs of the lodges; absent too are their white-gloved stewards dedicated to restraining the noisier elements amongst the bands and to preserving Protestant propriety. The majority of the band members are male teenagers or young men in their early twenties. This age range contrasts sharply with the largely elderly membership of the Orange Order.[3] Moreover contrary to popular opinion, the bands are completely organizationally independent of the Orange orders.[4] Most are democratically self-governing, annually electing a committee from among their members. This is entrusted with running the affairs of the band–handling fundraising for instruments and uniforms, deciding which parades to attend, and planning the musical development of the band. Most bands do, however, tend to have a somewhat older leader who is loosely in charge of the money and recruitment.

This parade, like the vast majority the band will attend in any season, has been organized completely separately from the official Orange institutions. Of the 30 or so parades that the bands will attend between now and the end of the marching season in early September, only some four or five will be associated with the marches organized by the Orange orders or Apprentice Boys. The rest are organized by the bands themselves. These take the form of competitions, annual parades and door-to-door collections. There are impromptu outings like the Eleventh Night bonfires which mark the start of the Twelfth celebrations throughout the province. (The largest Orange demonstrations each year are held on 12 July to commemorate the victory of William of Orange over James II in 1690. On the eve of 12 July ('eleventh night') bonfires are lit in celebration of the Battle of the Boyne.) And of course, when the occasion demands it, there are appearances at political meetings and rallies. In effect the bands have collectively originated a marching calendar of their own. This seems to be as much governed by youthful leisure demands as it is by the rituals of Loyalist tradition.

The lads arrive carrying brown paper bags stuffed full of cans of beer. A teenage punk in leather jacket and torn fatigues, with a bondage chain stretching from his ear lobe to his nostril, struggles to open a cheap bottle of wine with a drumstick borrowed from a band member. He offers the wine wrapped discreetly in a paper bag to various band members to swig. His dyed orange hair compliments the colourful jackets of the bandsmen – a symbiosis of subcultural style and Loyalist dress.

The older members of the more established bands arrive by car. Their elaborate regimental-style uniforms, expensive instruments and music holders testify to a more restrained musical tradition and social order. These are the competition-oriented bands, with 'musical directors', employing musical arrangements utilizing harmony and counterpart. The younger 'Blood and Thunder' bands usually use only single-key flutes which they play in unison, largely from memory. The repertoires of the competition bands include popular classics and military marches as well as the usual Loyalist favourites. Indeed they are in many ways indistinguishable from similar brass and silver bands to be found in working-class communities throughout the United Kingdom.

The youthful 'Blood and Thunder' bands are of a different character.

The bands from Nelson Drive and Tullyally arrive at the estate and form up on its perimeter. Each band is anxious to announce its arrival and does so with a volley of staccato drumming. Groups of supporters accompany the bands applauding them as they make their entry to the estate. They march into the centre of Irish Street to the starting point of the parade playing against each other at full blast. The combative Tullyally and Nelson Drive bands roar in tribal unison, after a whistle from their leaders, 'We are, we are, we are the Protestant Boys!' – a cry followed by vigorous whistling and foot stamping. This combative performance is not primarily musical in character and has perhaps closer similarities with the gestural activities of football supporters – and indeed these bands undoubtedly derive elements of their style from this

Fig. 4.1 The 'Sons' rehearse
(*Photo: Desmond Bell*)

source.[5] Local loyalties, teenage machismo and class sentiment fuse in this parading of Protestant identity.

These 'Blood and Thunder' bands are almost exclusively male though many of them do have girl flag-bearers. There are mixed and all-girl bands but these are either the more established 'competition' bands or traditional tartan-kilted accordion bands. Neither have the same association with the combative street politics of militant Loyalism. Indeed, it is most unusual to see a young woman playing a flute or carrying a side drum in a 'Blood and Thunder band'. And, in fact, the bands practise a rigid gender demarcation with girls relegated to non-musical activities like flag-bearing or carrying the collection boxes used in fund raising.

By the shops I run into Karen Hewitt from Curryneirin, a senior pupil at the local grammar school. She had come up to Irish Street for the parade. She nudges me in the ribs to indicate the noisy arrival of the Pride of the Valley, her local band, assuring me

> they're a good band if they take control of themselves, but if they go te the pub before, it'll be fightin' amongst themselves ... who is not walkin' right and who's not playin' right ... they'll just have to be separated.

Why, I asked her, was she so interested in the bands when the girls clearly were second-class citizens within this culture?

Karen: Something to do ... so it is ... There's nothin' else te do round here. I want te hear the bands. If I wasn'e there people would be sayin' 'God I wonder why she's not out tonight because we usually see her at them'; we're proud te be out.

As she explained to me, she used to carry the flag for the band but had felt awkward about doing this as she lived on a mixed housing estate:

Karen: I was carrying the flag for Tullyally but every time the bus [carrying her neighbours] was goin' past I was hidin' me face with the flag in case I knew anybody. Its bad enough walkin' with it but out *carryin'* the flag!

Me: Why's that?

Karen: I don't know ... well, next door is Catholics and over the other side is Catholic and I wouldn't like te be seen carrying the flag ...

Pride of the Valley had a reputation for being the rowdiest band in the town. Indeed only the past weekend some members had been involved in a major fracas with members of another band from out of town after a parade in the neighbouring town of Limivady. Yet, as I was to discover, a number of members of the band were going out with Catholic girls from the nearby Ardmore estate. The lads were keeping this quiet from their mates, but as Karen Hewitt put it:

> there's ones from Tullyally that was actually doin' the fightin' last year, goin' out with girls from Ardmore – And I don't know what they're going te do when the band's out at night down that way. Like one of the girls she's moved inte Curryneirin [a mixed estate where the band parades] and the boy will probably be up with the band! And he is one of the big Protestants from Tullyally!

What we have here is perhaps not so much sectarian prejudice melting in the heat of romantic passion, as a testament of the extent to which much of male youthful stylised aggression towards 'the other side' is a product of peer pressures and sub-cultural dynamics.

Karen was in the process of explaining to me the role of the flag-carriers within the bands when Keith Hope, bedecked in the vivid uniform of the 'Boys' and carrying his side drum, butted into the conversation to express his distaste at the choice of girls as standard-bearers. Keith was just fourteen and a pupil at the Irish Street school. What, I asked him, was his objection to the girls marching alongside the boys?

Keith: Cause it's too cissy lookin'. Some bands got wee girls flutin' an all but it doesn't look right with wee girls in the band. A flute band was always usually young fellahs like. If you're goin' te have a flag carrier you'd be better having a young fellah carrying it with dark glasses or something ... better than a crowd of wee girls wavin' the flag, disgrace themselves with that there. It looks more.

Me: More?
Keith: More military.
Me: Military?
Keith: Ye know more – more *Protestant* like!

In Northern Ireland, as elsewhere, representations of ethnicity involving the naturalizing of gender divisions are reproduced in and through subcultural display.

The disappearance of waged work is producing a crisis of gender identity for the working-class teenage male. His sense of masculinity has up until recently been anchored in the valorization of hard physical work and in the privileges claimed by the 'breadwinner' within the family. Unemployment and the institutionalized de-skilling involved in the state's Youth Training programmes have eroded the material basis of this gender identity. Undoubtedly the 'Blood and Thunder' bands provide an alternative and increasingly aggressive assertion of masculinity for the marginalized young working-class male. As Willis (1984) argues:

> One way for young men to resolve their 'gender crisis' may be an aggressive assertion of masculinity and masculine style for its own sake. Male 'power' may throw off its respectable cloak of labour dignity. It may give a physical, tough, direct display of those qualities not now guaranteed by doing productive work and being a breadwinner.

Loyalist street youth culture provides a terrain for these young men where traditional male values of hardness, bravado and physicality can be rehearsed and paraded. These 'markers of manhood' are now being constructed in the sphere of leisure at a time when traditional identities associated with the workplace and the wage packet are less available. The parades as a forum for youthful exhibition and stylized confrontation offer ample opportunities for exposure to physical risk and for the aggressive display of communal solidarities. As a public spectacle they provide a stage for the performances of recognisable skill and dexterity at a time when these traditional elements of working-class cultural capital are being eroded by unemployment and restructuring of the labour process. As Phil Cohen (1984) has argued:

> The practice of dexterity is no longer anchored to the sign of

manual labour; it takes place increasingly in leisure contexts, in the mastery of popular dance forms or video games for example. As a result positions of 'skill' and 'unskill' are no longer tied so rigidly to divisions of labour or their relations of generational transmission, but are negotiated primarily through the peer group.

Those who have witnessed the finely-honed skills and risk-taking routines of the drum majors of the marching bands with their intricate twirling of baton under leg and behind head and massive hurls high into the air to the delight of the crowds, or who have heard the precision volleys of the unruly teenage drum corps, can be in no doubt that the marching bands provide such a peer-group milieu for the parading of 'skill'.

Lining up behind Pride of the Valley are the Caw Sons of Ulster. This outfit is clearly a poor relation within the world of the marching bands. Its members wear knitted red pullovers and ordinary trousers, rather than the elaborate and vibrant uniforms of the more established bands.[6] Indeed, not all the band are even dressed uniformly. Their assortment of non-matching open necked shirts, and assorted jeans and trousers give the band a curiously rag, tag and bobtail appearance in marked contrast with the other bands. This contrast is heightened by the fact that several of the band are already the worse for drink even before the parade starts. A controlled stagger rather than a disciplined march is the best Terry Kelly, their leader and bass drummer, could expect from them.

The 'Sons' had originally been formed by the friends of a young Loyalist who had killed himself whilst fooling around with a homemade pistol. He had been immortalised in the original name of the band – the Robert Wray Memorial Band. This band had fallen apart, however, after much internal fighting. Terry, a thirty-year-old full-time member of the UDR, had somewhat reluctantly bowed to pressure from the young people from the estate to start up the band again. Now he was trying, apparently very much against the grain, to instil some discipline, both musical and social, into the ever wayward 'Sons'.

The 'Sons' hail from the Nelson Drive estate. This neighbourhood has gained itself an unenviable reputation within Derry for roughness. Increasing levels of unemployment and welfare dependency have bequeathed a social-problem profile to the estate which has a high turnover of tenants. The estate is a product of a spate of public house-building in Derry in the early 1970s which saw much of the working-class population of Derry, both Protestant and Catholic, decanted from the older inner city artisan areas to the new large estates located on green field sites on the periphery of the town. Protestants were relocated on the new East Bank estates. Catholics, for their part, transferred to the new areas of public housing which stretch out westwards on the city side of the town towards the border with the Irish Republic. Despite its public commitment to integrated housing, the actual allocation policy of Northern Ireland's Housing Executive reproduced and indeed intensified the sectarian territorialization of residential space.

The 'Kick the Pope' bands come from estates which are now almost entirely confessionally exclusive. An examination of the 1981 Census Small Area Statistics (100 metre-square grid)[7] revealed that of the some 1,300 persons living in the Irish Street area, less than 10 per cent were Roman Catholics. Similarly low proportions of Catholics to Protestants were also found in the data for the Nelson Drive area.

Interestingly enough, over half of the 'Sons' came from families relocated from the city side in the large movement of Protestants to the East Bank in the early 1970s. Many of these families who moved to Nelson Drive in fact came from one particular area on the city side – the Glen estate. This neighbourhood had been a mixed one with a Protestant majority up until the late 1960s. A spate of IRA attacks on Protestant members of the security forces living in the estate had led to a rapid exodus of Protestants in the early years of the current 'Troubles'. A significant number of these migrants had been rehoused in the new dwellings being built in Nelson Drive. A week spent in the local office of the Northern Ireland Housing Executive examining the records for housing lets for the period 1974–89 unearthed the fact that one in six of the current residents of the Nelson Drive estate had originally lived in the Glen. For the lads in the 'Sons' there was little doubt that the band kept alive their sense of association with their former locality. As Terry Kelly explained to me:

You could almost put it down to being a Glen band. All we've done really is move the band over here . . . It's still really a Glen band.

Similarly, as I got to know the lads in the 'Boys' better I discovered that for them too the band not only reflected a sense of local identity but indeed was an important resource by which the young reconstructed a sense of community subject to constant erosion under the impact of housing relocations and urban change. A significant number of the band, although they had been raised on the estate, were no longer actually living there. Irish Street had been built in the early post-war period and was completed long before the building boom of the 1970s. The estate could not accommodate the new families seeking housing in the late 1960s and many of the lads from the bands were now living in the newer more outlying estates. However, many still had grandparents resident there and still thought of Irish Street as 'home'. As Sammy Little, their leader put it:

Irish Street is likely a community focal point, from years and years ago . . . all the places I lived I always came back to here . . . like this is the place that can pack in the crowds on eleventh night like no other estate can. Every one knows this is the place te be.

Keith Hope, who did live on the estate, also identified this communal focus directly with the Twelfth celebrations:

Irish Street gets the most attention. Ours is the last bonfire lit, I think, and most of the time it's the biggest bonfire. Ye couldn't get moving in here on Eleventh night after eleven. After the pubs shut this place is just packed and I mean packed . . . Cause Irish Street's meant to be the hardest place, the best Loyalists. They all come to see our bonfire.

The band also signified a link with a place of origin in a time of change and dislocation. This link is forged in the most tangible of ways – in the ritual parading which, together with the graffiti, iconography and kerb paintings, now also largely conducted by the band members, sustains a symbolic demarcation of Protestant territory at a time when the material base of that community is being eroded.

Fig. 4.2 Musical dexterity
(*Photo: Kate Horgan*)

As John Clarke has argued regarding the skinheads in England:

> the skinhead style does not revive the community in a *real sense*
> [my emphasis] the post war decline of the bases of that community
> had removed it as a real source of solidarity, the skinheads had
> to use an image of what that community was as the basis of their
> style. They were the 'dispossessed inheritors'; they received a
> tradition which had been deprived of its real social bases. [   ]
> We would suggest that this dislocated relation to the traditional
> community accounts for the exaggerated and intensified form
> which the values and that community received in the form of the
> skinhead style.

Undoubtedly the cultural work of the 'Blood and Thunder' bands,
like that of the Tartan gangs which they have largely succeeded, is
best understood as a response by the young to the material decline
of Protestant working-class communality. Elements of the parental
culture are utilized as a symbolic resource and are combined with
specific youth cultural forms to achieve the reconstruction of a
mythic identity. As Carson Logue, a YTP (Youth Training Programme – a government sponsored scheme to create employment)
trainee from Nelson Drive, who I was to spend a lot of time with,
put it, pointing out the freshly painted kerbs at the entry to the
estate 'You are now entering Jaffa [Orange man or Protestant]
land, beware!'

Carson was often found hanging around with the 'Sons', sharing
'the crack' at their rehearsals and on occasions travelling away
with the band to parades out of town. He was not without his
reservations about the band.

Carson: They wanted me to march with them the night . . . but no
way; look at the shape of them – wild! But fair play te
them they're trying te get their point across.

Me: What point's that?

Carson: That they're not goin'te let the Taigs take over! Like
that's all they want te do!

Several hundred teenagers have by now gathered to support the
bands. They are adorned in Glasgow Rangers and Linfield foot-
ball-supporters scarves, some wear Union Jack hats and many are

carrying miniature Ulster flags. I see kids from all over the East
Bank that I recognize from the youth clubs. The older inhabitants
of the estate appear at their front doors, or lean out of open
windows to view the action and wave to passers-by they recognize.
This is clearly a communal celebration. The atmosphere of the
occasion lies somewhere between a street carnival and a military
parade, combining as it does youthful exuberance and communal
ritual with the ever present edge of potential sectarian confrontation.

The first band moves off on a route which takes it to the
southern perimeter of the estate where it borders with nationalist
Gobnascale. At this point it swings left before it reaches the
substantial police cordon barring its passage into the nationalist
area. With a few derogatory gestures towards the police the 'Boys'
at the head of the parade turn back into the centre of the estate by
another road. A symbolic gesture of defiance against police
interference in the right to march has been made. In fact the band
had made application to the RUC some six weeks earlier for the
right to hold this march and make a street collection, so the
demonstration of defiance against the RUC is a somewhat empty
one.

However, police restriction and control of band parades were
undoubtedly a source of considerable grievance amongst these
Loyalist young people. Billy Holmes, one of the fluters in the
'Boys' gave vent to his feelings on the RUC:

> If you're standing at a street corner the bastards are down on ye
> like a ton of bricks saying, 'what are ye doin' standing here? . . .
> What's yer name? . . . what have ye been doin'? . . . What are ye
> goin' te be doin'? . . . Where do ye live? . . . Who do you know?
> . . . When did ye last shite?' That's about the only question they
> don't ask . . . But at marches they just stand back, they do
> nothin' like . . . if you're with a crowd and you're drinking –
> even if you look like yer twelve – they wouldn't say anything te
> ye . . . they're scared te.

That year as the RUC, on the instructions of British government,
made a concerted attempt to reroute Orange marches away from
sensitive areas, the bands were to find themselves in a more
generalized confrontation with the police. As the bands threw

themselves into the front line of a sustained physical Loyalist challenge to RUC parade restrictions, a new slogan began to appear on the gables of the Protestant ghettoes: THE STREETS ARE OURS AND THAT'S A FACT – SMASH THE PUBLIC ORDER ACT. Loyalist political strategy and subcultural imperatives for the youthful repossession of public space had become conflated.

As the parade gets moving, lads and girls dance and clown about behind their local bands. Some wave wine bottles at the police in a gesture of defiant hedonism at odds with the dominant puritanism of their parental culture. The young people swarm over the public highways with the sort of licence only a Loyalist parade can provide. Police bring the traffic to a complete halt to make way for the parade. Motorists will be made to wait up to fifteen minutes while the bands pass. Clearly for young Loyalists this sanctioned dominance of the roadways, however brief, has an important symbolic value. This is partly derived from the territorial concerns of populist Loyalism but also from the contemporary concerns of youth to establish public space for social activity. These kids are being moved on every other day of the week from the shopping centres and public complexes of the city by these same police officers.

Tagging along behind the bands this youthful entourage perform a peculiar parody of the traditional Orange procession, clutching beer cans and wine bottles rather than the Lodge banners or bibles of their elders. A traditional form of the parental culture is here adopted by the young and invested with new functions and meaning appropriate to their generational situation. Many of these young people are now denied access to bars and commercial discos. They find in this vibrant street culture, with its intoxicating mixture of hedonism and martial discipline, an alternative milieu for their recreational needs. They can drink without sanction, mix with the opposite sex, indulge in displays of dexterity, musical skill and youthful bravado in a situation where the possibility of confrontation is never far away.

The bands, each accompanied in turn by a small straggle of denim- and leather-clad followers, rather than by the serge-suited denizens of the Orange lodges, tramp out of Irish Street in a carefully-planned route. This takes them through a number of adjoining Catholic neighbourhoods. The residents come to their doors to greet the marchers. Teenage girls rattle the collection tins under the noses of the householders encouraging them to contribute to the band fund for new uniforms and instruments. The band supporters beckon to the teenagers gathered by the doorways of the houses on the route, to join them in the parade. As the column of bands, flags and young beer-swilling supporters winds through the streets of the Protestant Waterside it swells in numbers. By the time it reaches the later stages, upwards of a thousand people are involved.

The parade gathers momentum as it approaches an interface with an adjoining Catholic area. Catholic youths gather across open ground in a spot which has seen regular stone-throwing confrontations over the past few years. This is a traditional 'shatter zone' and all the participants in this ritualized drama know it. The police look tense for the first time and quickly place themselves between the parade and the Catholic onlookers. However on this occasion the confrontation is highly stylized and harmless. The bands play up in defiant register. The drums are beaten in a frenzy, and catcalls echo across the divide. Threats and insults are mouthed but the parade moves resolutely on. This display, apparently so bellicose to the outsider, is conducted with great jocularity by the youthful participants on both sides. It seems, in fact, more directed towards their fellow marchers than to the outsiders on the other side of the police cordon. It appears to be as much concerned with sustaining communal solidarities as with expressing sectarian hostilities.

Again, useful parallels can be made between the skinhead style and Loyalist youth cultural practice. Clarke identifies the role of football support in providing a focal point for the organization of new forms of youthful territoriality for the skinhead 'mobs':

Football, and especially the violence articulated around it, also provided one arena for the expression of the Skinheads' concern with a particular, collective, masculinity with physical toughness, and an unwillingness to back down in the face of 'trouble'. The violence also involved the Mobs' stress on collective solidarity and mutual support in times of 'need'

For Loyalist youth there can be little doubt that the parades and associated street activities provide a similar focal point, providing a specific representational content to a universal youth subcultural imperative.

The parade, after almost two hours of tramping and playing, winds its way back towards Irish Street and its starting point. With a last flourish of drumming the bands break up and the crowds start to disperse. The older 'competition' band members pack up their instruments and leave the estate in their cars. The lads from the 'Blood and Thunder' bands hang around the shops chatting and drinking and exchanging drum riffs in groups of two or three side drummers. Eventually the flags are rolled up, flutes stuffed in pockets and bass drums abandoned as supporters and bandsmen alike head for the local pubs for a last drink. Some of them, emboldened by the evening's activities, have decided to make the hazardous journey across the bridge through 'enemy' territory in order to attend a disco in the Apprentice Boys Hall in the old walled city. And do so in full uniform! Another marching season has begun.

The Maiden City Protestant Boys: a profile

The band had been formed sometime in 1980 after the collapse of an earlier outfit the Irish Street Sons of Ulster, a band which had acquired something of a reputation for drinking and fighting. This original band had appeared in 1976 in the first wave of 'Blood and Thunder' bands which appeared across the province in working-class housing estates in the wake of the growth of paramilitary Loyalism after 1972. These early bands had attracted large numbers of male teenagers. The original Irish Street band had, for instance, some 50 teenage members. By the mid-1970s the bands had more or less replaced the Tartan gangs as the focal point around which Loyalist youth organized itself.

Some of the former members of the 'Boys' could remember the start of the Tartans in Derry. Cecil Knowles, originally from the Fountain, recalled the period:

One of our mates was in Belfast at a course and he stayed in the Woodstock Road and they had a Tartan gang who fought with other gangs through Belfast – other Loyalist gangs. And he arrived back from his course with his scarf and told us all about the Tartan gangs and would we be interested in starting a Tartan gang. So we started a Tartan gang in the Fountain area.

Everyone in the area was dressed the same – it was known as the 'White tartan' and we kept it strictly within the Fountain area.

Other gangs rapidly appeared on Protestant estates in the town, in Irish Street, Kilfennan and Nelson Drive. Very soon internecine gang war broke out between the rival areas. The Tartan style also spread to the Catholic youth in the Bogside who adorned themselves in a 'green tartan'. The gang violence became inexorably implicated in sectarian confrontation, with the Protestant gangs coalescing and large scale clashes with the Catholic Tartans occurring regularly in the town centre on Saturday afternoons.[8] The Loyalist gangs then formally amalgamated in a new super gang, the colourfully named Wolf Tartan. Cecil remembered this process well:

> We all met at dances on a Friday and Saturday night and fought among ourselves and we all decided that instead of doin' this we should come together and sort the real enemy out ... We all decided to meet in the Waterside one Saturday afternoon. We all met around Clondermot Road about 150 to 200 young fellahs and we all changed over te one tartan – that was the red Wolf tartan. And we marched over the town over to the Fountain area, where we had another meeting and then we all headed down the town looking for the other side ... we were looking to get revenge on them for some of the deeds they carried out.

Neighbourhood gangs of working-class youth had long existed in Derry and Belfast, as elsewhere. In the past, gangs drawn from adjoining Protestant neighbourhoods fought each other and staked out 'territories'. Since the 1970s a redefinition of gang loyalties has occurred and with it the reterritorialisation of space on a confessional basis. Boundary maintenance activity is now directly related to the sectarian divide.

The Tartans also had a more direct relation with political developments in the working-class Protestant community.

The Tartans began to appear at UDA organised parades, marching together as one gang and on occasions were involved in violent clashes with the police and army. The UDA, in turn, responsive to local complaints about the unruliness of these youths, imposed its own robust discipline on the gangs and managed to effectively break up the Wolf Tartan. On the other hand the gangs also proved a useful source for recruits to the paramilitary ranks. As Cecil recalled:

> At that time the UDA sealed off certain areas of the Waterside. The manpower to man these barricades was low so they [the UDA] approached members of the Tartans in each area to try and get it strengthened . . . and most of the boys did respond . . . and after that most of the boys in the Waterside and the Fountain in the gangs joined the UDA and the Tartans more or less faded out as a gang.

The relation between the gangs and the paramilitaries was a complex and fluid one. Organized Loyalism quickly became wary of the delinquent tendencies of the Tartans. The 'lads', for their part, were anxious to resist incorporation into the hierarchically-organised paramilitary organizations with their stress on martial discipline.

The Tartans soon declined as an autonomous adolescent sphere, their members taking their place with the adult Loyalist organizations, and the bands emerged to provide an alternative focus of youthful activity. They, in turn, underwent what could best be described as 'paramilitarization' of style. The wearing of dark glasses, carrying of flags associated directly with the UDA and the banned UVF, and amplification of the militaristic and combative style of the bands all testified to the extent to which the bands responded to the new militancy amongst Loyalist youth and the search for a successor to the Tartans. On the other hand, as popular support for the Loyalist paramilitaries waned in the late 1970s and the civil violence became focused on the struggle between the IRA and the security forces – in contemporary Derry only the most skeletal UDA organization now survives – the bands went from strength to strength providing for young people an alternative to paramilitary activity.

In Derry, at least, we found really no evidence of any active involvement any longer of the band members in the paramilitaries, though most of the members of the 'Boys' described themselves as UVF supporters. However, one of the younger members of the band who I had interviewed in depth on a number of occasions, is currently in prison serving a long sentence for discharging a revolver at a prison officer's home. As the court case revealed, he had been put up to this by an older man with connections with both the UVF and the United Kingdom neo-fascist party, the National Front. There seemed to be no evidence that the lad had in fact been a committed or trained member of the UVF; rather he was a well-known hothead who had embarked on the attack mainly as an act of bravado. Nor was the band implicated in his recruitment since the older figure, who was English and an ex-British soldier, was a part-time youth worker in a Community Centre with no real association with Irish Street or its band. Given incidents like this, many of the younger members were in fact highly sceptical as regards the Loyalist paramilitaries. These were generally regarded by the young as now marginal to events in the province. Most found the intricacies of the paramilitaries' political arguments difficult to follow, however much they liked their macho style.

The 'Boys' retained many of the elements of this paramilitarized style. Its older leaders however, had aspirations for the band to evolve musically and organizationally into a full 'competition' band playing more complex marching tunes beyond the traditional Loyalist corpus. Most of the bands do seem, over a number of years, to go through such an evolutionary development. They start off as large, unruly 'Kick the Pope' outfits whose teenage members are more interested in combative display and more responsive to subcultural dynamic than they are to either musical accomplishment or the proprieties of official Orangeism. Later they 'mature' into competition oriented bands.

The 'Boys' had begun with a large youthful contingent eager to be out parading on the streets but with little musical skill. The band started off with the basic one-key flute with its restricted range and, indeed, had only recently purchased the more elaborate and expensive five-key versions which permitted the playing of more complex marching tunes, involving parts. Similarly the band did not at first have tailor-made uniforms but only jumpers knitted by a local woman. Band suits and their accompanying accoutrements, lanyards, badges, leather belts, and plumes are expensive and it took the band considerable time and effort to raise the money needed to purchase these items. Sammy assured me that it cost over £100 to 'put a fluter on the street'. Though the lads paid a weekly subscription of 50p, most of the money had to be raised by street collections, by holding discos and collecting during the band's annual parade.

The drive to raise money, in turn, made the band, or at least its leaders, more responsive to community social control. As the bands get established and the average age of the members tends to rise, the bands become smaller as those less interested in the purely musical developments tend to drop out. At this point the bands either tend to fall apart as they abandon their subcultural functions or continue to evolve into more established 'competition' outfits. The young band supporters I spoke with were always either bemoaning the fact that a particular band, had, in their words, 'died down', or applauding the fact that a new 'noisy' band had appeared on the streets. Indeed it was clear that a certain tension existed between the older leaders in the band anxious to instil musical discipline and comportment in parades, and more responsive to community pressures to curb the wilder side of their members, and the younger rank and file more concerned with peer-group 'crack', generational autonomy and the rituals of militancy.

Of the 25 members of the band, all of whom were young men, approximately half were in their teens and, apart from the two older leaders in their late twenties, all the band were under twenty-four. Only Ian, the 'chairman' of the band, was married. The band also had a junior section of eleven to fourteen year-olds who assembled once a week to be taught the rudiments of flute playing but who did not march with the lads on parades as yet. As table 4.1 shows, almost half the band were unemployed and, indeed, of those with a job, five were working in government-assisted work schemes. A number of those unemployed had been so for a number of years. A third of the band had been through the YTP treadmill. Half of their fathers were unemployed and many had siblings without a job. All but two of the band had gone to non-selective secondary schools and the vast majority had left school with no or minimal qualifications. All of the band resided in areas characterized by high levels of confessional segregation; all but two lived in houses rented from the Housing Executive.

None of the band were members of a political party though most of the 25 when questioned said they would vote for the DUP – but

Table 4.1   *Social profile of the Maiden City Protestant Boys*

	Status of band members	Status of members' fathers
Full-time employed	10	12
Registered unemployed	12	10
YTP	1	
Full-time education	2	
Retired or permanently sick		3
Totals	25	25

not without reservations. Some of the older members declared a preference for the Ulster Loyalist Democratic Party, the political party founded by the UDA. Only three of the band were members of the Orange Order, although eight of their fathers were. More of the band, some nine, largely those in their twenties, were members of Apprentice Boys Clubs and seventeen of their fathers were in this organisation. Despite its name the band members were a relatively irreligious bunch with almost half of them never going to church and the rest attending less than once a month; none of them were involved in church organizations and only one ever attended a youth club.

Amongst the 'Boys' almost 60 per cent of the band chose to describe themselves as 'Ulstermen', with some 40 per cent choosing the British label.

In terms of attitudes towards segregation and integration, all but one of the band expressed a preference for living in an ALL-PROTESTANT neighbourhood. None said they would be happy to marry someone of the opposite religion, though two said they would be happy enough living next door to someone of the opposite religion.

Saturday 27 April

The second parade of the season was the annual parade of the Orange and Blue Flute Band from Newbuildings on the outskirts of

Fig. 4.3 Twelfth of July Parade
(*Photo: Londonderry Sentinel*)

Derry. Once a year each band organises a parade on its home patch to which it invites all the other local bands and selected bands from elsewhere in Northern Ireland. All the invited bands compete for various prizes provided by the home band which uses the occasion to raise funds by collecting in the streets and often organizing a disco after the parade. The well-established and resourced bands will issue printed invitations and often up to 50 bands will congregate for the occasion. Each host band has to wait nervously to see how many of the invited bands will actually turn up on the night as bands rarely seem to reply to the issued invitations and often only decide to attend after a discussion at their weekly practice. A band's standing tends to be judged by the number of other bands it can attract to its annual parade. As much of the street collection is done amongst the visiting bands themselves and their supporters, the more bands that appear then the larger the street collection will be.

Through this calendar of competition parades, a network of contacts stretching right across the province is built up between the bands. This widens the focus of their activity from merely local concerns to the more general political interests of the Loyalist community as a whole. In addition, these larger gatherings stimulate greater competition musically and stylistically between the bands. They generate excitement – new faces, new rivalries, novel musical arrangements and innovations, greater sexual possibilities.

Newbuildings was once a self-contained rural village, but with the proliferation of public house-building since the 1970s it has now virtually become a suburb of Derry. Like the other new 'Protestant' estates on the east bank periphery of the town it has become associated with hard-line Loyalism. Its band, which is a well established one, has close associations with the DUP. On this occasion it has managed to lure Ian Paisley to Newbuildings to distribute the prizes to the bands. The local government elections are coming up and the DUP are glad of an opportunity for a platform. Youthful hedonism and sober political purpose will meet head on tonight.

By seven o'clock a stream of young men and women decked out in Ulster scarves and Union Jack hats can be seen making their way along the long straight road that stretches from Derry, along the banks of the River Foyle, to the village of Newbuildings. The hired buses pull up in the village, and out onto the streets tumble an assortment of uniformed band personnel accompanied by their supporters who help them off with their instruments, flags and copious quantities of canned beer.

The bands show considerable entrepreneurial drive. They hire the buses themselves packing them with their supporters who they charge for the trip. They also purchase the beer in bulk from local supermarkets and sell it on the buses marking up the price to raise some money for their coffers. These away trips are very popular amongst the young, and for good reasons. As Margaret McAllister and Michelle Burke who are tonight hanging around with the lads from the 'Sons' put it:

> It's a night away from everybody who knows you. Nobody can say 'I seen your son and he was doin' this and he was doin' that'. By the time you're home your Ma and Da are lying in bed sleeping.

The away trips provide opportunities for excesses of behaviour which would not be tolerated on the band's home territory where the young are more subject to communal constraints and parental censure. For the younger kids in particular, these trips provide opportunities for drinking, merriment and sexual encounter not open to them via commercial leisure provision. As Margaret told me:

> Most of the time if ye go to discos you'll not get into the place. Ye have to be eighteen or twenty-one and no leathers and denims . . . ye have te dress up. Everybody feels more comfortable in their own clothes so if ye had te dress up it would seem wild.

Margaret McAllister and Michelle Doherty, final-year pupils at the Irish Street school, were keen rockers and were constantly clad in red-leather gear. They were happy to troop behind the 'Sons' and follow on to the rough and ready discos organized by the bands themselves at which dress codes were flexible! Though, as girls, they had to be careful when travelling away with the band:

The young fellahs are dying te get us away on these trips. They wanna get us drunk and all . . . But we don't drink. They all just get drunk and then they fight among the bands, throwing their jackets an' all . . . 'I'm leavin' your band.'

Not all the girls are so abstemious. By the chip shop three teenage girls dressed skinhead style, with cropped hair and a small tuft of longer hair worn at the back, are rapidly downing cans of cider beside the bus that has brought them from Coleraine. The lads from the 'Sons' stand around drinking and chatting up the visiting girls. Terry Kelly, their leader, is relieved that today at least most of the band are fairly sober. Two of his more unruly members have decamped to the Tullyally band – much to his relief:

If it's drinkin' and fightin' they want they've gone te to the right place!

Tonight the bands are drawn from both the surrounding rural area – Brady, Artigarvan, Killaloo, and from the urban working-class estates in the towns in the west of the province – from Limavady, Coleraine, Omagh, Garvagh, as well as from Derry itself. The rural bands have a wider age span amongst their members and include men in their thirties and forties. They are more staid in appearance and generally 'respectable' looking. The town bands are mainly teenagers. Their uniforms are like the members of the bands themselves, more raucous and brash. The supporters of the rural bands have come by car – families with the stolid, respectable look of Protestant small farmers and shopkeepers. The urban bands have come with legions of young and noisy supporters, many adorned in vibrant youth cultural styles.

Kids in heavy-metal, biker, mod and punk gear are to be seen amongst the crowd. These youth cultural styles mix and merge with the symbols of Loyalism in an expressive symbiosis. A heavy-metal kid proudly displays an Ulster flag transfer appended to the back of his studded denim jacket; mods in parkas adorn their billowing parkas with paramilitary stickers and with a red, white and blue target motif emblazoned with the motto ULSTER; a punk with brightly dyed hair backcombed into protruding spikes adorns his judiciously ripped denims with Rangers (i.e. Glasgow

Rangers, the predominantly Protestant Scottish football club) scarves. None of these kids dressed in these styles are cohering in discrete subcultural groups. Punks socialize with heavy-metal kids, mods with bikers. Nor does a particular band seem to have any association with any particular style. The Maiden City Protestant Boys, who are by now starting to assemble to join the parade, have members and supporters who embrace rocker, new-wave, punk and mod styles.

Does this incoherent panopoly of styles mean that these young people are merely involved in an imitative stylization with no subcultural 'reality' behind it? John Clarke (1976) has warned us about fetishising the surface elements of, and objects of, subcultural style. As he argues:

> the generation of sub-cultural style, then, involves differential selection from within the matrix of the existent. What happens is not the creation of objects and meanings from nothing, but rather the transformation and re-arrangement of what is given (and 'borrowed') into a pattern that carries new meanings, its translation into a new context, and its adaption.

These transformations – of elements of both the parental culture and generational style – anchor potentially universal and commercially homogenized styles in a specific subcultural experience. For young working-class people the subculture is always a transaction with their parental culture and an appropriation and reworking of youthful consumption styles. As Clarke notes:

> working class youth sub-cultures take some things principally from the 'located' parental culture: but they apply and transform them to the situations and experiences characteristic of their own distinctive group life and generational experience (in Hall and Jefferson, 1976).

The bands, with their own regimented style, seem to mediate between youthful style and 'traditional' Loyalist culture. A noticeable degree of interaction exists between the bands and their loyal audience, a personalistic bond which distinguishes the youthful 'Blood and Thunder' bands from the rural and older competition bands. In the context of the decline of the formal institutions of

Orangeism in the lives of young working-class Protestants, the bands have now become the most important agency in the reproduction of populist Loyalism across the generational divide. Indeed, it is precisely the partial generational autonomy of the bands as a youth cultural milieu that enables them to perform this key role in cultural reproduction.

As the bands congregate at the starting point of the parade, groups of side drummers from different bands engage in drumming duels, exchanging triplets, rolls and paradiddles; voice and response, phrase and refrain, climaxing in rapid unison-playing of rhythmic volleys. I see Keith Hope from the 'Boys' discussing the finer points of drumming technique with some of the side drummers from the out of town bands. Keith had learnt his drumming in one of the traditional pipe bands that his father had been a member of, but was having to adapt his style to the more robust demands of the 'Blood and Thunder' milieu. As he tells me:

> I'd rather be in a flute band. In a pipe band ye go down the street an' all yer friends laugh at ye. In a flute band, a Loyalist band, ye play more Ulster stuff like. Its Protestant music, its just your music.

This drum duelling is the nearest the musicians come to breaking out of the rigid musical discipline of their martial music. The strict marching tempo of the parade, hammered out on the bass drum, provides few opportunities for syncopation, embellishment or improvization for a generation that spends most of its time bopping to the rhythmically-sophisticated, and improvisationally open, dance musics of black America. As if in compensation for this, the drums come to play the primary expressive role in the band's performances. They provide the only real variation in the dynamics of the music. In the flute bands, especially any 'Blood and Thunder' band worth its salt, the flutes are often almost inaudible alongside the explosion of sound coming from the side drums and bass drummer. This form of instrumentation – the flutes playing in unison and the bass drum anchoring and constraining the tempo and dynamics – does not lend itself to musical innovation or individual virtuosity.

It is perhaps more in the adaptation of the marching style itself on the streets that youth attempts to breathe some life into established tradition. We can list these stylistic innovations – the subversion of the military marching style in the exaggerated swagger and rhythmic shuffle of the fluters; the weaving dancers of the cymbal players who jaunt, crissing and crossing, through the ranks of the rest of the band almost in the manner of a country set dance; the antics of the bass drummers who attempt a form of wild dancing which takes some of them careering into the crowd at each side of the road, causing cries of delight from the audience; the vigorous, synchronised swirling of the flags by their bearers; the drum majors providing a touch of pure circus as they hurl their stocky decorated batons high into the sky above the crowd, catching them to great applause. Each young band may have two or even three of these stick-bearing aristocrats of the streets. Similarly they will usually have more than one bass drummer. The Orange order, anxious to curb the unruly character of some of the bands, has attempted to restrict them to carrying only one bass drum on parades and has also attempted to curtail the baton-throwing feats of the drum majors. It has not been conspicuously successful in this.

The Order, concerned to avoid any direct conflict with the authorities, was in fact trying to impose its own code of conduct on the bands. This, as well as aiming to curb youthful exuberance on the street and excess off it, was also attempting to stop the bands carrying flags – particularly paramilitary ones. The lads in the 'Boys', like those in the other bands, expressed considerable resentment about this intrusion in their activities. The code was viewed as another example of Orange timorousness in the face of government pressure. Robert Eakin, one of the side drummers, had no doubts about the failings of 'the Orange':

They're turnin' tail. They're not taking a strong enough stand. They're not standin' with the ordinary people in the street. You've got the bandsmen, like, we're prepared te make what stand we can, showing people we're going to be there if they need us.

Of course, as most of the parades that they and the other bands now attended had nothing to do with the Orange orders, the lads couldn't see how the code could be enforced anyway. The 'Boys' did usually respond to the request of local lodge, LOL 1007, to accompany them on the big march on the Twelfth but they were in no way bound to do so. The bands would continue to do their own thing and that night I was to see a number of bands carrying the standard of the banned UVF, a purple flag with a single small orange star in one corner. That spring (1986) the 'Boys' were parading without a colour party, but by the next marching season, they were fielding three male flag-bearers, carrying the Union Jack, the Ulster flag *and* the standard of the illegal UVF.

Whatever this array of flags signifies about the complexities and contradictions of Protestant ethnicity – other bands carry the Scottish flag, some carry the standard of the Young Citizens Volunteers, (a junior section of the UVF) with its green shamrock and red hand of Ulster – the choice of flags is also a testament to the generational independence of the 'Blood and Thunder' bands from the official Orange institutions.

The parade snakes around the village, weaving through the streets of the housing estate. Somewhere along the route Paisley and a DUP contingent of election candidates have joined the parade in front of the first band. Clearly Paisley aims to use the parade as an election rally. A DUP stall selling Ulster badges and paraphernalia, and distributing election propaganda, has been set up at the centre of the estate. As yet, trade is slack.

The march ends with the host band, the Orange and Blue, lining up at the front of the crowd to applaud each band as they complete the parade circuit. Flags swirl, drums deafen and batons soar higher than ever as the parade comes to a climax. Again the tight constraints of Protestant propriety and the martial discipline of the Orange march are threatened with being blown apart by the youthful exuberance of the players caught up in the gaze of their audience.

Paul McGrath, one of the lads from the 'Sons' who I spoke to at their Tuesday night practice session the week after this parade, caught the mood of the marchers well:

> It's everybody watching *you* and clappin' *you*. You feel real proud of yerself. Like at that parade at that Newbuildings march at the end, all the crowd were clappin' and cheering . . . It's a bit of a joke really but you feel really good.

For someone like Paul, now unemployed after serving his time for three years as a motor mechanic, the band and the parades provided one of the few sources of self-gratification in his life.

As the bands reach the end of the parade circuit Paisley positions himself at the finishing line. He is clearly determined to be seen by as many of the marching bands and their supporters as possible and to identify with their activity. The young marchers seem relatively little concerned with this political dimension super-imposed on their parade. The dismissed musicians continue to play in small groups exchanging volleys which punctuate the falling darkness. Others head off to the nearby pub or to the chip shop for refreshment after the exertions of the night.

A small crowd gathers around a stage which has been erected by the shops on the estate. Only a fraction of the crowd who watched the parade stay on for the political speeches – despite the fact that on this occasion a television crew shooting material for a documentary on 'political extremism' in Ulster[9] gives the occasion potentially some extra interest. The crowd is mainly composed of the very country folk who provide the backbone of Paisley's political support. However, despite the authority of Paisley within the Loyalist community, the attitude of the crowd is less than attentive, indeed almost irreverent.

The cameras, with their carefully chosen angles, will later represent Paisley on the television screen as the charismatic mass orator swaying a duped and volatile mob. They will fail to capture the smallness and intimacy of this essentially domestic occasion and its preoccupation with youthful pleasure and communal celebration. Indeed, only Paisley with his huge physical presence and thundering voice which triumphs over an appalling makeshift public address system, commands the attention of the onlookers. He too senses that this is not the occasion for political seriousness and delivers a light hearted speech, full of self-parody. He praises the bands for their 'steadfastness':

I know that it's spring and dark winter is past when I hear the sound of the Protestant marching bands. It warms my heart to hear Protestant feet marching once again. For it is the marching bands that are keeping open roads for Protestants to walk upon.

Paisley, despite his by now polished media persona, remains

constrained by the forces that brought him to power in the first place. He is still required to be at the head of – and to be seen to be at the head of – the street actions of militant Loyalism. Indeed, as political commentators have noted (Taylor, 1978) Paisley's leadership is based neither on simple charisma nor on a specific election programme, but rather on his ability to 'personify and represent the populist elements within the Protestant community', and by his 'willingness to defy the law to put into practice Protestant principles and demonstrate symbols of Protestant culture and power.'

The lads from the 'Boys' have been watching Paisley's performance from the side of the stage. They are less convinced of his credentials as a militant leader. Many of them see his intervention tonight as political opportunism.

The 'Boys' now declined the invitations of the local DUP party organization to accompany candidates on election rallies. The party had been deaf to appeals from the band for donations for new uniforms, as indeed had been most of the other Unionist notables in the town. This had made the band even more jaundiced about parliamentary Loyalism. As Sammy noted, it was ironical that the only positive reply to their request for donations came from two Catholic businessmen (who owned pubs the band frequented).

The 'Sons', considerably more hard-up than the more established 'Boys', did take up the offer of the DUP to accompany its candidates in its vote-seeking perambulation in the East Bank estates. The £50 offered for this service would come in handy in paying off the finance company debt on the instruments. One evening next month I witnessed the 'Sons' leading a DUP contingent through Irish Street. They were unmercilessly subjected to hoots of derision from some of the lads from the home band gathered, as ever, by the shops. For a few moments it looked as if a fracas might break out between the local lads and the intruders – much to the embarrassment of the po-faced DUP stalwarts. The surly independence of the younger bands, their unruliness and indeed sheer unpredictability, make them awkward allies for the stiff-collared puritans of the Unionist political machine.

Indeed, in mid-May the 'Sons' themselves were to give ample demonstration of this. The DUP planned a night of glory after their advances in the local elections and arranged a victory parade through the Waterside area to celebrate. The 'Sons' had been hired to provide the musical accompaniment for the proceedings. I arrived at the shuttered shops in the centre of Nelson Drive, from where the parade was to set off, to discover that half the band had not turned up. Terry Kelly, thoroughly sickened, was stuck with a pile of uncollected band pullovers over his arm, trying to explain the situation to the irate dignitaries of the DUP.

Apparently a feud was in full swing within the band. At their weekly practice two days before the planned victory parade, a major row had blown up between Terry and some of the more wayward members of the band about their drinking on parades. Half the band had privately decided to bring Terry's drive for greater discipline to grief by boycotting the victory parade. While Terry attempted to appease the DUP stalwarts, swearing that this was it, he was definitely 'putting the band off the road, permanently', the missing members were – I was later to discover – lying around in the long grass up by Maggy's Lane (where the bikers met to drink) with bumper bottles of cider, overcome with laughter.

Tonight, here in Newbuildings, as dusk falls, the DUP hopefuls renew their appeal for support in the coming election. Most of the young bandsmen and their supporters have however already voted with their feet and have abandoned bass drum and flag to pile into the disco.

3 June: Annual Parade and disco of the Maiden City Protestant Boys, Irish Street

By the time of the annual parade of the Maiden City Protestant Boys, the marching season was well underway. On the open spaces on the Loyalist estates the younger children were already starting to pile up materials for the traditional Eleventh night bonfire, still more than a month away.

The lads from the band were congregating in front of the shops with a crate of beer. Some of them were carrying white plastic improvised collection tins made out of old plastic paint containers, ready for the planned street collection. They confided in me that they expected fewer bands than they had actually invited as there were also parades at Newbuildings and Limavady that night.

Certainly the 'Sons' would not be in attendance – they had not been invited. While this usually would probably not have stopped them from coming, the ongoing row within the band over discipline was still festering. Terry had managed to get rid of another two of the more unruly members of the band. They had, in fact, been arrested for throwing missiles at the incoming train from Belfast, and it seemed the police were also questioning them about a range of other acts of paramilitary-inspired vandalism, including spray-painting Loyalist slogans on Housing Executive property and breaking into a Catholic primary school and causing considerable damage.

Terry was trying to recruit some new younger members to replace this delinquent element and, indeed, later in the night I was to meet Carson Logue who informed me that, on the basis of an appeal from Terry, he was going to throw his lot in within the band. His brother, an ardent Loyalist now living away from Derry, had taught him how to play the flute. Carson felt that with a few practices with the band he'd be able to go out with them for the Twelfth parade.

Terry had decided to keep the band out of parades and concentrate on practising and breaking-in the new members ready for the big parade on the Twelfth of July. To raise morale in the band he had ordered brand new red berets with distinctive badges which he hoped would have arrived by July. In somewhat of a coup he'd managed to arrange a contract with an Orange Lodge from County Down for the Twelfth parade. The Lodge, which had never actually seen the 'Sons' perform, had already offered to pay the cost of the bus for the band and give them a £100 on top to lead them out on the Twelfth.

Over in the community centre the trophies provided by the band for the competitions are on display. The visiting bands crowd around a makeshift bar selling cans of beer and soft drinks. The bar is of course totally illegal. It has no licence for the sale of alcohol – but it is an important source of income for the home band. A uniformed member of the band collects the money and dispenses the cans. Others sell tickets for a raffle.

Some nine bands have actually turned up for the night, somewhat less than Sammy Torrens, who had sent out the invitations, had hoped for. Bands have, however, travelled to be here from Omagh, Coleraine and Limavady. The parade moves off on a route identical to that followed in the April outing. The full range of marching bands can again be clearly witnessed – from, at one end of the spectrum, the noisy and unruly Pride of the Valley with its youthful membership and combative style, through the 'Boys', in the process of transition to a more musically accomplished and decorous future, and the spick-and-span William King Memorial from the Fountain, which has long since abandoned its raucous 'Blood and Thunder' origins, to, at the other end of this evolutionary scale, a musically-accomplished older competition band like the Hamilton Flute Band, with its elaborate arrangements and studied sobriety.

At the weekly practices of the 'Blood and Thunder' bands each new tune is learnt partly by ear and partly using rough musical charts. A band's repertoire will usually consist of around 30 songs. The notes used in a particular tune are written out in sequence in alphabetical, rather than notational, form with no representation of duration or dynamics. New members sit with the more experienced members playing joining in in unison till they master a tune. Until such time, they are borne along by the musical momentum of the mass of established proficient members – melodic safety in numbers. These musical practices are pretty rudimentary in comparison with those of the competition bands. Of course, it is their basic simplicity that both facilitates a wide basis for recruitment to the bands and minimizes the pressures on the less musically-accomplished to leave. In the bands, questions of musical competence are somewhat secondary, for most of the younger members, to their social functions. Indeed, the musical practices of the bands both reflect and sustain social solidarities within the band.

Tonight there is much interest in the appearance of a new flute band from St Johnston, just over the border from Derry in the Irish Republic. They come from that small area in east Donegal, the Laggan, which still has a significant Protestant population and in which Orangeism was traditionally strong.

In the short speeches after the prizes are handed out they were welcomed as our, 'exiles from Donegal'. Sammy Torrens was in fact still coaching them in the rudiments of flute band technique and made the ten-mile journey into the Republic once a week to attend their practices and help out. A local Loyalist political figure, asked by the band to distribute the prizes, sounds a familiar warning, in welcoming the St Johnston band, and invokes an old image of encirclement:

We were squeezed out of Donegal; it's up to you to make sure we don't get squeezed out of Londonderry. We have to defend our faith and our traditions.

As ever the young grow restless as the speeches are made – short though they may be. Already the girls are hanging around the door of the community centre arrayed in pastel cottons, eager to know when the disco will start. And for the lads, the serious drinking has already begun.

Some of the lads break away from the prize-giving to launch a hail of stones at a local bus which passes by the centre of the estate on its way up to the local hospital. It was not entirely clear why they had done this – apart from the obvious fact that some already had 'drink taken'. One band member offered the excuse that, 'it was probably all Fenians on it', as he reckoned that all the residents of Irish Street would have got off at the previous stop.

There was undoubtedly a distinctive delinquent element on this as on other estates, some of whom had been in the bands at one time or another. I had already met some of these kids at the youth club adjoining the estate – or, to be more precise, hanging around outside. They had been banned by the headmaster from entering the club and the school premises for fighting whilst at school, and for organising a mini-riot in the school playground after classes one afternoon. This had ended in a sortie of Protestant pupils stoning a number of Catholic homes located beside the school.

In each of the estates loose gangs of male teenagers cohered around a range of sectarian-motivated, if random, delinquent activities. These gangs claimed elaborate titles like Natrats, Fountain Zulu Tartan Rule, Irish Street Tartan etc. In fact these labels seemed to serve as flags of convenience. For, on other occasions the same lads from Irish Street called themselves Maiden City Loyalist Youth, a name with an uncomfortable similarity to that of the band, just as the Fountain kids claimed the alternative title West Bank Loyalist Youth.

These Loyalist gangs rested on patterns of peer-group association established elsewhere – particularly in the marching bands. Indeed, the membership of the gangs and the bands overlapped to a considerable extent in the 14–18 age range. The gangs, unlike the bands, seemed to possess no enduring gang structure. 'Membership' seemed to largely consist of wearing the established symbols like tartan scarves or Ulster, Linfield or Rangers scarves, engaging in sporadic acts of graffiti-spraying and vandalism, including sectarian-inspired attacks on Catholic property, or simply being around when bother broke out with Catholic rival groups and being prepared to join in the 'brickin'.

Though these gangs often utilize paramilitary references to 'legitimize' random acts of vandalism, directed in a haphazard way at the nearby Catholic population, there was little real evidence that more than a handful had any real organizational involvement with the paramilitaries. Indeed their identification with Loyalist terror groups like the UVF, UFF and PAF seems one conducted largely at the level of the imagination.

Typical of these kids was 'Rats', now aged seventeen. He had been an irregular school-attender and, indeed, was eventually to be sent for a spell at a Juvenile Training Centre outside Belfast because of his truancy and defiance of school authority. He had returned to school for the last couple of months of the school year. Shortly after leaving school at the age of sixteen, 'Rats' had got involved with the police for brawling and suspected vandalism. After a series of official cautions, he had once again been committed to the training centre for a short period. Released once again he had agreed, somewhat reluctantly, to take up a place in the Maydown YTP. As the marching season warmed up skirmishes between the Irish Street lads and kids from Gobnascale were becoming more common. Stone-throwing between the two camps across the *Top o' the Hill* divide between the two estates was carrying on until late at night as the summer months began and the school holidays got under way. 'Rats' was at the centre of this 'brickin' and had, it seemed clear, been involved in a number of incidents of vandalism directed at nearby Catholic families. The most notorious activity of his gang had been an early morning assault on the house of an elderly man which was located right in the middle of the shatter zone between Irish Street and Gobnascale. The man's windows had been broken and the slogan IRISH BASTARD scrawled in paint on the man's front door.

Somewhat perversely, 'Rats' actually ran around with a Catholic girl from the Ardmore area who I was to see with him around Irish Street. Whereas he would not be able to show his face in the adjoining Catholic estate – on the one occasion he did in the summer he was to get into deep trouble – 'Rats' felt quite relaxed about moving about in the exclusively Catholic Ardmore estate located some two miles distant. Like many of the young people I met he was quite capable of being in the thick of sectarian rioting, focused on the physical and ideological boundaries of his own immediate neighbourhood, and yet engaging in friendly relations with individuals from the 'other side' well removed from his local territory.

In September I met him at the youth club hobbling on crutches. It transpired that, blind drunk, he had wandered into the Catholic Gobnascale area and been seized by a number of young Republicans. 'Rats' had earlier been warned by the IRA about his delinquent activities and that night was subjected to a brutal punishment attack. He had been threatened with a loaded gun and had concrete blocks dropped on his legs before being dumped at the edge of Irish Street. 'Rats' was remarkably blasé about this ordeal, claiming he couldn't remember much of what happened. Luckily no real damage had been done to his legs and the general view around the estate was that he had it coming to him.

By ten o'clock the disco is in full swing – or at least the girls are. At this stage they are dominating the dance floor, jiving in pairs in the manner so beloved of young women throughout Ireland. As the homogenous disco music gives way to the sounds of heavy metal, the lads gather in circles to engage in the long-established ritual of 'headbangin' (a pseudo-aggressive dance form) and the girls retreat to the ladies' toilets. Another arena becomes subject to male domination. A supporter of the band performs a frantic punkstyle dance responding to the strains of Sid Vicious' version of 'My Way'. The young bandsmen enter the fray, pogoing up and down, their epaulettes flapping to the beat of the music in frenetic scenes which depart from the usual etiquettes of coolness which dominate the commercial disco floor these days.

Interspersed amongst the disco-hits and punk-medleys are Loyalist paramilitary ballads on record. All join in on the choruses of 'Soldier of the UDA', punching the air in clenched-fist salute. One of the older members of the band takes the microphone from the disc-jockey and gives a tuneless rendering of the morose ballad of 'Sergeant Lindsay Mooney', a song identical in its melody and poetics to a popular Republican ballad. As the young audience grows restless he leads them in a spirited delivery of 'Derry's Walls – We'll Fight and No Surrender!', a tune which every Protestant child in Derry learns at their mother's knee.

Preparing for the twelfth

By early July the school holidays had begun. At the centre of the estates, on open ground piles of wood, discarded household furniture and tyres are being stacked in preparation for the Eleventh night bonfire. The pile is getting higher and higher by the day as the younger children spend their days scouring the area for flammable material. On most of the Protestant estates the younger teenagers had built makeshift huts beside the bonfires. As the Eleventh night grew nearer and the bonfire began to take shape, some of them, indeed, were staying out all night and sleeping in these huts, ostensibly to guard their bonfires from possible marauders from the nearby Catholic estates. Keith Hope had spent a number of nights like this:

> ye stay out to guard the bonfire 'cause they come down and try to burn it on you like. All the wee boys and the big boys sit out in the hut since about seven o'clock till we leave in the mornin'. Any Taig does come down to burn it ye chase them away. We stay in the hut all night playing cards an' all and walk around the streets every so often.

Clearly, with the end of the school year and the start of the long summer break the Orange celebrations provide an exciting focal point for youthful street activity, filling otherwise empty and unstructured days and evenings. The groups guarding the bonfires, mainly younger teenagers, are joined by the older lads in the late evenings after the pubs shut. They were starting to repaint the kerbs red, white and blue and had organised to go round the doors of the estate collecting money for the paint. A paint-bombing war appeared to be in full swing and a group of Catholic kids had managed to penetrate into the estate one night and throw paint over an elaborate mural painted on boards that had been erected on a gable wall. The following night 'Rats' and some of the other lads launched a return strike on 'Gobna':

> about two or three in the mornin' we went out and painted the kerbs, red, white and blue ... Then we went down to the *Top O the Hill* and done a lot of paint bombin' itself like. Up there we smashed a few windows like ... right enough we had drink in us that night.

This, in turn, incited a group of Catholic youths to attack the entrance area to the estate and a number of windows were broken and two cars burned. Things were threatening to get out of hand, and each night now the police landrovers stationed themselves between the two factions up by the school. The nightly confrontations began to take a familiar ritualized form. Sandra Brolly took a poor view of the bellicose attitudes of the lads in Irish Street, partly because she had a Catholic boyfriend from the Catholic Creggan estate. Yet she was a keen spectator at these riots and wasn't averse to throwing the odd stone:

> At night they all come up from the shops lookin' for a fight, the ones from Irish Street. Then they [the kids from Gobnascale] say, 'To hell with that there, we're not taking that', and they come up and brick back. But . . . we usually join up at the end of the night and brick the cops. We *all* hate the cops . . . but then when they leave we'd just be brickin' each other again.

The older lads in the bands take responsibility for erecting bunting, flags and arches. Some estates have formal arch committees which raise money for these decorations in door-to-door collections. Again, the band members tend to dominate these. Nelson Drive had erected the same elaborate Orange arch for the past few years at the entrance to the estate. This was maintained by a local joiner and stored each year in his garage. Carson Logue, now rehearsing regularly with the 'Sons', and involved with the other lads from the band in kerb painting – and by the sounds of it in paint-bombing – was helping with the decorations. He recalled with great amusement the erection of the arch, demonstrating that Loyalists are not without some sense of humour:

> we were putting it up but the poles [supporting the arch] were too weak . . . The weight of the arch when you were pulling it up was tremendous . . . every time ye pulled the arch up on the pulleys the poles kept bending . . . in and in . . Now this is no word of a lie . . . I swear on me mother's life . . . we were just done putting up the arch and the first car to go under it . . . there was a priest in it, honest te God, a yellow Ford car . . . and Jesus didn't the arch fall and almost killed a fellah, Jimmy Cairns. He

was in Hospital for three weeks with a broken shoulder! . . . This is no word of a lie!

At one time in Loyalist neighbourhoods the decoration of the streets would have involved the whole community and would have been entrusted to the senior members of the community. Now, with the structures of Protestant working class communality considerably eroded, it is the young people who provide the manpower, and the bands the organization, for this activity. As one of the leaders of the William King band from the Fountain told me somewhat wistfully:

> Years ago in every wee street there'd be three or four arches. Now there's only three or four in the whole area, ye know. Everybody done there own wee street then, now you have a couple of dozen men (from the band) that does the whole area.

The bands have now assumed the key role in sustaining a sense of Protestant identity which expresses itself in a sense of exclusive community rooted in a particular local territory. Jonathan Bryce, a seventeen-year old member of the William King who devoted his days to painting an enormous and elaborate mural to commemorate the band on the boarded up shops in the Fountain explained to me:

> it's the band that keeps this estate goin' – keepin' people's heads up and proud of their tradition and history. It's the band that keeps the people together.

The marching season and the build up to the Twelfth brings a heightened concern with Protestant identity and difference. These ritualized practices in which the young play such a significant part – the bonfires, paintings, parades and accompanying confrontations – are the specific means by which an exclusive Protestant identity is represented and renewed in the Loyalist mind. Karen Hewitt from Curryneirin, when I asked her what the ideological term 'Ulster' meant to her and how it differed from the more neutral designation, 'Northern Ireland', gave a perceptive reply:

> Sometimes it doesn't mean anything if you see someone writing

ULSTER, say at Christmas or something . . . but when it comes
up to the Twelfth it seems to mean more to everybody. Ye see
more people writing, ye seem to notice it more. Like if ye went
past a fence now you'd begin to notice it cause its coming up to
the Twelfth . . . I don't think Ulster is meant to be a place . . . it's
just meant te be the Protestant people. You know the Waterside's a place . . . but ye wouldn't call ULSTER a place. Its the
North of Ireland but it isn't any particular place – it's just
Protestant.

It is the street-active young who now play the key part in the
ritualized representation of a Protestant 'imagined community'.

Eleventh night

Around five o'clock in the afternoon I arrived in the Fountain to
find the local kids putting the finishing touches to their bonfire.
This is now a massive monumental structure over twenty feet high,
profiled against the ancient walls of the planters' city. The Fountain is the last remaining exclusively-Protestant enclave on the
West Bank. The area was substantially redeveloped in the early
1970s. The maze of tiny labourers' cottages and red-brick terraces
which sustained such a vibrant community life in the past was
replaced by a severe complex of flats and maisonettes. The almost
military austerity of the contemporary concrete buildings serves to
reinforce the impression of a garrison under siege. Following
street confrontations in the early party of the 'Troubles', the estate
is completely fenced-off from the adjoining Catholic Bishop Street
area.
    During the redevelopment, many of the original residents left
the Fountain to settle in the new estates on the East Bank and the
neighbourhood's population was significantly depleted. One of the
older residents of the area recalled the Twelfth celebrations of the
past, a memory against which the malaise of the present could be
measured:

The Fountain now is not the same as it used to be in the olden
times. Always up in the wee street where my father lived – there

were only eight houses in it – you had bonfires goin' and lovely arches. There used to be competition between the rivals of the streets. We had a big horn up – we still have the records – and we had dancing on Eleventh Night. They were wild about waltzin', so they were, they used to dance till all the hours of the morning ... I don't know how they marched the next day. And on the Twelfth Night they'd be as bad again. But for the old street itself – it's all changed. I think I have only one neighbour now who used to be in the old street. I don't know where they all went to. The people's all gone.

Despite the fact that the estate lies outside the city's walls, in the minds of the young Loyalists it is now located, symbolically at least, within the beseiged planters' city. The Fountain has become, within the youthful imagination, a last bastion of Protestantism in the overwhelmingly Catholic cityside of Derry. Like Irish Street on the East Bank, the Fountain has become the spatial focal point for the celebration of Loyalist rites. With its location in the shadow of the city walls, surrounded by Nationalist Derry, it has acquired a particular significance as a physical referent of Loyalist communality.

Many of the original residents – or their teenage children – return to the neighbourhood to enjoy the bonfires and merriment on the two bonfire nights in July and August, and to attend the annual Relief of Derry parade organised by the Apprentice Boys in August. In this some 15,000 marchers pass through the area. On these occasions, as the crowds flock into the estate, the Fountain is reborn. The planters' city is reclaimed again – if only for the day.

Precariously perched at the top of the gigantic bonfire is Jonathan Bryce, a recent school leaver from the grammar school, and two of his friends, waving a huge tricolour. Not, I hasten to add, a conversion by Loyalist youth to the politics of Irish nationalism, but preparations for an auto da fé. The top of the bonfire was also festooned with a colourful array of Sinn Fein election posters. These had been secured in a daring raid in the early hours into the strongly Republican Bogside area. They had been ripped down from street lamp standards (the lads had also paint-bombed a Republican wall mural with Orange paint). These posters, together with the tricolour, were to be put to the torch later that night. The flag had been especially made by Protestant workers in one of the city's shirt factories and smuggled out past the security gates.

These young people actively reject an Irish identity. Yet they are perhaps less certain of who they are in national terms. As we have argued, Ulster Loyalism does invoke a specific and exclusive ethnic identity – 'the Protestant people of Ulster' in its political discourse. Yet it does not clothe its claims in the apparel of any distinctive nationalism. Loyalists increasingly find themselves at odds not only with Irish nationalism but also with the British state and British public opinion. A Protestant identity, if it is to be more than just an assertion that Unionists are not Irish or some sort of vague set of platitudes about British heritage, requires the symbolic resources and mythic representations of Loyalist populism. As the social basis of this Loyalist communality erodes, youth cultural work demarcating the symbolic and spatial boundaries of the imagined Protestant community becomes more central to the reproduction of this populism. Here in the Fountain an event like Eleventh Night is almost entirely in the hands of the young. They celebrate the rites of renewal for the community as a whole. One of the young men from the Fountain put it this way:

> It's about the only day they show who they are. Any other day you wouldn't know who they are or what they are. But up around here in August they all mix, they're all out like. Aye, there's more life about it in August. In any other month you wouldn't see anybody.

By eleven o'clock the first of the bonfires in Nelson Drive is lit. Then Bond Street, Tullyally, Faughan Valley and last, around midnight, the Fountain. The lads douse the bottom of their bonfires with petrol and the edifice explodes in sheets of flames to the cheers of the large crowd now assembled. The onlookers scream in delight as the tricolour catches and withers in the fierce blaze. Some of the band have brought out a few flutes and side drums and they accompany the merriment. They have all brought ample supplies of beer and wine. Without their distinctive uniforms and military formation the band members merge and fuse with the youthful crowd. Tomorrow they will have to be up early to make the journey with the Orange Lodge to the Twelfth parade in nearby Portstewart.

Down in Nelson Drive, Terry has led the 'Sons' (casually dressed in leather and denim jackets) for an impromptu parade around the estate to gather support for the bonfire celebrations. The dissension of the recent past is now behind them. They too will be up early tomorrow to climb on the bus heading to Comber in County Down. Ahead lies the challenge of representing their neighbourhood in the big parade in the east of the province.

But tonight, for all the bandsmen and their supporters, there are opportunities for excess. The bottles of vodka and cheap fortified wine are passing among the crowd, the banter between the lads and the girls is as sharp as ever. Already groups of young people are sitting gathered around the fire. Many will spend the entire night by its dying embers swopping stories and reliving past adventures. Some of the wilder ones will gather up by the School at the Top O the Hill trying to goad the Gobnascale youth into an anniversary confrontation. . .

> We'll Fight and no surrender
> And come when duty calls
> With heart, and hand and sword and shield
> To guard old Derry's walls.
>
> (traditional)

5

Youth and Ghettoization in Northern Ireland

Introduction

In this chapter I trace the impact of sectarian ghettoization on the lives of the young in Northern Ireland. Drawing on the fieldwork conducted in Derry, I plot the effect of increased political polarisation on the sensibilities of working-class teenagers. This chapter examines how youth cultural practices reflect the ghettoization of social life and, indeed, reinforce the divisions between young Protestants and Catholics.

A point of comparison

Once my field work commenced and I began to spend some time with the young Protestants of Derry it didn't take me long to realise just how different were their experiences of growing up to my own as a teenager over twenty years earlier. Old school friends who were now teachers in the town's secondary schools expressed the view that attitudes amongst the young had hardened since the 1970s. Young Protestants, I was told, were less willing and less able to socialize with young Catholic people; they were more likely to support militant Loyalist political parties and stances. It was felt they were generally less tolerant towards those with different religious and political beliefs, and that explicitly sectarian attitudes seemed more prevalent. The 'Troubles' had left their mark.

The mid-1960s had seen a considerable improvement in inter-communal relations in Derry. The IRA campaign waged from 1956–9 had been a dismal failure and the Nationalist Party, to which the majority of the Catholic population gave their political allegiance, was being incorporated into political life at Stormont.

Militant Republicanism seemed an anachronism. Moreover, Unionism under the leadership of O'Neill was promising modernising change if not actual reform. Derry, situated as it was, on the border, and with its natural hinterland spreading into County Donegal, seemed set to profit from the improved political relations and increased economic cooperation between the two states in Ireland. For many young Protestant people reared in the more liberal post-war climate, Orangeism seemed an arcane residue of a troubled past. It was convenient for many to embrace the illusion that Northern Ireland was, in the context of the British post-war social democratic settlement, evolving into a 'normal' modern liberal society.

Local grievances about how the area was faring economically in comparison with the east of the Province were aired by both Protestants and Catholics alike. Unemployment in Derry was running at over twice that of the Belfast region. Despite this, Unionist industrial location policy continued to favour the eastern part of the province to the detriment of the area west of the Bann, with its predominantly Catholic population. Indeed, in 1965 there had been a concerted cross-sectarian campaign of protest against the government decision to locate the proposed second university for Northern Ireland in the Protestant market town of Coleraine rather than in Derry which already had a long-established university college. As a teenager I can remember attending a crowded meeting in the city's Guildhall called to protest against the university decision. At this Unionist and Nationalist had actually sat together on the platform.

The Stormont Election of 1965 saw a Liberal candidate of Protestant background gather sufficient cross-sectarian support to come within 1,000 votes of unseating the sitting Unionist member. And indeed, Protestant liberals were prominent in the early days of the Civil Rights movement.[1]

A survey of youth conducted in Derry in 1969[2] indicated a significant shift amongst teenagers away from blanket support for Nationalist and Unionist political parties and positions towards cross-sectarian parties and social-issue politics. A third of the representative sample questioned declared their intention to vote, when they had the opportunity, for Liberal or Labour candidates. Indeed, less than a third expressed support for the traditional Unionist and Nationalist parties. The same survey indicated that over 70 per cent of the young people surveyed were in favour of integrated schooling, and an even greater number (85 per cent) felt that youth club provision should be 'inter-denominational'.

By the sixties the ripples of the global post-war economic boom were at last reaching Northern Ireland. Unemployment was at its lowest for many years. Significant differentials between Protestant and Catholic levels of unemployment remained however, as did regional variations. Derry, with its population now almost 70 per cent Catholic, still had the highest rate of male unemployment for a town of its size in western Europe. In 1971 23 per cent of Catholic males were out of a job, compared with just 8 per cent of Protestant males.

By the mid-1960s the government had managed to lure to the town a number of large multinational companies. British Oxygen and the giant Du Pont company opened large plants as the artificial-fibre sector boomed. School-leavers with technical education – both Protestant and Catholic – could look forward to semi-skilled and skilled employment and apprenticeship training[3]. The extension of British welfare state provision to Northern Ireland had also played its part in raising living standards. It had been most dramatically felt in the extension of access to both secondary education and university study.

Schooling, of course, remained religiously segregated, both at the primary and secondary level. However, at least amongst the children of the middle classes attending the town's four single-sex grammar schools, recreational mixing was becoming more common. Moreover, the town's large technical college drew its students from both sides of the sectarian divide. Those destined to enter skilled manual jobs or office employment had ample opportunities to form cross-religious friendships – which they often did. The 1969 youth survey, conducted before the 'Troubles' had really begun to have significant impact on residential patterns in Derry, found that at that time almost 60 per cent of the young people questioned said they had friends across the religious divide. Significantly, it was in the 'intermediate' schools at the bottom of the tertiary hierarchy, (secondary moderns in England) that cross-religious mixing was least advanced (only 45 per cent of the intermediate school sample 'were friendly with anyone of the other religion'). These intermediate schools were attended largely by the sons and daughters of the Catholic and Protestant working class, the social stratum that was also most residentially segregated.

However, the city centre provided an important intercommunal meeting place which facilitated daily interaction and communication between Protestant and Catholic in what remained, by British standards, a small town. Young Protestants and Catholics eyed each other in city-centre cafes and picture houses. They increasingly crowded into the same clubs and dance halls. They tramped through the Bogside to the Brandywell Showground to support the same football team – Derry City. As Eamon McCann (1987) has argued:

> Derry has been a divided city for generations but Derry City has always been a determinately unifying force. When the club was founded a proposal to name it 'Derry Celtic' was quickly rejected on the ground that it had obvious associations with the Catholic-Nationalist community. [ ] The Board of the new soccer club founded in 1928 was the only institution of any significance where Unionists and Nationalists operated agreeably together, which they could manage only on the basis of a firm understanding that politics would never enter into the matter.

Nor did politics enter courtship behaviour in the town in the 1960s. Young Catholics and Protestants did date and there were real opportunities, for those prepared to avail themselves of them, to explore, via the erotic encounter, the culture of the other. In this apparently more favourable political and economic climate, shared youth cultural interests – rock music, fashions and styles, and common sites of pleasure – were able to provide a non-sectarian habitus beyond parental traditions and prejudices. As the mods and rockers took to the beaches of Brighton and beat their feet to the sounds of American soul music, the teenagers of Belfast and Derry flocked to the Antrim resort of Portrush. The teenage bank-holiday skirmishes there seemed in mimetic unison with youthful exuberance elsewhere and untainted by sectarian animus. We rocked to the native sound of Van Morrison, Sam Mahood and the Interns . . . a corner seemed to have been turned. The hedonistic and cosmopolitan impulses of the young themselves seemed to have unravelled the disabling mythologies of 'tradition'.

This improvement in community relations in Derry may, in the context of the continued Unionist maladministration of the city, have been somewhat deceptive. As the former editor of Derry's Catholic newspaper was to comment in retrospect:

> One of the peculiarities about Derry was that the political cleavage was mitigated by surprisingly good personal relations between Protestant and Catholics. Through the forties, fifties and early sixties, the communities had their demarcation lines, but cooperated socially and in sport, and the sectarian riots that were endemic to other areas of the North were almost unknown in the city. Perhaps the bonhomie was responsible to a dangerous degree for the Protestant miscalculation of the depth of Catholic feeling about the unjust political framework (Curran, 1986).

Youth in the 1980s

The mods were to return to the streets of Ulster in the mid-1980s. But now the target motifs on the back of their distinctive parkas were decorated red, white and blue *or* green white and yellow according to the religious background of the wearer. The leather jackets and denims of the heavy-metal kids were emblazoned not only with the demonic icons of electric rock, but also with paramilitary initials and emblems. Indeed, many of the youth cultural styles were now exclusively appropriated by the young from one 'side'. In mid 1980s Derry, the skinheads' style was practised solely by Catholic youth. And the Protestant teenagers who were regularly involved in street skirmishes with the self-proclaimed 'Rossville Skins' from the Bogside area of the town, identified the distinctive denim garb, boots and razored hair of the 'skins' as *ethnic* rather than merely subcultural markers. Subcultural style was now assimilated within the dynamics of sectarian conflict.[4]

Sectarian division: a taken for granted reality

How accurate were the assessments of teachers and youth workers concerning the supposed declining tolerance amongst the young? What role are youth subcultural practices playing in the formation of sectarian sensibilities?

When we examined in depth the attitudes of young people in Northern Ireland, what was striking was not a display of personal prejudice but a begrudging recognition of the naturalness and inevitability of sectarian conflict.

The young are often ambivalent and fatalistic about the sectarian milieu they live within. As one interviewee commented when asked about multi-denomination youth provision:

Ah, I would mix but I don't get the chance . . . if you mix . . . you don't only expect trouble from the other side – Catholics – but you also expect some from your own people that maybe live in the same street as you. Because they maybe would hit you because you were playing with a Catholic. They don't like it, they don't play, so maybe they'd hit you. Maybe you'd get hit by other Catholics. It's the same for the other person if he mixes with them. I'd like to mix, but I find it easier if you didn't mix and just kept to yourself.

Two school-leavers further explored this facticity. First youth:

Well I never fought wey them. I never had to. I threw stones and all at them like, but I never has anything really against them, 'cause to me I would like to get mixed community groups – both sides – and see what they are like. That's what should be happening. I mean it's no use doing it now with the likes of fifteen-year-olds, but it's the kids of five te ten that's growing up in it, and I would like to see them getting on well with Catholics. Going away wey' them, letting them ones see what they are like. Most of the kids think that every Catholic is an IRA man.

Second youth (discussing his actual experience of a mixed holiday):

I mean going away wey' them . . . well look at the time that we went te Holland – sure we went up te the airport, there was this row between this Catholic and Protestant, it was cooled down and over. We got to Holland, we had no problem at all. Back again, they came over into our estate for a night and we went

over to their estate for a while. One night we went over te their
estate and we got stoned. Ye know, ye can take them away
alright, but its coming back, ye just come back te the same
thing. Y'd have te take them away and keep them.

This willingness to participate in sectarian street violence and
belief in the widespread inevitability of such territorial conflict, yet
expressed preference for 'getting on well with Catholics' may
strike some readers as somewhat paradoxical. Yet this was a
common response amongst the young working-class people we
talked to. In my opinion, it is futile to attempt to reduce these
complex representations of the young, on even such an apparently
simple matter as 'getting on' with Protestants/Catholics, to
the one-dimensional responses of the attitudinal survey, with its
simplistic search for indices of prejudice and tolerance. Attempts
to treat sectarianism as a structure of personal prejudice, rather
than as a habitus of social and ideological relations governing the
lived experience of youth (and their elders) are misconceived.

Youthful reactions to the sectarian conflict cannot be simply
calibrated along a scale of personal prejudice. We require a
framework of interpretation which can relate youth collective
practices to the material situation young people in Northern
Ireland find themselves in today – one characterized by economic
marginalization and ghettoization.

To treat sectarianism as a structure of personal prejudice
capable of quantification by objective psychometric measurement
is of course to operate within an interpretative framework – a
distinctively ideological one. This methodological approach re-
duces sectarianism to a pathology of individual sentiment. It
conspires with 'official' definitions of sectarianism in deflecting
attention from the political realm. At the same time, it scapegoats
the working-class child, or his/her culture, community and 'traditions', identifying these as the origin of sectarian conflict.

Sectarian polarisation and 'territory'

This is not to deny that there has been a significant shift in levels of
expressed tolerance amongst the young. Sectarian attacks on the
young by the young have, as Cairns (1987) documents become

more common. Young lives have been lost in these sectarian clashes. Cross-sectarian bonds provided in the past by sport, music and dancing have unravelled. In the unresolved political crisis in Ulster the costs of the resulting inter-communal violence, which has left over 2,000 dead, have been disproportionately borne by the working class concentrated in the confessional ghettoes.

It is evident that there is an acute awareness amongst young people in Northern Ireland of the sectarian spatialisation of residential space. Our school survey revealed the restricted mobility which so governs the recreational and social activities of secondary-school pupils in the Derry area. This restricted mobility was particularly pronounced for working-class boys from public housing estates – those most likely to be involved in street gangs and territorial clashes with young Catholics.

Derry is located close to the border with County Donegal in the Irish Republic. Indeed, its proliferating suburbs now extend right up to the border. Derry people – or at least the Catholic population, are used to crossing the border on a daily or weekly basis. Many young people from the West Bank housing estates regularly stroll over it. When we asked our sample of young Protestants how often they crossed the border, we found that a quarter of those from the secondary schools had *never* crossed the border or crossed it 'once only' in their lives. A further half said they had crossed only a few times in their lives. Grammar school pupils were more likely to have crossed the border regularly and only 5 per cent of these had never crossed it. This could perhaps be explained by the fact that their school is located on the West Bank of the city, less than a mile from the border, and of course more of their parents are likely to possess cars. However, within the city itself, working-class kids from the non-selective secondary schools seemed more constrained by territorial demarcation.

The 1970s saw the exodus of large numbers of Protestants from the city side of the town in the wake of the civil disturbances and heightened sectarian tension in the town. Since then the river has come to be perceived, by Protestants, as the dividing line between the two communities. In reality this does not quite accord with the demographic facts, as there is a substantial Catholic population resident in the Waterside area of the town, just as there is still a small Protestant population on the city side of Derry. Protestants, however, perceive the city side of the town, on which is located the commercial district and local government offices, as being demographically and politically dominated by the Nationalists. Accordingly they see much of the city side as a 'no go' area for them. Sectarian spatialisation in Northern Ireland is not primarily about establishing whether a simple confessional majority exists in a particular area. Rather, it is about power and dominance – which political symbols and whose political presence will predominate. Today, in Derry at least, Protestants are on the retreat and young Loyalists have become hyper-sensitive to sectarian spatialisation.

Indeed, in our survey 37 per cent of those questioned admitted that they knew the city side of the town 'not at all' or 'not very well'. Moreover a quarter of male pupils of manual working-class parents attending the secondary schools declared that they 'never' or 'very rarely' crossed the bridge which links the two 'sides' of the city (the corresponding figure for female, grammar-school pupils living in private housing within non-manual occupations parents was significantly lower at 4 per cent). Indeed, girls seemed considerably more mobile across perceived territorial boundaries. They regularly visited the city side for shopping and were prepared to traverse the bridge in the evenings to go to the pictures and attend dances. In general their 'life maps' were less determined by a sectarian categorisation of every day life.

For example, 31 per cent of our sample as a whole said they had 'no Catholic friends at all', with a further 20 per cent saying that they had 'very few' Catholic friends. However, girls were more likely than boys to have Catholic friends. Indeed, they were more favourably disposed to living in mixed-residential areas and to contemplate living next door to or marrying Catholics. Again, I am not claiming that they are somehow more tolerant or less prejudiced than their male counterparts, but that their very marginalisation from youth sectarian subculture and its boundary-maintenance activities frees them to a greater extent from the strictures of identity and territory. Largely excluded from the masculinist and ethnically expressive world of the 'lads' they were also largely absent from the ritualised sectarian confrontations which so dominated male experience.

Indeed, many of the girls were more than aware of this 'freedom'. Karen Knox a seventeen-year-old girl from Curryneirin, one of the few remaining mixed-housing estates in Derry, told me of her boyfriend's problems:

Paul doesn't go over the town. They're all scared of the skinheads an' all. They don't do nothin' to the girls. Paul was only over once last year to get his fishing licence. Just in the car, out of it and straight home. You couldn't ask him to go over the town at all. I wouldn't miss it ... I go over every Saturday morning to the shops and we go over at night (with her girlfriends) to the pictures ... ye never see any trouble.

'Trouble', as Karen reported, was as likely to come from your own side:

Everybody in Curryneirin is nearly goin' out with somebody from Curryneirin, even if it is mixed. It doesn't bother you, you're just that used to having them around ye. The wee boys would probably fight with him, you know, but the other wee girls wouldn't say much. You get the odd one ... Like my friend she's goin' out with a [Catholic] boy from Ardmore and there was this girl from Tullyally and she say's to her 'I heard ye were going out w' a Fenian', and my friend denied it, you know. And she says, 'Well, I saw ye in the car with him and the next time we see ye w' him we're going te give ye a hiding' ... But I think it's all talk – the girls ye hardly ever see fightin' ... but it *is* the boys.

There was considerable evidence that male power, in the form of organised teenage harassment, was exercised against both young women and young men who infringed the sanctions against fraternisation and indeed miscegenation with Catholics. The lads' perceptions of sectarian territorial boundaries had, of course, been forged in most cases by direct experience of regular clashes between rival groups of Protestant and Catholic youths.

In Derry most of the 'lads' obviously perceived it as too dangerous to cross the bridge into the city side on their own. Many had tales to recall of sectarian bother encountered by themselves or by their friends. When they did cross the bridge they did so en masse to attend parades or to go to the dances organised by various Loyalist organisations in the Apprentice Boys Memorial Hall located in the heart of the old town overlooking the Bogside. On these occasions there is safety in numbers and the young make their way back to the Waterside through a carefully selected route which takes them on most of their journey homewards through safe Protestant territory. On occasions stragglers did meet difficulties. Ronny King, an unemployed seventeen-year-old, recounted in a matter of fact way his experience of being accosted by a group of Catholic youth on his way home from the 'Mem':

> Usually on a Friday night coming back from the 'Mem' the Catholics have the run of the town – over the top of it anyways, but I was over in the wrong territory one night and ended up gettin' this [baring his stomach to reveal the trace of a scar for all to see]. They asked me where I was coming from ... knew I couldne' say the 'Mem' so I says 'dance in Laurence Hill' [location of a predominantly Catholic YTP]. Then they asked me where I was going ... I says 'Drumahoe' ... 'Where in Drumahoe?' they says ... I says 'Ardmore' [a Catholic estate] and then ran off towards the Bridge.

His interrogators must have been not all convinced by his account because they pursued him, and on catching up with him he was seriously assaulted and left semi-conscious in the street.

As Derry has become increasingly subject to religious residential segregation, where one lives has come to be seen as the best diagnostic clue to one's confessional background. The young are acutely aware of these codes of territory and identification and indeed play a key role in policing them. In Derry, certainly, it was the young Protestants, very much a minority in a predominately Catholic town, who seemed most fascinated by these codes. Keith Hope assured me:

> It seems that the Catholics can't tell who the Protestants are most of the time unless they know them ... I could ... A Protestant could walk round town and not be ... you know they wouldn't know what you are ... He could go into Catholic bars ... but if a Catholic comes over here then you know them straight away.

I probed somewhat further:

Me: Surely you only recognize them because they are wearing school uniform or something or some other distinguishing wear?

Keith: Naw! . . . you see plenty of boys walkin' past the *Top O the Hill* . . . like you'd know he was a Fenian like just by lookin' at him, the way he dresses or something like that. You're walking down and you see if he keeps on looking over at ye an' all and what's the shape of him like.

Me: And you can really tell?

Keith: Well you know most of them by name up there [in Gobnascale] by now. Ye know them by name shouting in the rioting an' all. You see them places – the ones who go over te Stewart's Supermarket – and you hear them shouting the boy's name and ye get a good look at him and get te know his name, then you see him at the Top O the Hill. They know our names . . . like they'd shout Hey Spud ye fat cunt', or something. They know that's Spud just be listening to us shoutin' 'Spud come on now'. And then if they seen him over the town they get him.

It became clear that in so far as Keith and his mates could 'tell' it was not because they had developed some sophisticated capacity for reading ethnic cues and discriminations, but because regular interaction – albeit largely antagonistic – did occur between rival gangs of Protestant and Catholic youths, and specific territorial boundaries could be drawn by the young which distinguished definitively between insider and outsider.

Many of these young people were actively involved in staking and defending sectarian territorial claims. Individual skirmishes quickly develop into more generalized and long term confrontations between sectarian gangs. As one of Keith's mates told me:

If you go out and get a hiding from five people then you'll go out and get five people and give them a hiding and then they'll get five people and so on . . . You never get one fightin' one – its a whole estate against another estate, back-ups all the time. One day there's a boy McGilloway from Nelson Drive, he got a touch coming home from school . . . then he rounds up a whole dose of boys from Nelson Drive, went in [to the adjoining Catholic estate] and in about five minutes there's about eight boys from the Triangle [Catholic area]. Ten minutes later the police were out.

The major focus of these clashes is the perimeter areas of the 'confessionally pure' housing estates they live on, or in the 'shatter zones' which have appeared in Derry since the mid-1970s at the interface of Protestant and Catholic areas. It is possible to identify fairly clearly the topography of sectarian space in Northern Ireland – the areas regarded as confessionally clear and distinct and therefore safe or dangerous depending on your religion, 'flashpoints' where adjoining confessional ghettoes meet, and neutral areas where commercial or mixed residential neighbourhoods provide reasonably safe routes for travel.

One of the youth clubs where I was working was attached to a secondary school in the somewhat unfortunate situation of being located in the middle of one of these 'shatter zones'. Clashes between Protestant and Catholic youths had regularly occurred both after school and in the evenings as the young people made their way to and from the club. In turn these lads came to experience the sectarian categorization of residential space as a reality *sui generis*, a taken for granted fact. Keith was amazed at my ignorance of these matters:

See if I bumped into them [Catholics] in here I'd give them a kickin' like – same way they'd try to give me one down there. See ye get te know them like. We know better not te go down there into the *Top O the Hill* [district] and the Taigs know better than te come in here. Ye just have te look after yer own street like.

The paramilitary graffiti and painted kerbs provide the symbolic resources to sustain these territorial claims and demarcations. These boundaries are afforded an objective, factual basis by the young. I asked some of the young people from the Irish Street about why they painted their kerbs red, white and blue and what it meant. As one of the bandsmen told me:

It just to show that we're Protestants, that this is a Protestant estate. To show it's not Catholic – like they wouldn't walk into it with a tricolour 'cause its red, white and blue over the kerbs. Same you'd know a Fenian estate and stay out of it – green white and yellah'. Ye'd know better than te walk down it wey' a Union Jack around ye or something.

Half the young people we surveyed expressed a preference for living in a neighbourhood that is *all Protestant*. Those living in public housing estates were significantly over-represented amongst those opting for a confessionally pure neighbourhood, as were males in comparison with females, and, indeed, working-class lads in comparison with middle-class ones. I would argue it is in the context of a ghettoization process sustained in part by the boundary maintenance practices of the lads themselves, that the attitudinal responses to questions of residential segregation are intelligible.

Interestingly when our respondents were asked the more personalized question, whether 'they would be happy to live next door to someone of the opposite religion', a much lower number percentage of the total sample answered 'NO'. Young Protestants' attitudes to Catholics seemed to be often the product, not of individual prejudice, but of their active involvement in subcultural activities of 'defence'.

Integrated education?

As our survey revealed, there had been a significant decline in support for integrated schooling amongst the young Protestants of Derry. In 1969 almost half of Protestant pupils declared their support for mixed schools. When our sample were asked 'What sort of school would you like to go to?' (i.e. religious composition), overall less than one in five declared a preference for integrated schools. Again, attitudes on the issue of integrated schooling seem to flow not from individual prejudice but from territorial anxieties sustained by school peer-group pressures. As there are in fact no integrated schools in Derry[5] and few elsewhere in Northern Ireland, young people have no actual experience of integrated education. They assume the worst possible scenario for mixed schools:

'Boots' Brown: Naw ... wouldn't like it. Dead against it. Sure there'd be fights steady.

Fred Johnston: Sure look, there's three Catholics in our school, sure they get wealed [hit] everyday ... just around the school ... kicked around.

Ronny King:

We'd a Catholic young fellah' in our class. Paul
McKay ye call him . . . sound young fellah . . . we
might hit him like, ye know not really bad like . . .
One day we were all sittin', every one of us
started te drum [Orange tunes] . . . the worst class
in the school and we all started te drum . . . and he
cracked up and broke all our pencils, so we just
pulled him te the ground and hit him an' all . . .
He's not bad like . . . he's not bitter. It was just
because he was a Catholic when we were at
school.

In 1969 there had been overwhelming support amongst the young
in Derry for inter-denominational youth provision. In 1986, we
found very little support amongst young Protestants for this.
Despite the rhetoric of the Youth Service about promoting tolerance and mutual understanding amongst the young, youth club
provision remains largely segregated. Indeed I encountered only
one Catholic teenager amongst the combined membership of
almost 200 in the two clubs I attended. These two clubs, like many
others, were purpose-built youth wings attached to already segregated secondary schools. This of course meant that their clientele
was largely drawn from former pupils and, accordingly, was
exclusively Protestant. Similarly, the new youth and community
centres on the city side of the town were exclusively Catholic in
their membership. In Northern Ireland any 'community' form of
provision, located as it is at the heart of the confessional ghetto, is
bound to attract local kids from only one side of the divide.

Political attitudes

How had these teenagers' political attitudes changed? Northern
Ireland is not only a highly-polarized society, but also a highly
politicized one. Young people are not immune to these forces.
Indeed, as our survey indicated they were in many cases likely to
hold apparently *more extreme views* than their parents. When
asked about which party they would vote for if they had the
opportunity, the sample indicated overwhelming support for parties usually associated with extreme Loyalist positions in the

spectrum of Northern Ireland politics (71.4 per cent declared support for the militantly Loyalist DUP, with only 8.1 per cent declaring for the supposedly 'more moderate' OUP). Pupils from manual working-class backgrounds attending the non-selective secondary schools were considerably more committed to the DUP than middle-class pupils from the grammar school (over 80 per cent of the former as opposed to 47 per cent of the latter were DUP 'supporters'). The 1969 survey had indicated considerable support for non-confessional parties amongst the young. In our survey, support for the 'middle of the road' Alliance party was in the order of 5.3 per cent, with slightly more pupils (7.3 per cent) indicating they would support the neo-fascist National Front if they were to stand in elections![6] Some 57 per cent of our sample identified Dr Ian Paisley, the charismatic leader of the DUP, as the politician who, in their opinion, 'had done the most for Northern Ireland'.

Significantly, girls seemed less attracted to 'extreme' parties than boys. They were under-represented in support for the DUP and National Front and significantly over-represented in support for the OUP and Alliance Parties.

I attempted to tease out the different perceptions working-class lads had of the competing Unionist parties.

Richy Baker: For the first time the other night I seen it on TV, a DUP man and an Offical Unionist man having an argument – for the first time I seen it – like I didn't realise there was such a big difference between the two of them. I just made up my mind like that there – DUP that's the side I was on. The next local elections now'll be the first time I'm votin'. . .

Ronny King: Paisley's the only man who's going te turn round an' speak for us.

Richy: That's right . . . Like who else have we for te argue yer point? . . . I wouldn't care if we were independent of the British government tomorrow as long as Ian Paisley was prime minister!

Ronny: I hate the sight of the Official Unionists, hate them. If I go home and see one of their posters I climb up and pull them down.

As other commentators have argued, militant Loyalism involves elements of a putative class identity. It is also strongly masculinist in its ideology and organization. Women have most often been relegated to the sidelines in its confrontational style of politics. In the eyes of these young men the DUP – despite its, in fact, solidly petit-bourgeois membership – is seen as articulating the concerns of working-class Protestants. The aura of restrained violence and images of masculinity offered by militant Loyalist politics may have a certain attractiveness to marginalized young men.

National identities

Politics in Northern Ireland focuses to no small extent on issues of national identity. How did our young people identify themselves? Have national-political identities changed also?

We asked them: 'Which of the following terms best describes how you think of yourself: Ulster man/woman, Irish man/woman or British man/woman?' Not surprisingly less than 5 per cent described themselves as Irish. In 1966 Richard Rose asked a similar question about identity in a province-wide survey of social and political attitudes. Almost a third of Northern Ireland Protestants (no specific figure for young people is available) expressed an attachment to an Irish identity. The majority of our sample (60 per cent) identified themselves as British, with 35 per cent describing themselves as 'Ulster' people.

Almost twice as many males as females identified with the Ulster label, and almost twice as many young people from manual occupational backgrounds as from non-manual backgrounds. The Ulster identity, with its association with militant Loyalist politics (in our sample 87 per cent of Ulster identifiers declared support for either the DUP or the National Front), finds its constituency of support amongst male, secondary-school pupils of manual working-class backgrounds.

National identity in Northern Ireland is, as I have argued, a complex affair. Protestants, as we have seen, do not in essence express their ethnic distinctiveness in *national* terms. However the rest of the world, by and large, does and we expect people in Ireland particularly to do so. Protestants often seem to display some degree of uncertainty about their national identity, seemingly unsure as to whether they are 'truly' British, Irish or something else – perhaps 'Ulster people'. Political identities in territories with unresolved national questions tend to be relational. Protestants' uncertainty about their national identity becomes particularly significant when Catholics in Northern Ireland seem to them to be so certain about theirs. As Carson Logue from Nelson Drive reflected when I asked him about his sense of nationality:

> Well, I'd *like* te call myself British, a British person like ... but ye look deep into it, like, I *am* Irish ... because – Northern *Ireland* like. Ye don't hear the English going around and sayin' 'I'm British', they'd say 'I'm English' ... like the Scottish. I'd like te classify meself as a British person – if anybody ask me my nationality I'd turn round an' say 'British' ... I hate calling meself Irish, meself like ... but it's a thing ye have te face up till. Its the truth, ye look at yerself, yer living on one island.

Militant Loyalism as a cultural and ideological practice attempts to address some of these 'contradictions' experienced by Protestants in being British in Ireland. Amongst many working-class Protestants – particularly it seems young ones – the Ulster identity is a favoured one. With its aggressive assertion of Protestant self-reliance and identification of a precise community of political association – the 'Protestant People', the Ulster identity has won a place within the youthful imagination.

As one lad commented discussing his form's reaction to a particularly boring geography lesson:

> the teacher showed us the map of the world and said, 'there's Ireland, there's England ... we says te her, 'What we wan'te know is, where's *Ulster!*'

Loyalism and school counter culture: the boys in the band

For many non-academic kids, Loyalist symbolism and sentiment functions also as an important cultural resource for the construction of a school counterculture. The brandishing of football scarves identified with Protestant teams – Linfield and Glasgow Rangers, self inflicted tattoos of paramilitary initials, the flouting of school rules forbidding the wearing of political badges, the chanting of Loyalist slogans and singing of party songs, and the muffled drumming with ruler and pencil simulating Orange marching bands, are both a testament to working-class resistance to official authority and a youth collective expression of Protestant ethnicity.

Ronny King and 'Boots' Brown had both been in the non-academic stream in secondary schools. They recounted the following incident to me:

'Boots': See when we were at school, this is no joke, see the Newbuilding men, they *were* UVF, you seen Drumahoe and Tullyally and they were UDA. Boys like that wearin' UDA badges and UP THE UVF and then the teachers tried te take them off them ... They wasn't actually inte nothin' like, just badges they wanted te wear.

Ronny: Aye ... One teacher Kerr from over the Bogside there, walked inte the class one day and there was a ween o' boys singin' songs – ye know Orange songs – te get him mad like. I walked in wey a pile of badges on. I didn't put the badges on because we had him last four periods: I put the badges on because I'll wear badges if I want te. If ones said te me 'Do ye support them?' I would say 'Aye!' You know what I mean, like, not because I'm in them but I support them. I know they'll do nothin' for me, but I support them. And he reached for me and a couple of boys and says, 'Youse are singing, youse are going te the [Head's] office.' An he pulled the badges off me coat so I went over and took the badge back and pinned it on 'Naw, no way, I'm keepin' me badges up!' I just sat down in me seat and everyone started te throw wee bits of perspex we had te cut up inte shapes. One hit him and he came up – I was sittin' at the back of the class, never fired nothin', me and Gordon McGregor just doing our work. He just reached for me and pulled me out of the chair and hit me – so I just sunk the head on him, so I did.

On another occasion a group of Loyalist inspired pupils had gone so far as to break into a school on Eleventh night to remove school desks and furniture to burn on their bonfire!

The entrenched internal selection and differentiation processes characteristic of these secondary schools sustain a distinctive school counter-culture amongst the 'low-achievers'. This 'nonconformist' sub-culture sought to actively undermine school authority and to provide an alternative set of focal concerns for these young people. From this non-academic group comes the most vigorous support for the marching bands and for militant Loyalism can be located.

In our sample, over a half of all pupils at non-selective schools declared that they were either supporters or members of a particular marching band which they named. Significantly some 70 per cent of pupils in the lowest academic stream in the non-selective secondary schools were members/supporters. On the other hand only 21 per cent of those in the grammar school said that they were either supporters or members of a band.

We have identified a crisis in the generational reproduction of Protestant identity. This crisis, as I have already suggested, has many dimensions – political, economic and spatial; the changing and more insecure relationship of Unionism with the British state; the erosion of Protestant privilege in the labour market and council chamber; the decline of traditional Protestant working-class communities and the Loyalist culture they sustained. In particular, within the lives of many working-class teenagers, there has been a decline in the importance of the traditional institutions of Protestant socialization.

Firstly, there has been a steady lessening in the religiosity of young working class Protestants. Figures available from the Presbyterian church indicate that between 1969 and 1979 the number of children attending its Sunday Schools in Northern Ireland declined by some 35 per cent. In the Londonderry Presbytery it declined even more – by over 40 per cent. This higher figure, in an area where regular church attendance was the norm in most Protestant families up until recently, is perhaps in part due to the population moves that have occurred within the town. As the Protestant population drifted across to the river during the 1970s to resettle in the East Bank of the district the congregations of the Protestant churches located on the city side became depleted. There were a number of sectarian attacks on these long-established Protestant churches which further reduced the numbers attending. Some of the churches relocated in the East Bank area, but their growth has not compensated for the overall loss of families attending Protestant churches in Derry.

The Presbyterian church in Derry reports a decline of some 13 per cent in the number of families registered in its churches over the period 1970–80, probably a considerable underestimation of the loss.

Our survey revealed that less than half of the fifth-year pupils attended church on a regular basis. Amongst older kids who had left school the figure was undoubtedly dramatically lower. Not surprisingly working-class pupils attended church services less regularly than their middle-class counterparts and were less likely to be involved in church organizations. There had also been a decline in membership of uniformed organizations like the Boys Brigade and Boy Scouts with their traditional Protestant and social-imperialist ethos. Up to the mid-1960s, Derry had sustained some twelve scout troops and at least six companies of the Boys Brigade which drew recruits from working-class families, as much as from middle-class ones. In 1985 we found that three times as many pupils were now members of non-church based clubs as of uniformed oranizations, with less than one in five of working-class lads involved in *any* church organization.

Many of these young working-class people, however, preserve the vestiges of their Protestantism, although they are now outside the social networks of the traditional churches. As Paul McGrath told me:

> I went this time last year ... I just went down to the church, don't know the name of it, did my communion and that was me. It's boring just listening to yer man shoutin' his head off. Jesus, it's wild boring. You canne sneeze or nothin'.

In UK terms, this seems hardly remarkable. The decline in church attendance and falling membership of the uniformed youth organizations has been steady since the War. Northern Ireland society however has been somewhat more immune to the process of secularization. Amongst the Protestant working class the numbers regularly attending church have certainly diminished sharply since the 1950s. Yet, even Protestants who are not church attenders themselves think it important that their children attend Sunday Schools and receive bible instruction in school. Indeed, Protestant identity, although not reducible to religious commitment to the reformed faith, does – in the absence of any universalistic and democratic political ideology of nation or class – still depend on religious representations as markers of the ethnie.[7]

In the current political context some young Protestants are responding to the declining influence of the traditional Protestant denominations, by moving towards the strident evangelicism of Paisley's Free Presbyterian church. This has an overlapping membership with the DUP and has resurrected the traditional fusion of Protestant fundamentalism and populist Loyalism that was such a potent cultural force in Ulster in the second half of the nineteenth century. Some of the lads I interviewed, like Ronny and Richy, attended to hear the militant political sermons which are a feature of that congregation. Their interests in doing so seemed secular rather than sacred, involving some sort of a search for political answers rather than for spiritual uplift.

As Richy Baker commented when I asked him why he attended the Free Presbyterian church though he was an episcopalian:

> Well ... the Free Presbyterians are the most Protestant of the lot. I'm not a Free Presbyterian myself but I'd say they are the most *loyal* bunch. Perhaps it's because of their ministers. In my eyes they seem to be *the* Protestant church of the lot, like.

Some of his other mates were less enthusiastic about this fusion of politics and religion and had some anxiety about the rigid puritanism of Paisley and his followers:

Eddy Finlay: If we had Ian Paisley as prime minister we would have no drinkin' or anything...

Jim Baird: [indicating agreement]: There would be fuck all...

Eddy: I don't agree with their religion, the DUP; their politics – aye! ... but not their religion, not this business about Sunday...

Jim: No swimmin' pools, no leisure centres, nothin' like that...

Ronny King, who in these discussions invariably adopted the most 'extreme' Loyalist position he could think of at the time, attempted to justify the DUP sabbatarian policy in the political and territorial terms that he thought might appeal to his hedonistic companions:

Ronny: But they're trying to make a Sunday out of it, cause that's the *Fenian* day . . . ye have te see that like. It's the day the Fenians go out te enjoy themselves – that's what Paisley's against . . . the Fenian Sunday. The DUP know that if they close these places down some Prods are goin' te disagree with it but it's the Fenian's day . . . ye got to stop the Fenian day. . .

[N.B. In Ireland, Sunday is traditionally the major day of recreational activity for many Catholics.]

Over the past ten years there has been a significant decline in the membership of Protestant youth in the formal institutions of Orangeism – Junior Orange Lodges and the Apprentice Boys Clubs. Less than one in ten of our sample, for instance, said they were involved in these. Ten years ago similar surveys[8] indicated that one in four Protestant secondary-school boys were members of these organizations. This declining membership amongst the young is partly attributable to the political fragmentation within Unionism. The Orange Order has traditionally been closely allied with the Official Unionist Party and is officially represented on its governing body. The DUP on the other hand has long been at odds with official Orangeism and has promoted the more populist Independent Orange Order and more recently the Apprentice Boys as a vehicle for Loyalist organization. The Orange Order remains strong in rural areas where its continued role in social life, organizing dances and socials, gives it still a certain currency amongst the young. In the urban areas it has largely lost these functions and its capacity to attract young working-class recruits.

Since the early 1970s many working-class teenagers have been more attracted to the physical-force militancy of the paramilitaries. On the other hand there is no real evidence of any widespread involvement of young working-class Protestants in the paramilitary groups. However, by the mid-1980s these organizations themselves had suffered a considerable decline in membership and political influence. The young, in turn, had become more aware of the dangers of too close an involvement with 'terrorists'.

Certainly the bands and many individuals continued to declare verbal support for the UDA or UVF. Some of the bands are quite explicit about their identification with the UDA or UVF and, despite opposition from the Orange Order and threats of possible prosecution from the police, carry the flags of these paramilitary groups in parades. Individual youths continue to brandish paramilitary insignia and adorn gable walls with paramilitary slogans and initials. As we have seen, this identification and the sense of bravado it generates provides a significant focus for school counterculture. But the lads have become wary about being unwittingly used – as a previous generation of teenagers were in the 1970s – by their paramilitary elders. Indeed, many of the young were as sceptical about the Loyalist paramilitaries as they were about Unionist politicians in general. As 'Boots' Brown commented when asked about the paramilitaries:

We have the UDA, the UVF, the UFF, Third Force ... what did they ever do? Nothin'! They never do nothin' in seven years. Why don't they do something, take on the Provos [Provisional I.R.A.] and red [clear] them out? They're useless, all talk.

Nor have the Unionist political parties been any more successful in attracting young members. The Young Unionists remain a small rump of middle-class debaters – in Derry they seemed to have no members at all. While the DUP seems to be unable, despite having a somewhat younger membership than the staid OUP, to sustain a youth wing of any importance. Indeed, in many areas it seemed to depend on the marching bands to mobilize a network of youthful support to assist during elections in postering and the parading and posturing activities that pass for canvassing in Northern Ireland.

In the late 1980s, however, it is the marching bands with their expressive display of Protestant identity and difference, via a potent mixture of martial music and Loyalist symbolism, that have become the most important mobilizing agency for Protestant working-class youth. They are now playing the key role in the reproduction of militant Loyalist culture and ideology across the generations.

We thought it might be useful to re-examine our survey data to see if any significant relation could be established between membership and support of these bands, and a profile of attitudinal response associated with a sectarian categorization of everyday life. Did the young bandsmen and their supporters differ in any marked degree in their attitudes from other young Protestants *not* involved in these networks? If such a difference in response could be established it would lend credibility to our view that peer-group associations and youth cultural associations play a key role in the genesis and reproduction of ethnic identity; an ethnic identity so closely bound up, in the troubled Northern Ireland situation, with a sectarian habitus for youth.

We examined the pattern of response, from our sample and the band-member/supporter populations within it, to a number of specific questions addressed to the following topics: cross-religious friendships, attitude to residential segregation/integration, attitude to educational segregation/integration, declared support for political parties and national identity. We have already discussed how our young people in general responded in these areas – how did the band members and their supporters make out?

While 31 per cent of our sample as a whole said they had *no* Catholic friends, 43 per cent of band/members declared they had no Catholic friends (the corresponding figure for non-members was much lower at 28 per cent). Similar but less significant differences were apparent for band-supporters and non-supporters. When the variables of social class and school type were controlled, significant differences in the friendship patterns of members/supporters and non-members/non-supporters *still* obtained, suggesting that membership and support of these marching bands played a determining role in the formation of segregated friendship patterns, and more generally in the sectarian categorization of everyday life.

Thus, while half the young people questioned expressed a preference for living in a neighbourhood that is all-Protestant', some 67 per cent of band-supporters, as opposed to only 32 per cent of non-supporters, opted for residential segregation. Significant differences were again apparent in the responses of band-members/supporters on the question of educational integration. Altogether less than one in five of the pupils declared a preference for integrated schools. Some 87 per cent of members and 84 per cent of supporters expressed a preference for schools with an 'all-Protestant' intake, with fewer non-members/non-supporters supporting this preference (59 and 46 per cent respectively).

Not surprisingly, band-members/supporters were over-represented in those who supported militant Loyalist parties. Some 80 per cent of members declared support for the DUP and a further 18 per cent supported the National Front – even though they do not stand for election in Northern Ireland and, as far as I could see, had no organisational presence in Derry. Again, non-members were relatively less attracted to extreme parties.

Perhaps most interesting is the response of band-members/supporters to our questions about national identity. The most enthusiastic support for the Ulster identity comes, as we might expect, from these young people, with almost half of members and 44 per cent of supporters choosing the Ulster label in preference to either a British or Irish identity. On the other hand, less than a third of non-members choose the Ulster identity.

These responses of the young need to be placed firmly within the context of the economic marginalisation of the young in Northern Ireland and how this shapes their lives. However, this fine combing of our survey data does seem to support our contention that it might be more appropriate to understand the sectarian categorisation of every day life held by many young people in Northern Ireland in terms of the influence of peer-group associations and youth-cultural practices rather than by reference to either some clinical theory of individual pathology or overly-deterministic theory of generational cultural transmission.

Conclusion

After 20 years of civil unrest, political instability and polarization, youthful attitudes *do* appear to have hardened. It would be strange, given the corrosive nature of the conflict in Northern Ireland, if they had not. Yet perhaps the effects of the 'Troubles' on the sensibilities and practices of the young cannot be assessed independently of a more general understanding of the 'new social state of youth' in the 1980s. For there is evidence that Northern Ireland is not unique. In other pluralist societies the economic marginalization of working-class youth had also been accompanied by manifestations of racial intolerance. Youth-cultural practices which generate stylized hostility to outsiders – particularly ethnic outsiders – are to be found amongst white working-class youth in other parts of the UK, in parts of France and in the US. These youthful assertions of white ethnicity have interacted in a complex manner with the growth of racism. The 'nationalism of the neighbourhood', as Phil Cohen (1988) calls it, is not reducible to a structure of personal prejudice but must be understood as a form of regressive ethnicity which arises as a youth-cultural response in specific material situations. We need to more clearly identify the political, economic and cultural conditions under which youthful ethnic representations and practices degenerate into racist outcomes. The obligation of the critical researcher surely is to illuminate the situations in which the youth-cultural habitus sustains regressive forms of ethnicity. To do this in the Northern Ireland context we must now examine in greater depth the economic marginalization of a generation.

6

Economic Marginalization and Blocked Inheritance

Introduction

Mass unemployment has severed young working-class people in Northern Ireland from the social links that the world of work provides. It has separated them from an occupational culture that bound together the generations and, as a class culture, mediated to some extent the sectarian divide. Today young people are spending longer in segregated schools and are proceeding onto largely segregated forms of Youth Training provision. On the dole queue their lives are becoming increasingly privatized as they drop out of the social sphere of work and are excluded from the sites of commercially provided recreation. For young Loyalists the collapse of work has compounded a problem of blocked inheritance. Protestant privilege and patrimony have been eroded. Adjustments are having to be made. In Northern Ireland, as elsewhere, the removal of opportunities to enter skilled employment and the occupational culture it provides, has threatened long-established social and gender identities. In turn new 'solutions' to address this crisis in cultural reproduction are being explored by young Loyalists.

Deindustrialization

By 1988 the unemployment rate in Northern Ireland stood at 20 per cent, a significantly higher rate than in any other region in the UK, and over three times the rate in the favoured south east of England. The ratio of unemployed to job vacancies is such that some 80 workers are chasing every job available. Over half those unemployed have been so over a year. In Derry the male rate of unemployment (33 per cent) remains significantly higher than the

171

Northern Ireland average, as does the number of those experiencing long-term unemployment (over 60 per cent of the district's registered unemployed are receiving Supplementary Benefit).

Young people have been disproportionately affected by the rising levels of unemployment in Northern Ireland. They are also over-represented amongst the long-term unemployed. Between 1974 and 1981 youth unemployment rose by a massive 320 per cent so that by 1981 there were almost 15,000 unemployed young people in Northern Ireland.

The crisis in the Northern Ireland economy has manifested itself in a drastic decline in manufacturing employment. Since the early 1970s not only have the region's traditional industries continued to decline but, in addition, the multi-national firms attracted to the province in the 1960s and 1970s have also shed labour or indeed pulled out altogether. In a few short years the biggest complex of artificial fibre manufacture in Europe was virtually dismantled by the closure of ICI, Courtaulds, and Enkalon. In Derry the Hutchinson plant (owned by Courtaulds) closed down and the Du Pont factory, with £20 million of state aid, rationalized its production, transferring fibre manufacture into other products and substantially cutting its workforce. Even these technologically advanced plants were not immune to the recession. Similarly, electronics, telecommunications and engineering also suffered severe job losses.

Derry experienced a particularly large loss of traditional manufacturing employment after 1972.[1] This was largely due to a decline in the district's long-established shirt industry. Over 1,400 largely female jobs potentially available to female school leavers were lost between 1972 and 1978 alone. Women working in the shirt factories had traditionally dominated manufacturing employment in the city. However, after 1973 they were rapidly losing their leading position in manufacturing employment.[2] Increasingly women were finding employment, often on a part-time basis, in the service sector, and male dominance in manufacturing employment was firmly asserted. Most of the shirt and collar factories, once so central to the local economy and the town's occupational life, now stood empty. The Star Factory, Rosemount Factory, Tillie and Henderson, Ebrington Factory all closed their doors.

These red brick and sandstone monuments to machinofacture were to be put to new purposes in the 1980s. Tillies, in which over 800 women had laboured, cutting, stitching and finishing shirts for an Empire, has become a snooker hall and commercial 'recreational centre'. A number of the other buildings have been used to house government-sponsored 'youth training', 'community enterprise' and 'small business initiatives'. The youth of the Bogside preempted the appropriation of the Star factory by the corporate state – by burning it down.

There were at the same time also considerable losses of male jobs in the mechanical engineering and electrical engineering industries as a series of multi-national companies pulled out of the area at the end of the 1970s. This led to a drastic reduction in the availability of apprenticeships for male school leavers after 1974. Apprenticeship training, whether employer-based or located in the Government Training Centres (GTCs), has given way to the generic vocation preparation provided by the YTP schemes. Yet surveys of school leavers indicate that a majority of working-class male school leavers still aspired to follow their fathers into skilled employment through the traditional avenue of the craft apprenticeship.

In Northern Ireland the young entering employment have been concentrated in certain sectors of the economy particularly affected by the recession. As occupational surveys indicate,[3] the young enter jobs traditionally requiring few qualifications – such as clothing and footware, construction, distribution and services, particularly catering. They are under-represented, on the other hand, in the public sector or at least in the salaried part of it. This sector, as we have seen, was the only expanding area of employment in the 1970s. For the young in Northern Ireland, as elsewhere, economic restructuring has meant marginalization within the labour market. Young Protestant working-class males in the past followed in their fathers' footsteps to gain entry into an aristocracy of labour. De-industrialization has meant a rapid erosion of a traditional patrimony of occupational skill and advantage. With the disappearance of craft apprenticeships this group of young people are now exploring alternative codes of cultural inheritance and communal heritage no longer dependent on the vicissitudes of the labour market.

Youth unemployment

To accurately gauge the extent of marginalization of the working-class youth of Northern Ireland from the world of waged work we need only to examine the labour market statistics available from various government sources. The 1981 census provides the most extensive source-data on economic activity for the 16–24 age range.[4] In Northern Ireland in 1981, and the unemployment crisis considerably worsened after that, less than one in three of males in the 16–18 age band was in paid employment. In 1971 almost 60 per cent of this group had been in waged work.

A more detailed picture of what is happening to Northern Ireland's school leavers is now available from a cohort study conducted by the Northern Ireland Department of Finance's Policy Planning and Research Unit (Table 6.1). This study traces the activities over 18 months of a representative sample of almost 3,000 young people from the province's secondary schools (secondary and grammar) who reached the age of 16 in 1983–4 school year and were thus eligible to leave school in June 1984 (or the Easter of that year).

Table 6.1   *Cohort activities, percentage: Oct 1984–Oct 1985*

	October 1984	October 1985
Full-time education	55	39
YTP	21	11
Full-time employed	17	38
Unemployed	6	10
Other	1	2
Totals	100	100

Source: *PPRU Cohort Study*, 1986.

These figures indicate that some 40 per cent of the cohort eligible to leave school opted to stay on, a higher percentage than elsewhere in the UK. Only 38 per cent entered full-time employment. Moreover one in five of young people are either registered unemployed or on a YTP scheme. In fact of those who left school at the first available opportunity almost a half are either unemployed or YTP trainees.

Another useful data source is provided in the 1984 Continuous Household Survey also conducted by the Department of Finance. This source confirms the extent of the marginalization of the young within the labour market apparent from the 1981 Census figures. It also provides us with an invaluable source of information on the relation between religious background and economic activity.

As Table 6.2 shows for the 16–18 age group, unemployment is roughly the same for Catholics and Protestants. Approximately a quarter of each group are either registered unemployed or on a government 'training' scheme. On the other hand one in three Protestants compared with one in five Catholics is in employment. However, for those in the 19–24 age group, a massive leap in the percentage of those unemployed occurs for Catholics. Almost a third of those now beyond both the secondary school cycle and youth training provision are without a job. For Protestants there is a relatively modest rise with less than a fifth of this age range unemployed. These differentials indicate the continued disadvantage of young Catholics in the labour market. Virtually a third of Catholics between 19 and 24 are unemployed compared with just 19 per cent of Protestants in this age range.

Table 6.2 *Employment status of 16–24 year olds, percentage*

	Catholic			Non-Catholic		
	16–18	*19–24*	*16–24*	*16–18*	*19–24*	*16–24*
Working	22	46	37	33	64	52
Unemployed	18	32	27	17	19	18
Youth Training	7	1	3	7	0	3
At school/FE college	50	8	24	41	6	19
Keeping house	2	12	8	1	9	6
Permanently unable to work	0	1	1	0	1	0
Single parent	0	1	1	0	1	1

Source: Eleventh Report FEA 1988

Nor does it appear to be the case that Catholics suffer more from unemployment because they are less educationally qualified on average than Protestants. When we examine the level of unemployment experienced by Catholics with educational qualifications we still find them significantly disadvantaged in comparison with Protestants of the same level of qualification (Table 6.3).

Table 6.3 *Unemployment rates for those with a qualification* and those without, percentage*

	Protestants		Catholics	
	Males	*Females*	*Males*	*Females*
Qualifications	10.8	9.4	26.1	15.5
No qualifications	20.3	12.1	42.2	18.0

* CSEs and above   *Source: Eleventh Report FEA 1988*

The evidence indicates that Catholic school leavers are less likely to find jobs than their equivalently qualified Protestant contemporaries. For recruitment to both unskilled and skilled jobs the continued existence of nepotistic recruitment practices ensure that the correct religious background is at least as important a 'qualification' as academic certification. In addition the evidence suggests that when Catholic school leavers do manage to find jobs they are more likely than their Protestant peers to find unskilled ones. John Darby's 1979 survey of school leavers in the Derry area, indicates (Table 6.4) the dramatic under-representation of Catholic school leavers amongst those entering skilled employment.

Table 6.4 *Percentages of Catholic and Protestant school leavers in skilled and unskilled employment, selected schools, Londonderry area*

	Roman Catholic school leavers	Protestant school leavers
Skilled	45.3	73.9
Unskilled	54.7	21.8
Unclassified	0.0	4.3
Totals	100.0	100.0

Source: J. Darby and D. Murray (1980)

The same survey revealed the over-representation of Catholic school leavers amongst those who entered the Youth Training schemes. Catholics were four times more likely to end up in these schemes than Protestant leavers. The education system has, it seems, been no more successful in tackling the problem of religious based inequalities in the labour market in Northern Ireland than it has in addressing racially-based ones in Britain.

Moreover, the fact that more young people are staying on at religiously segregated schools and for longer periods has itself implications for the reproduction of sectarian division. As we have seen, both the formal segregation of Northern Ireland's children in the primary and secondary sector and the informal peer-group culture of the secondary school play their part in this reproduction of sectarian division. In addition, early leavers are increasingly ending up in training schemes also subject to significant levels of sectarian segmentation. At perhaps the most formative age in their lives there are now fewer opportunities available to young people for inter-religious mixing than there were in the past when more young people were in employment.

Mixing at work

The young people I spoke to were in no doubt as to the value of the work context in providing opportunities to meet and mix with the 'other side' and thus to challenge the sectarian sensibilities often acquired at school. As Michelle Doherty, an apprentice hairdresser, concluded, on the basis of her six months' experience of work since leaving school:

> In work it's just buried; when you're in, you're in te work, and that is it. It's just not religion that's brought up. You know when you're at school you build up a barrier against Catholics wey' everybody else. But when ye get out of school it's really a different matter when ye get te meet Catholics. There's nothing wrong wey' them at all. Ye get te know them, what they're like. Y've heard that much about them that ye just, ye know when ye leave school, ye say, 'Oh God he's a Catholic or she's a Catholic – stay clear o'them,' but!

The Government Training Centres (GTCs) predate the YTP era and have preserved in their organization some elements of traditional industrial work culture. In the centre in Derry young Catholic and Protestant men did work along side each other. Protestants however were very much in the minority in the

GTC constituting less than 20 per cent of the total number of trainees.

Ronny King, whom we have already encountered as a leader of militant Loyalist opinion amongst the Drumquin youth club members, talked of making friends across the divide in the Training Centre:

> Down in the Training Centre ye done all yer work, you never talked about it [religion and politics]. If you'd one boy – say a real rowdy boy – ye get them everywhere – he might bring it up. I seen me tellin' those boys to shut up. Like ye really work, get to know each other and go out an'all. I was the only Prod in the group, but I went out with them . . . dead on like. I didn't know who was a Prod and who was a Catholic, never bothered me like. I knew if I started any crack I'd lost me job like.

In this 'work' situation youth cultural practice seemed to have, for once, unhitched itself from sectarian identity. As Ronny recounted:

> Ye have te get te know boys . . . I was going to get wealed one day and there was thirty Taigs backed me up and that's true. One day I was goin' te get hit in the toilets and this boy Quigley came in and said te a boy if ye hit him ye know what y'll get. You make friends like that they'll all stick up for you. I would see me sticking up for Catholics in the Training Centre – ye know they were wee soft boys ye could take the hand out of easily, boys who couldn't look after themselves. I see me standing up and looking after boys like that.

Ronny, despite his own 'extreme' Loyalist views, had weathered the initial taunting and abuse from his Catholic fellow trainees. He persevered to establish a number of real friends amongst the Catholic lads. One of these in particular had stood up for him when he was threatened and he and Ronny had become close:

> I had two great pals, like, they were Catholics and we got on the best and even see me goin' out at nights with them. And one of them was a boy Quigley and he actually got involved. Maybe he was in it and I didn't know it. He was blew up tryin' to do an Ulster bus – ye know, leave a bomb outside for the troops going

by. And the other boy he's up for shootin' a soldier, a Brit, up in the Brandywell. You know I . . . I couldn't believe it. When I heard [about the explosion] I just sat in the house, nearly felt like crying, ye know.

Ronny's complex emotions as regards 'integration' are, need one say it, not reducible to a psychological index of 'prejudice' and 'tolerance.' For the young, at least, holding certain political views which those outside Northern Ireland at least might regard as 'extreme' does seem quite compatible with getting on well with individual members of the opposite religion. The banter and ideological repartee characteristic of the GTC did seem to provide a sheltered context of some sort for a certain type of political and social dialogue between young working-class Protestants and Catholics.

Schooling and the labour market

However, today the young are increasingly staying on beyond the minimum leaving age in segregated schools. They are doing so largely in response to the difficult labour market situation and the subsequent inflation of employer's expectations as regards the qualification of job applicants. It remains the case that relatively higher numbers of young people in the province leave school with *no* qualifications than elsewhere in the UK. As late as the school year 1977–78 almost a half of those leaving school at the age of sixteen did so with no recognized qualifications.[5] The situation has improved since then with more pupils following courses leading to recognized awards. By 1984, the number leaving school without qualification had dropped to a quarter. However the value of some of these, particularly the CSE award, has undoubtedly been eroded in the credentials race, and accordingly there has been no significant redistribution of educational opportunities within the school system.

Northern Ireland's secondary schools have been successful in motivating their pupils to pursue these new courses of accredited study. Yet, clearly, significant numbers of pupils following these courses will still find themselves unemployed at the end of their school careers.

Our own school survey indicated that secondary pupils were increasingly pessimistic about the possibility of finding employment. Sixty percent of them admitted that they were 'unsure' about getting a job on leaving school. Yet, almost all of these pupils still rated school success as 'important' or 'very important' in determining their chances of employment. Most pupils seem to accept the doctrine, promulgated daily by the school, and now underwritten by the Department of Employment, of a 'tightening bond' between educational attainment and occupational success. Indeed, only a quarter of these pupils expressed any interest in leaving school before they were sixteen. Not surprisingly those declaring an interest in leaving school were largely concentrated in the lower 'non-academic' streams of the secondary schools. Over half these pupils would opt for leaving school early if they could. As we have seen it is amongst this section of pupils that the most enthusiastic support for the marching bands, and more generally for militant Loyalism, is to be found.

Ronny King was in many ways typical of this group. He had been in the lowest stream of the Drumquin secondary school and was to leave school without any real qualifications. At school he had often been in trouble and had played an active part in a Loyalist-infused school counterculture. He had played a key role in the oft-recounted youthful rampage on a Loyalist Day of Action which had seen a baker's van hijacked and overturned and its contents scattered over the road. He had demonstrated his daring to his companions on many occasions, running along school corridors smashing panes of glass with his bare hands. He had led the local gang in many forays with the lads from Ardmore. However, Ronny, now almost nineteen, was still unemployed after spells at a number of different Youth Training schemes. He was now the first to admit these rituals of classroom resistance were powerless before the hand of fate dealt by the labour market. As he commented somewhat wistfully when we discussed his experience of school:

School was alright. But exams an'all I didn't just make better of it, I just done nothing. Just went to school for a good day's carry on ... just carrying on, and down the office [to the Head] and gettin' a whalin' ... If I was in a top class I'd a wanta work but the way I was, I was in a low class and I knew I wasn't gonna ...

I knew, anyway, all I could do was CSEs. A CSE grade one is only worth a GCE grade 3, so they were'nt goin' to be any good to me anyway you know ... But ... if I was back at school now I'd no way carry on; just sit down and work ... if I got the chance. Because ye need exams an' all if ye want te get a really good job or ... anything. You've nothin' te look forward to now, like, just on the dole ... hope ye get a job ... just keep trying till one comes up.

Experiencing unemployment

For many of these young people a vocabulary of social equality, and a consciousness of class injustice is largely absent. They experience the inequalities of opportunity and their economic marginalization largely in terms of individual failure. Indeed they are taught to do so. The everyday practices of school and training scheme embody a meritocratic ideology of education and a deficit model of working-class culture to explain juvenile unemployment. This represents both educational inequality and unemployment as originating in the personal failures and inadequacies of the working-class child, or their family and culture.

The new vocationalism which now infuses the educational system throughout the UK has a distinctive rationale. This reflects the ideological dominance of the new Right with their missionary zeal for promoting the 'enterprise culture'. Young people, Cohen argues (1984)

are being invited to discover in their own cultures a generic lack of motivation, discipline or skill. Increasingly, in schools, as well as on training schemes, they are being asked to see in their predicament not a structural effect, but rather a personal cause or incitement to improve themselves and prove to the world that 'anyone can make it if they try'.

In Northern Ireland, as Richard Jenkins has documented (1983), the very fatalism of Protestant working class culture itself reinforces this trenchant individualism. Educational failure and unemployment are explained in terms of the struggle of individuals daily with the wheel of fortune.

I discussed the problem of coping with unemployment with Ronny King and Carson Logue one evening. Carson perceived the problem as one of personal commitment in the job search effort:

> Aye that's the problem with unemployment today. People apply for one job and they get turned down and they says 'We'll more and likely get turned down for the rest, aw hell', and they give up. That's what's wrong w' unemployment, not enough stand on their own two feet. You've gotta keep pushin' and pushin' to get a job. Your not goin' te get a job if ye don't try hard enough.

Carson, a trainee at the East Bank YTP scheme, had not as yet had to face the dole queue. Ronny had. He had also felt the frustration of applying for scores of jobs and getting nowhere. In addition he had also experienced numerous hassles with the Department of Employment trying to get his welfare benefit payments. This had made him somewhat more sceptical about the self-improvement rhetoric of the Youth Training industry. He was feeling his way towards some sort of collective response to the problems of being unemployed and a claimant. He felt Protestants needed to be more aggressive in pursuit of their entitlements:

> Protestants have te learn te stand up on their own two feet, 'cause they're not going to get nothin'. They have te tell – should it be the Housing Executive when you're married or should it be the Bru [Unemployment Benefit Office] or anywhere else – ye have to stand up on yer own two feet and fight for it like.

Loyalism, however, provides few resources, either ideological or organizational, for coping with the problem of long-term unemployment now affecting the Protestant working class. Protestant culture remains strongly influenced by a Calvinist theology which emphasizes individual responsibility and the work ethic. The evangelical tradition which has been such a force within Protestantism in Ulster continues to embrace a demonology of individual failure, and hands out harsh judgements to those who fall from grace. Long-term unemployment remains a relatively recent experience for many sections of the Protestant population and Protestant working class communities have found it perhaps harder to make a collective readjustment to 'hard times' than their Catholic neighbours.

Without subscribing to the tenets of a Culture of Poverty Theory, it is clear that the Catholic community has over a long period had to cope with high levels of unemployment. It has developed certain cultural and organizational resources in order to do so. Building on a strong voluntarist tradition within the Catholic church, a web of welfare and cooperative groups – advice centres, credit unions, tenants' groups, community groups – have sprung up to serve the needs of this economically marginalized community. In turn, a whole stratum of community entrepreneurs with considerable organizational skill in managing the interface between their community and the British welfare state has appeared. Many of these gained their political experience during the rise of the Civil Rights movement, which undoubtedly led to a general radicalization of the Catholic working class. John Hume, the current Westminster MP for Foyle, is only the most famous representative of this reformist nationalist tradition which continues to coexist in tension with the older physical-force tradition of Republicanism. This voluntary stratum has indeed been encouraged by the British government representatives in its role as a mediator between the state welfare apparatus and the marginalized Catholic working class.

As a result of the growth of this community movement and, more generally, because of the political resistance to official authority of the nationalist community since partition, the usual 'ideological effects' of welfarism – the privatization and stigmatization of the unemployed and claimants – are considerably less marked than in the Protestant community or indeed elsewhere in the UK. Of course the very pervasiveness and enduring nature of unemployment within the Catholic community has played no small part in 'normalizing' the experience of unemployment. There is some evidence that unemployed Catholics suffer less of a fall of self-esteem and social status in their community than do Protestants in theirs.[6]

They are certainly more likely to see the problem of unemployment as a political problem than are Protestants. Catholic youths may have greater recourse to political 'explanations' of their unemployment, perceiving it less in terms of individual failure and more as a problem of an inequitable and unjust system facing them. In my experience, any young unemployed Catholic in Derry is able to give a closely documented account of the operation of British discriminatory capitalism. It matters little whether this is an accurate account of the situation, the point is that it functions within popular consciousness to place blame fairly and squarely with the British state rather than with the individual. Within the Protestant community there is no equivalent network of cooperative and self-help organizations mediating between the state and the subject of welfare. As an unemployed Protestant you are on your own not only before God but also before Mammon. Nothing equivalent to the Civil Rights radicalization of the Catholic population occurred during this period within the Protestant working class. The fragmentation of the Unionist bloc and the emergence of the Loyalist paramilitaries as a political force in the early 1970s did see the emergence of a new cadre of working-class political leaders. Some of these took an active interest in the sphere of community action and cooperativism, while their colleagues conducted a pogrom against the Catholic community. There was, however, no more general ideological shift within the Protestant working class towards a politics of radical reformism which might have provided an impetus to push working-class Loyalism beyond a politics of resentment.[7]

In so far as young Protestants do seek a political explanation of unemployment they of course quickly find themselves caught up in a maze of ideological contradictions.

In a discussion with Ronny, Carson and some of their friends from the Drumquin youth club, I posed the question of the responsibility of the British government for mass unemployment in Northern Ireland. I got conflicting answers:

Keith Hope: Thatcher's good te us. She'll not be beaten. See the Hunger Strikes they'd [the Labour Party] given in to them.

Eddy Finlay: [dismissively]: Thatcher?

Me: And the Conservative economic policy?

Carson Logue: Well right enough Maggy Thatcher is a bit te blame. Spending it on all these missiles and all this here, the money is being wasted stupidly. Like the miner's strike – look how much money went into the policing of that there, millions of pounds every week ... millions of pounds wasted that could have been goin' for jobs.

And these big judges gettin' pay rises. Why do they need pay rises for? They've got their own nice big house, they own their house and four cars and they're gettin' more! Its not goin' te make them richer than they are, cause they're the tops already. Fifty thousand pounds a year a judge is getting. What's the average salary, well wage, an unemployed person is gettin'? Bet ye it don't even mount up te nine hundred pounds!

Ronny joined in the now heated discussion to add his indignation:

Ronny: There's the Queen and the Princess look at the money they're gettin, the money she's gettin' for clothes. Too much money spent on them two. They don't bother about the unemployed, Maggy Thatcher an' all. They worry about the judges an' all, higher class people. Cause they do, they class themselves as higher class people. They think too much bother over here, she doesn't think about us like, she just thinks about her people over there.

Eddy: The government looks upon *us* as the problem. They don't care about us, it's just a problem they have on their hands.

Keith: Aye ... the 'Northern Ireland Problem'.

These young Protestants belong to a generation which has now come to age in an era of mass unemployment and which is witnessing the unravelling of the traditional relation of Unionists with the British state. Some of them are groping towards a political understanding of the problems they face. As they do so they are increasingly coming up against the limits of their parental political tradition.

The youth training courses

As in Britain, all sixteen-year olds who have left school and cannot find a job are guaranteed a year's 'vocational preparation'. The Northern Ireland Department of Employment does not give a similar guarantee to seventeen-year olds but in practice most seventeen-year olds who wish to participate in the Youth Training Scheme are able to do so. In April 1986 there were nearly 10,000 young people involved with the YTP scheme, almost one in six of the sixteen–eighteen age cohort.

Indeed both the government's career service and the career teachers in the schools are finding their roles reduced to counselling young people in preparation for entry to these schemes. Career Officers report that 90 per cent of vacancies now notified to the Careers Service are under the YTP or other government-assisted schemes. The YTP scheme has become a bridge – or perhaps the better term would be filter – selecting and feeding early school leavers into the labour market. Effectively other entrances to employment have been closed off for these young people.

With figures made available by the Careers Service in Londonderry we were able to plot the destinations of the 1987 cohort of school leavers in the two Protestant non-selective secondary schools we had earlier surveyed and whose former pupils we interviewed in the two youth clubs.

These figures confirm the virtual collapse of employment possibilities for the contemporary school leaver in the Londonderry

Table 6.5   *Destinations (at 1 October, 1987) of Protestant secondary-school leavers (Londonderry cohort 1986–7)*

	Male	*Female*	*Total*
Returned to school	7	28	35
Entered full-time Further education	7	19	26
Full-time employment	11	31	42
Registered unemployed	7	6	13
YTP (total)	78	16	94
comprising:			
East Bank WPU	*52*	*13*	*65*
GTC	*24*	*0*	*24*
Other	*2*	*3*	*5*
Unknown	2	10	12
Totals	112	110	222

Source: Job Centre, Londonderry

area. Just 10 per cent of males entered full-time jobs although 30 per cent of young women did (largely due to a recruitment drive by a local shirt factory). Seventy per cent of young men entered the various schemes, the majority into one particular YTP scheme.

In 1979 John Darby had found that less than 10 per cent of the Derry Protestant school leavers had entered government-assisted schemes (in Darby and Murray, 1980). When one compares the results of these two surveys conducted eight years apart, one can begin to appreciate the speed and extent of the economic marginalization of young Protestants. One can also speculate how the new social state of Loyalist youth might shape their cultural practices and sensibilities.

Ally Hetherington and his two mates had all been YTP recruits. Mickey McKay had now found himself temporary employment in a meat packing plant. The three of them regularly complained about the limited options facing them as school leavers:

Interviewer: Did the careers teacher ask you what you wanted to do after school?

Ally: She just asked you where ye wanted to go – te Maydown or Glennie Barr's [i.e. the Government Training Centre and the East Bank YTP scheme]. Just go down there and if we hear of a job going we'll come down and tell ye. I haven't been offered a job yet and I've been down there nearly eight months.

Mickey McKay: I was down there longer than you and I got offered just one job . . . I don't know what I'm going to do after I get paid off.

Ally: Sittin' on the Bru just.

Rob McNab: Ye canne go on the Bru now 'till you're eighteen. . .

Mickey: I'm not going back into the Training Centre . . .

Tony (emphatically): Ye canne go on the Bru!

Mickey (now very agitated): I'm *not* going back into the YTP's not *one* of them, and I'm not going to the *Tech* (technical college) either.

Ally: You should go and do the year's course (on social learning skills) in the Limavady Tech, Mickey.

Mickey: Les (a youth worker) was on to me, trying to get me to go down there but I won't . . . I wanna get a *job*!

Most of the young people I talked to were very scathing in their assessment of the YTP scheme. The local Work Preparation Unit that most of them were offered places in was known universally as 'Funny Farm'. The tales of walls built, demolished and rebuilt, of endless metal skips welded, and of other futile exercises in pseudo-occupational 'training' conducted in the Unit were legion.

The instructors in the GTC trained to teach craft apprentices are now struggling with the new pedagogies concerned with 'social and life skills' for young people the state deems 'unemployable'. Many continue to cling to the older forms of skill instruction, attempting to preserve the formal elements of craft training and the rituals of apprenticeship now bereft of any utility given the absence of any actual institutional passage to skilled manual employment for these young people. Discipline seemed a major problem for the Units. For, the young trainees quickly realise the futility of much of the scheme's activity. Ally and his friends gave vent to their feelings:

Ally: Its a pit! Don't like the way they're organised. They don't really care about ye ... It's not only that the instructors don't care about ye. Nobody cares about ye ... Just hang around all day and act the cunt. That's all ye do, honestly.

Interviewer: What's wrong with the instructors?

Mickey McKay: Not strict enough ... say ye took a couple of days off like they'd say nothin'...

Ally: Say if ye act the maggot, say throw Swarfega around or that there, you're up to the chief. He sits ye down and gives ye a lecture, say nothin' then back te yer class. Sometimes ye get a final warning ... then ye get another final warnin'.

Mickey (caustically): Tommy Nealy had thirteen warnings!

On the other hand some of the young people in the YTPs were happy to conspire together with the instructors to attempt to preserve the ideal of craft apprenticeships in the post-industrial era.

Carson Logue who was now a trainee in the Work Preparation Unit, where he was getting some training in joinery, often described himself as 'serving me time as a joiner' although the course, like all the programmes in the Unit, involved no actual apprenticeship qualification. From the first time I had met him he had talked enthusiastically about becoming a joiner:

> I really got interested, as soon as I seen the joinery and done a wee bit of it meself. I says te meself 'This is the stuff for me, I love this here.' It's good work like ... I passed me CSE in woodwork ... I'd love te think meself gettin' on as a proper joiner now.

Indeed such was his level of commitment that he had borrowed the money from his father, a boilerman at a local hospital, to order himself an elaborate joiner's toolkit from a mail-order firm. One day, several months after I had originally met him, he told me proudly that he had been 'taken on' as an apprentice by an experienced tradesman. This was partially true. But as I was later to discover he had in fact been placed by the Unit for a period of work experience with a Community Enterprise scheme. The craftsmen he was working under were not part of a commercial firm, but rather themselves employed on short-term contracts on a state-assisted enterprise scheme converting an old shirt factory for use as small business units. There was no way that such a placement could give rise to a real job or chance of a genuine apprenticeship. And, indeed, after a number of weeks working on this placement Carson came to realise this. Disappointed he opted for a placement which involved the humbler task of humping bales of paper for a retail stationery company. This he judged more likely to lead to a possible job.

Somewhat later he explained his decision to me. His options, as he put it, were running out:

> I wanted te be a joiner ... like I had me heart set on it but I'm seventeen now and when I turn eighteen it'll be too late then because the apprenticeship for joinery is really supposed te start at sixteen ... its a four year apprenticeship that you do for joinery.

As elsewhere in the UK, this training provision has served to disguise the severity of the youth unemployment problem. What the schemes certainly have not been able to do is to solve the problem of youth unemployment. The epithet 'Job Creation' has been quietly dropped from the title of the schemes. In Northern Ireland some 30 per cent of the 18–20 age cohort remain unemployed. This is the age group which has progressed beyond the Youth Training provision and hence is – with the exception of students – fully integrated into the labour market. The YTPs in Northern Ireland, like youth training schemes elsewhere, have functioned essentially as state-sponsored instruments of social discipline for the marginalized young. They attempt to regulate the bodies, minds and self-images of young workers in preparation for their integration into the new, 'flexible' and 'cost-conscious' labour market. Whatever their manifest educational objectives the schemes undoubtedly provide a 'training' in low-wage expectations. Ally Hetherington described to me the problems he had budgeting:

> I get £30.15 a week, travel allowance an' all like. If I take a day off at all that's £25.00 [he was attending out-patient clinic at the local hospital regularly]. Then buses, fiver a week. I have to put another fiver a week back for meals there … need two to three pounds to keep goin' at the Tech [one day compulsory attendance at local Technical College]. I give me mother a tenner some weeks, then fifteen other weeks to save a fiver for me like for clothes an' all … I have te save up till the summer te get one decent holiday – like for one day, that's about the height of it down te Portrush – its impossible!

In this context any 'real wage' from an employer is likely to be seen as an improvement:

Mickey McKay: I can't complain about the money in Foyle Meats [where he is currently temporarily employed]; some weeks I was getting £41.00, that's the least I ever got. Other weeks I gettin' £49.00 and £50.00 even.

Mickey was well paid. For as the PPRU survey revealed the average weekly take-home pay for those school leavers working full time in November 1984 was just £37 and indeed half of those questioned earned under £36.

Those on the dole like Ronny King often tried to supplement their inadequate income by doing a part-time job on the quiet:

> gettin' the milk and unemployed that's the only way te make a living, a milkman and drawing the dole ... now the purty [potato] gathering's started and I'll be doin' purties perhaps next week ... its the only way to make money.

Many of these young people had held part-time jobs while at school, working in shops, or delivering milk and newspapers. In the summers many were involved in casual work in the farms which lie just outside the city limits. Indeed as the PPRU survey revealed, nine out of ten pupils from Northern Ireland's secondary schools had some experience of part-time or summer employment *before* they left school – a statistic which challenges the frequent assertions by the manpower service bureaucracy that a major deficit in today's school leaver is their ignorance of the world of work. The young people I talked with knew all about low-paid, low-skill, low-security jobs – precisely the sort of jobs that would be available to them as school leavers.

But even part-time jobs were now getting harder to find – not least because employers were substituting both part and full-time workers with YTP-placed trainees whose labour cost them little or nothing.

With the disappearance of the wage packet for many of these young workers, access to commercial leisure – traditionally a site of cross-sectarian meeting in Derry – is minimized. The street and the Loyalist parade provide an alternative, but confessional, focus for juvenile recreation:

Ally Hetherington: Ye can't afford te go te a pub like, one pint and ye'd be skint. We can't afford te go to the Broomhill [dancehall] or anywhere like that by the time we'd pay for the door, we'd have nothin' left ... Just running around the streets ... The parades, that's a day out for us without having te spend te much – ye get a carry out. Ye get a day out an' thats it.

Another response to the problem of exclusion from the commercial world of leisure is the 'wall party'. The Drumquin lads met on the weekend evenings from the early spring to the end of the Autumn in an abandoned and burned-out house previously occupied by a Catholic tenant with Republican connections who had been intimidated out of the area. There they drink beer and exchange stories into the small hours, 'get a wee fire goin' and yarn away, come out of the pub like with a few cans an' all, eighteen or nineteen of us, the crack's great like, just lie against the wall . . . its great!' The participants in the 'wall parties' seemed to be mainly older teenagers, but on occasions after the pubs shut they would be joined by older youths in their twenties. Something similar happens in urban centres throughout Ireland where marginalized youth, anxious to get out of overcrowded homes but with little money for commodified pleasure, have their 'cider parties' around makeshift fires on whatever open spaces they can claim. The younger teenagers were also experimenting with solvent sniffing, and sweeping up after youth club discos I would regularly find scores of discarded typist correction fluid bottles.

These drinking parties have attracted the attention of the police both in the North and South of Ireland. Indeed as I write, a major 'moral panic' is being orchestrated by the media in the Republic of Ireland about teenage outdoor-drinking parties.

Many of the young people I talked with felt they were being harrassed by the RUC. Ally described how he was regularly stopped and questioned when out with his mates:

Ally: They said we were 'loitering with intent', like we were only goin' over the field . . . and they tried to accuse us of drinkin' . . . which we weren't doin' at the time [*guffaw*]

Carson Logue: At that time!

Ronny King also expressed his resentment at the systematic police surveillance which young people had to face.

They stop ye and fuckin' question ye up and down 'What were you doin'? Where are ye coming from? Where are ye goin' to now? Where were ye last night?' . . . an all. See if they get te know ye, when they get yer name, yer in bother man. I see me stopped many's a night walkin' the road. You could just turn round and say 'None of your fuckin' business!' but.

These confrontations lead to more general resistance to the presence of the police:

Ally: Like we call them the filth . . . They're not well-liked around here. You look at the likes of Nelson Drive, Irish Street and the Fountain [all Protestant estates], cops everywhere, 'meat-wagons' [police land rovers] in all the time . . . Do you ever see them when you go through the Bogside? Naw!

Carson: If they see a crowd of young fellah' they'll go over and hassle them and try and pick a fight with them . . . and, then when they'll pull them into the meat wagon and its 'down the station mate'.

The 1970s saw a massive expansion of the RUC in response to the civil unrest. The British government's decision to 'Ulsterize' security policy meant replacing soldiers on the streets with heavily-armed police. Undoubtedly this has meant Northern Ireland is a much more heavily-policed society than it was before the 'Troubles'. The young are particularly likely to be subjected to stop and search procedures by the police. If they gather in any numbers they are likely to be moved on.

In addition, the RUC has developed a sophisticated Juvenile section. This seeks to prevent juvenile delinquency by attempting to substitute tutelary interventions for judicial process in the handling of juvenile misdemeanour. This section works together with the schools, social work agencies, and corrective institutions regulating the lives of the street-active young. Young people are undoubtedly subject to much greater levels of police surveillance than in the past. Much of this surveillance is conditioned by police concerns about the potential involvement of the young in street disorders. An examination of the *official statistics* on recorded juvenile crime held by the RUC Juvenile Liaison Branch for the Londonderry area revealed that almost a third of prosecutions of children in the 11–17 age range which had occurred in the 1981–3 period were for Public Order Offences. This category includes disorderly behaviour, loitering, rioting, and organizing or participating in illegal parades. The upshot of this 'preventative' policing strategy is that probably more young people are subject to police surveillance and corrective action than in the old rough and ready judicially-led system.

Youth training and the reproduction of ethnic and gender difference

In Northern Ireland proportionally fewer girls than boys take up places within the YTP schemes (Rees, 1980). The PPRU Cohort Survey found that 70 per cent of the school leavers who entered YTP were male. On the other hand, more girls stay on at school after the age of sixteen. The Job Centre statistics for our Derry schools also showed that girls were more likely to stay on at school beyond the minimum leaving age. Those that entered employment were taking up jobs in Derry's shirt factories.

In Derry, as elsewhere, the desire of young women to remain at school may well reflect both the diminishing job opportunities available to them as women and also the inflation of educational credentials within the labour market. Secretarial and clerical jobs remain at the top of most female school leavers' list of acceptable employment. But nowadays employers demand higher qualifications from applicants. In addition, girls' preference for staying on at school also undoubtedly reflects their unfavourable perception of the YTP provision with its largely masculinist orientation, and consequently male recruitment pattern (Rees, 1980). Many find it better to stay on and try for the qualifications which provide a passport to white-collar employment than run the gauntlet of artisan machismo at the YTPs. As Margaret McAllister, a seventeen-year old pupil who had returned to the Irish Street school for an additional year after failing to find a job the previous June told me:

> Whenever you go to look for a job and ye look at the 'classified ads' its all 'one year's experience wanted'. There's nothin' really for school leavers now at this time. I was lookin' today at a secretarial job and it says 'one year's experience'.

Interviewer: Do they count the YTP as experience?

Margaret (somewhat cynically): Aye, they classify *that* as 'experience'. The Careers Officer advised us to do it, to go down [to the scheme] but its not very nice surroundings.

Interviewer: Why's that?

Margaret:　You're just thrown in like a builder's yard. Its alright

for ones doing mechanics and all that there ...
maybe the offices are different?

Girls are recruited into these centres (in the WPU Margaret refers
to, which I visited on a number of occasions, some 20 per cent of
the trainees are in fact female). However they are placed into
rigidly-defined areas of 'women's work'. In this scheme and many
others this means providing the catering and secretarial services
for the unit. The YTPs both in their formal sexual division of
labour and in their informal, overtly chauvinist, work culture
reproduce the gendered organization of the labour process to be
found in the 'outside world'.

Moreover these schemes replicate not only the gender but also
the ethnic differentiation of the young within the labour market.
Although not organized on a confessional basis they tend by their
very location to serve either Protestant or Catholic areas, but not
both. Accordingly many of them end up effectively religiously
segregated.

For example, in Derry at present there are three major work
preparation schemes which provide YTP 'training' for the young
unemployed. Two of these are located on the predominantly
Catholic, city side of the town. Less than 5 per cent of their
trainees are of Protestant origin. The other scheme is the one
located on the East Bank of the town already identified by our
respondent as 'Funny Farm'. It is located besides a long-established industrial estate in what could be designated 'neutral
territory'. Its trainees are approximately 60 per cent Protestant
and 40 per cent Catholic. However some 75 per cent of its staff are
of Protestant origin. This gives the Unit a distinctively 'Protestant'
ethos, in many ways amplified in the public mind due to the
appointment to the Unit of a manager formerly having a strong
association with militant Loyalism. Almost half of the male school
leavers from the two Protestant non-selective secondary schools in
our survey sample choose to go to this unit. Two thirds of those
who end up in the YTP net opt for it.

The fears of young men – both real and imagined – about
encountering sectarian intimidation in the workplace or having to
travel through 'hostile territory' to get to work, undoubtedly limit
the geographical scope of job-search activity. The effects of the
sectarian territorialization of urban space in constraining labour-

market mobility in Northern Ireland are well documented in the case of Belfast[8] and go some way towards explaining the under-representation of Catholics from the West Belfast ghettoes in industrial employment in the city. Rather less is known about the situation in Derry. But as the Fair Employment Agency has argued on the basis of its study of local government employment (1987), 'there is a strong reluctance of Protestants to apply for jobs on the City side of Londonderry'.

Some of the young people I interviewed had in fact taken up places in the city-side training schemes and crossed the bridge each day to travel to work. Carson Logue had been one of only two Protestant trainees in one of the smaller city-side schemes. He was anxious to relate his story to me – and to any other person in the youth club who would listen:

> They found out I was a Protestant and started giving me a lot of hassle. I'm a strong believer in my religion like, we used to have arguments an' all and I think that sort of led to it ... I went over to the Templemore Sports Complex with the group every Friday to play football and always wore a Rangers top. I gotta lot of hassle about that like – tried to rip it off me like – got a few hidings meself. That's why I left there and went to Funny Farm.

Carson had admitted to me earlier that he had actually been quite happy in the city-side scheme and not really minded the cross-religious banter. Indeed there seemed to be some evidence, according to some of the youth workers I talked to, that his parents, staunch Loyalists, had put considerable pressure on him to leave the scheme when they discovered he was the only Protestant in his group. However such accounts of hassle and conflict, suitably embellished for rhetorical effect, are listened to by younger school kids and undoubtedly reinforce their reluctance to join schemes where Protestants are very much in the minority.

Ronny King, as we have seen, had accepted the challenge of entering the GTC where Protestants were very much in the minority. However he described how his teachers in school had not encouraged this move.

At school teachers said to me 'You couldn't go to the training

centre, you'd be at the other kind.' But I was in there for a year.
I met the teachers again playing football one day. They couldn't
believe me – a couple knew I'd changed but other ones thought
I'd really had bad in me and have it with me for the rest of me
life. But I wanted te go out and prove them wrong and prove I
could work with anybody no matter what religion. And I done
it!

The city-side units are characterized by their emphasis on social
education and by the personal-growth orientation of their training
programmes. The tutors talk a lot about the importance of
providing a training for life which will allow the young to cope with
the problems of unemployment. They see this as a realistic
accommodation to the chronic job situation facing Catholics in
Derry. The East Bank scheme, for its part, concentrates much
more on basic vocational training and industrial skill education. It
lays great stress on 'good work habits' and has been significantly
more successful than the city-side schemes in placing young people
in jobs. In effect the scheme is in English terms a 'Mode A' scheme
significantly better connected to the local labour market than the
two schemes attended overwhelmingly by Catholic school leavers.
The local organization of YTP provision is, largely unwittingly,
replicating the long-term sectarian inequalities of opportunity in
the labour market.

Ronny's career

We can perhaps form a more concrete impression of how young
working class people in Northern Ireland are experiencing
marginalization if we recount for a moment the experience of one
young person we have already encountered – Ronny King.

Ronny, as we have seen, had been a natural leader amongst the
'lads' in the non-academic stream of Drumquin Secondary. He had
orchestrated much of the classroom resistance to school authority.
Ronny left school at the first opportunity with the Easter leavers,
having turned sixteen. He had no qualifications but was already
street wise.

A relative had offered him a job in a small scrap business which
had won a contract to dismantle the Hutchinson's Fibre plant. This

had recently shut down with the loss of 500 jobs. For ten weeks Ronny earned good money, some £60 a week, and was able to give his sister who he lived with at least £20 a week for his keep. There was also money for clothes, booze and dancing. When the scrapping contract expired Ronny was let go, and had his first experience of signing on the dole.

After some four weeks in which nothing had turned up, he was persuaded by the Careers Officer in the Job Centre to accept an offer of a place on the East Bank YTP. His income had dropped now to just £23 a week and he had to reduce the money he gave his sister, something he felt 'cat' about as her husband was also unemployed and money was tight in the household. Gone too were the luxuries he'd previously enjoyed.

However at first he was happy down at 'Funny Farm' and enthusiastically followed a course in french polishing. But he still had his heart set on an engineering apprenticeship. His father, when he was alive, had done a bit of french polishing but had found it difficult to find regular employment. Ronny was more than aware that this was a potentially precarious livelihood, 'How many french polishers does a town like this need?' he asked.

Although there seemed some chance he might be offered a job with a small furniture restoration firm, Ronny decided to apply to the Government training Centre to follow a basic industrial skills course. This, he hoped, might lead eventually to some sort of engineering apprenticeship with an employer. His income remained the same, though now he had also to meet the costs of attending the local technical college one day a week as part of his course. The months rolled by and he applied himself diligently to his training. For the first time in his life he worked alongside young Catholics and, as we have seen, surprised even himself by making friends across the divide. He had an opportunity to reassess some of his previous attitudes towards 'the other side', largely acquired at school. While at the GTC he applied for numerous apprenticeships with engineering firms but nothing came of it – jobs in the industrial sector were by now few and far between in Derry.

Having reached eighteen he left the Centre and, too old to return to the YTP, signed on. In the next few months he applied for scores of jobs. On occasions he was called for interview to the Job Centre. He sat through long, searching interviews and successfully completed tests only to be told by the manpower officials that as he had not been on the dole for a year he was not in fact entitled to apply for government-assisted jobs – the only ones advertised on the notice boards.

Nine months later and with his nineteenth birthday coming up, he had found nothing. Things were getting more difficult 'at home as his sister and her husband split up and his inability to contribute more to the already stretched household troubled him even more. He was earning a little bit of extra money delivering milk but didn't know how long this would last. In desperation he had sent off for the application forms to join the Army. Having met someone home on holiday from Australia where they now worked, he also toyed with the idea of emigration – but as he admitted he had no skill to sell. In truth he did not know what he would do. . .

Since I left the GTC I've applied for everything under the sun. Engineering, joinery, anything . . . I'm not what you'd call the best joiner but I'll have a go at it. Salesman or something like that there. Ballymena, Portadown, Enniskillen, where ye stay up there all week and only come down at the weekends. Nothin'. Been all the dole almost a year. Looking for jobs not getting no success I feel really cat about it.

Its not the young people themselves that's te blame. For when young people leave school, what there in front of them? Dole first. What's there then? YTPs. What's there then? GTC. What's there after it? *nothin'*! Fifty-fifty chance *nothin'*!

Marginalization and disinheritance

It is, I think, in the context of this economic marginalization faced by the Protestant working-class young, with its accompanying crisis of reproduction of occupational and communal, social codes, that youthful sectarianism is, intelligible.

As Phil Cohen (1988) has forcefully argued, within working-class culture the notion of 'skill' involves a complex set of representations which is not reducible to purely occupational questions. It also involves ideas about social and gender status and about both the autonomy and class identity of the waged worker.

The notion of 'inheritance' which the young working-class male holds is of course still concerned with the preservation of a patrimony of occupational skill. But both unemployment and the youth-training schemes erode the social and economic basis of working-class skill and autonomy – the latter through its pseudo-vocationalism and low-wage ethos and sustained assault on working-class culture.

But the notion of inheritance also involves other aspects of a communal heritage now threatened by the restructuring of the working-class in the current crisis. Indeed, the tenacity with which, as we have seen, young Protestant lads cling to the hope of becoming a 'tradesman' as the actual opportunities to do so drastically decline, suggests that for them much more is at stake in abandoning the idea of 'serving one's time' than a choice of job.

However as the codes of cultural transmission of working-class life start to break down under the impact of unemployment and changes in the labour process, representations of heritage are no longer tied primarily to the workplace. In turn, other more organic formations of heritage start to predominate within the lives of the young. These tend to crystallize around exclusivist images of community, and violent assertions of territory. Cohen (1988) identifies three features of this ideological structure:

> First it is centred on quasi-biological construct of community, where destinies are fixed to origin, and the 'consanguinity' of labour power is anchored to strategic images of kith and kin. When people talk about being born an Eastender, or having coal 'in their bones', they are talking about an apprenticeship to this kind of inheritance. Second, this patrimony constructs places of origin as sites of special, quasi-magical forms of ownership and control. You become an 'Eastender' by demonstrating that the East End belongs to you. Third, the assertion of this kind involves strategies of social closure which define all those who are held to lack such 'ethical' credentials as outsiders and a potential threat.

Male working class youth, as we have seen, have historically played a key role in sustaining this sense of imagined community. Increasingly they are playing a key role in policing, what Cohen calls, the 'ethical credentials' of local community. In the case of Northern Ireland this means the policing of confessional boundaries.

Through these territorial activities, Cohen argues:

> a distinctive body politic is constructed, one which allows working-class groups to exercise certain forms of local jurisdiction over and against each other and to invent themselves as a local 'ruling class' without either adopting bourgeois values or challenging their hegemony.

Its not hard to see how this analysis might contribute to our understanding of youthful sectarianism in Northern Ireland.

By the early summer of 1985, as a new marching season got underway and Loyalist opposition to the Anglo-Irish process began to build, Ronny began to hang around with some of the 'hard men' of the area with shady connections with the Loyalist paramilitaries. He travelled with them to attend the banned Orange marches that ended in violent confrontation with the police in Portadown. There he met and talked with hardened UVF members and bought and read their radical fascist paper *Combat*. His remaining friendships with Catholics unravelled and his bitterness against the nationalist community grew appreciably. It seemed possible that he had been directly involved in the intimidation of Catholic families living close by.

Postscript on Practice

It seems appropriate to make some comment about current educational and and youth-policy matters in Northern Ireland in the light of my ethnographic findings. Together with other youth ethnographers I have a commitment to a style of sociological writing that seeks to intervene in contemporary debates about youth policy by bringing to bear critical theoretical perspectives on educational and youthwork practice. Surely social researchers are under some obligation to trace the implications of their ethnographic findings and theoretical reflections for schooling and youth work practice?

In the Northern Ireland context, however, one is particularly resistant to the temptation to prescribe policy 'solutions' to identified social problems when perhaps *political* answers are more appropriate. At times writing about Northern Ireland can be a particularly sobering and depressing affair. A political stalemate since 1969 and the resulting corrosive cycle of state and para-military violence have left their mark on all of us. In this study we have traced the effects of the polarization between the two communities on the everyday lives of the young in Northern Ireland. For intellectuals, too, horizons have been lowered. We no longer look naively to enlightened social science to provide policy 'solutions' to the 'Northern Ireland Problem'. Indeed British policy in Ireland under the Conservative administration has seemingly itself abandoned the search for ameliorative political solutions. Earlier government commitments to eradicate sectarianism within the existing political order in Northern Ireland have given way to a series of crisis-management strategies focused on security imperatives. The Anglo-Irish Agreement is just one of these.

In the late 1980s the British government sought to reduce the 'Northern Ireland problem' to the law and order objective of 'defeating the terrorists'. Social policy took a back seat. Militant

Republicanism, for its part, despite its forays into municipal and parliamentary politics since the Hunger Strike period, remains ultramontane in its political strategy – all issues, economic, social, civil libertarian, have a tendency to evoke the same fundamentalist response – 'BRITS OUT!' For the strategists of Sinn Fein, socialism, as ever, must wait. That is, wait until national liberation has been achieved by the military phalanx. In turn, the labour movement rent by sectarian and political division, has become marginalized and impotent. Academic analysis with little or no purchase on either government thinking or oppositional politics drifts into metaphysics and idealism.[1]

In this context the 'radical reformism' which has informed the critical debate on social policy in Britain and which underlay the strategy of radical welfare politics practised 'in and against the state', is absent.[2] In policy debates in Northern Ireland the stakes are always higher.

The British state has, since 1972, represented the problem of sectarianism in Northern Ireland as, in essence, a social problem. Its origins have been located in the 'irrational prejudices' and 'tribal animosities' intrinsic to Irish culture itself. British imperialism has thereby attempted to absolve itself of its direct responsibility for the raw political situation it bequeathed to Ireland as a result of the partition settlement. Sectarianism has been treated within the policy discourses of the state as a structure of personal prejudice and not as the result of an unresolved, post-colonial political situation. As such, the problem is adjudged to be best addressed by a carefully managed dosage of personal enlightenment delivered by the educational apparatus. In short, the education system is expected to compensate for the failures of the polity in Northern Ireland – an impossible task which hard pressed teachers rightly baulk at.

When the issue of young people and sectarianism *has* been addressed in Northern Ireland, the attention of social commentators and policy makers has focused almost exclusively on the role of the province's segregated school system in institutionalizing and reproducing sectarian attitudes and divisions amongst the young. In turn, youth provision has been largely motivated by social-control imperatives. Its claim to additional state funding has rested, to a large extent, on its perceived potential to combat 'the destructive influences of paramilitary organizations'. The youth service in Northern Ireland has embraced, since the late 1970s, the diffuse objective of promoting 'tolerance and mutual understanding among people and a willingness to communicate in a society with diverse traditions and outlooks'. However, in reality, youth clubs and organizations remain religiously segregated, and youth leaders have continued to be reluctant to confront the issue of sectarianism amongst the young or to develop informal educational programmes to address the problem.

Moreover, within the sphere of formal schooling the British state, despite its rhetorical promotion of 'education for mutual understanding', has been slow to act. The sociological effects of segregated schooling are by now well documented. Indeed they were well understood years ago by the enlightened administrators who sought to introduce an integrated schooling system into Northern Ireland in the years directly after the creation of the Stormont state – and who so signally failed in this endeavour.[3]

With the creation and successful development of a small number of integrated primary and secondary schools outside the state-controlled sector, a prototype and living example of a non-segregated sector is already with us, tried and tested. Indeed the apparent unwillingness of successive British administrations to act decisively on the question of educational segregation is a telling sign of Whitehall's general lack of resolve to tackle the institutional basis of sectarianism in Northern Ireland. As we have seen, few advances have been made in remedying the disadvantaged position of Catholics within the labour market, and the government has remained hostile to arguments, from whatever source, that positive discrimination schemes are necessary to improve the position of Catholics.

Any administration in Northern Ireland faces, of course, strong and well-organized opposition from the Catholic hierarchy to any change in the current segregated school system. A Loyalist lobby against integration also lurks in the wings. On the other hand, Margaret Thatcher and the Tory government have not balked at confronting both Republicans and Loyalists where issues of 'principle' were held to be at stake. Moreover, as we well know, this Conservative government appears to have a somewhat lukewarm commitment to public education provision throughout the UK. Conservative educational policy in Northern Ireland remains tentative on the segregation issue. It continues to vacillate between a global enthusiasm for extending parental choice, particularly to those who are able and prepared to purchase private provision for their children, and an instinctive caution in its dealing with the entrenched religious and political interests which continue to block moves towards universal integrated education in Northern Ireland, as they do any introduction of comprehensive schooling.

Accordingly, integrated education will be dealt with on a voluntary basis. Parents will in the future have the right to send their children to specially-established integrated schools – if such schools are available in their neighbourhoods. Such integrated schools, like denominational provision, may attract state financial support. In other words the integrated provision will remain a marginal element within the overall, still segregated schooling system. In effect it will be available largely to those middle-class parents in non-ghettoized areas who have the organizational and financial resources to initiate integrated school projects.

In the context of a lack of government resolve to tackle the problem of segregated education, educationalists concerned with combating sectarianism amongst the young have found themselves severely constrained. One response has been to turn to curriculum innovation and inter-school cooperation across the sectarian divide to overcome the institutional obstacles to educational change.

Following the work of the Schools Cultural Studies Project (SCSP) at the University of Ulster, attempts were made in the 1970s to develop and implement a secondary-schools social studies curriculum which could address the 'cultural divisions' in Northern Ireland society. This project aimed to combat sectarian prejudice at school level by encouraging pupils to explore the diverse political and cultural traditions of Ulster and to compare the Ulster conflict to that found in other 'trouble spots'. The project would, at a more general level, encourage developments in multi-cultural education for 'tolerance.' At the same time a network of participating teachers and schools was set up to establish educational links for both pupils and teachers across the sectarian divide and to provide a curriculum focus for the other educational exchange schemes between Protestant and Catholic schools which have mushroomed since the early 1970s.

Central to this project, like many of the equivalent cultural

studies projects in England concerned with 'multicultural education', were two key assumptions. Firstly, that the teachers participating in the project could function as cultural 'change agents',
coming to constitute 'an elite group to spearhead change throughout the education system'. Secondly, that sectarianism (or racism)
amongst the young could be understood as an armature of
personal prejudice which could be stripped away by a cognitive
pedagogic strategy. Each of these assumptions can be questioned.

All the historical and sociological evidence suggests that radical
educational innovation and teacher action of the sort envisaged in
many multicultural curriculum projects can only be sustained in
the context of more general patterns of social emancipation and
progressive social change. For example, the successful post-
Second World War struggle in Britain for the implementation of
child-centered pedagogy in the primary school, and for the introduction of comprehensive schooling at the secondary level, were
inextricably bound up in the, albeit limited, political success of
British social democracy during this period. Conversely, the
eclipse of social democracy has occasioned an erosion of popular
support for 'progressive' educational principles and practices. The
forced halt on the onward march of labour has been accompanied
by a 'down turn' in the struggle for progressive education.

As the SCSP was to discover, political support for the liberal
aims of its social studies curriculum existed only within the
originating university (higher education is the only part of the state
system which in fact *is* effectively integrated). Within segregated
schools many headmasters, sensitive to local political pressures,
remained somewhat hostile to crusading teachers who sought to
introduce controversial issues into the curriculum and who were
prepared to act as standard-bearers for integrated education. As it
turned out, most teachers involved in the Coleraine project were
more than aware of their political vulnerability and lack of
institutional support. Most opted for a lower profile role as
'technical experts' in curriculum development. The cultural studies
curriculum, in turn, became identified with children already labelled
'less academic'. Few teachers felt confident enough to fulfil the
role prescribed for them by the university researchers as 'genera-
tors of a sectarian critique' or 'cultural change agents'. They were
in effect out on a limb. Indeed, the best the project could do for
these teachers was to provide, in the words of one researcher, 'an

umbrella protecting teachers against the falling hail of stress, injustice, alienation and violence' of school life in Northern Ireland's segregated and regressive schooling system.[4] A worthwhile, if idealist, strategy for changing hearts and minds by patient curriculum innovation and inspired pedagogy was dashed on the jagged reefs of political reaction which reinforced rather than challenged British educational policy in Northern Ireland. The decision to impose a 'national-core curriculum' on Irish schools, along with the rest of the Bakerite baggage of educational 're-forms', with little cognizance of the specific needs and sensibilities of Northern Ireland's schools, further circumscribe teacher initiatives in tackling sectarianism in the classroom. As far as history and social-studies teaching in Northern Ireland are concerned, it will further diminish the teaching of Irish history. This is already deplorable in Protestant-dominated secondary schools where curricula designed for English children are often slavishly followed. Ulster's young people will continue to learn their history off gable walls.

We can also question the assumption that sectarianism, like racism, is a matter of personal prejudice. As Phil Cohen (1988) has shown this assumption is widely held by 'multiracial' educationalists:

> The most popularly-held theory about the causes of popular racism is still that it is the product of ignorance and/or irrational fears. This is often linked to a deficit model of working-class culture. The common sense of the staffroom is that 'those kids' don't know any better than to be racist because their parents or peers have not equipped them with the intellectual or experiental resources to think any differently about difference.

Sectarianism in Northern Ireland is not the same as British racism – it achieves its exclusivist effects less by reference to an explicit ideology of genetic or cultural difference, and more by popular cultural practices of territorial demarcation and communal identification – yet there is little doubt that the same link between the deficiencies of working-class culture and sectarianism is made by many teachers. Indeed, as the researchers involved in the SCSP reported, a number of head teachers in particular expressed the view that, 'lower ability children tend to be more bigoted and that intelligent children do not need cultural studies'.[5] And the project teachers had to continually struggle against attempts to restrict the new curriculum to the less academic (and often working-class) segments of the school population.

As the university researchers of the SCSP were to discover, working-class pupils remained, in fact, relatively impervious to social-studies proselytizing. Protestant pupils seemed particularly resistent to the pedagogical assault on their traditional world view. As we have seen, they have made considerable subcultural investment in Loyalist tradition. As project teachers reported, pupils following the cultural social studies curriculum left their newly nurtured 'tolerance' behind them at the classroom door. One teacher commented in exasperation 'they'll give a liberal response because that is what I want, and keep their own narrow-minded views to themselves'.[6] Given the fact that Loyalist popular culture remains for these pupils an important resource for the construction of a school counterculture, this duplicity is hardly strange.

Cohen (1988) has identified the difficulty in using teacher authority to challenge white racism in English schools. Pupils assailed by the teacher because of their expressed racist views may come to outwardly conform to teacher's expectations, but at the same time inwardly rebel against teachers' proscription of racist attitudes and behaviours.

This kind of Jekyll and Hyde racism, which is a function of teacher pupil interaction, may then connect up with wider patterns of split perception. The attempt to censor the popular culture of racism through disciplinary means thus encounters a whole series of resistances which may produce a whole series of unintended side effects.

The teacher's intervention may in fact further cement the already existing link between popular racism and school counterculture. From the pupils' perspective their duplicity in the classroom may seem entirely justified. Carson Logue had experience of an enlightened cultural studies curriculum in the YTP scheme he had attended. He described his resistance to his teachers' efforts:

The tutors tried to get us together, like, that was the idea of Youthways, to get people together, like ... but what the tutors were trying to do ... they were trying to draw us away from our beliefs an' all and thinking nothin' like – I stood an' I says, 'no one is going to change my beliefs or anything like that there, I don't care what they say about good relationships, but my beliefs is still there, like, and nobody's going to take them away'.

Sectarian practices amongst the young are too often approached within such programmes from a perspective of high moralism – the flip side of which is usually a deficit model of working-class culture. Orange popular culture certainly fosters hostility towards Catholics. But it does more than this. It also functions to encourage localistic loyalties, provide public and recreational space for the marginalized young, and furnish the symbolic resources for the construction by the young of a distinctively Protestant sense of community for an increasingly beleaguered people. That is why the young cling to its arcane representations.

In the ethnography reported here we have explored the central role that the marginalized young now play in the maintenance and renewal of Loyalist 'tradition'. Perhaps now we are in a position to understand the emotional and subcultural investment which young working-class Protestants like Carson have in Loyalist popular culture. Hopefully we are now also in a better position to understand their resistance to the existing cultural studies programmes.

Teachers and youth workers in Northern Ireland have to date experienced a real dilemma when faced with the expressed sectarian views of their charges. Should they attempt to banish all political argument and ethnic display from the hallowed walls of the educational precinct? Or do they have a social responsibility to engage with populist sectarianism and encourage a critical dialogue between and within the two 'traditions', with all their strengths and shibboleths? Should school provide a neutral and civilized haven from the political rancour and sectarian bigotry of the adult world by banishing all political discussion? Or, should young people be facilitated by the educational system in their critical interrogation of their culture of origin?

In effect, prohibition of 'political talk' and evasion of controversial issues are the preferred strategies of most schools and youth clubs in the province when confronted with the popular cultural 'politics' of their pupils/members. After all, argue many teachers, the adult world in Northern Ireland has not shown itself to be particularly adept at addressing or living with the very real political and cultural differences that separate the two communities in Northern Ireland. Why, these teachers ask, should the school or youth club be expected to tackle the apparently irresolvable? Education cannot compensate for society. Is it not better that schools and youth clubs function as the 'time out' of Ulster society?

The problem remains of how to critically engage with sectarian behaviours and attitudes which are enshrined within popular cultural forms, like the marching bands, and which daily threaten the order of the classroom and the playground. The problem remains that for most of these young people the official culture of tolerance stops at the classroom door.

Teachers and youth workers know well enough that their pupils invest much time and energy in the subcultural arena. Despite this, any mention of politics and identity is generally banned from the school and youth club. In the English school with its multi-ethnic composition, silencing racist discourse in the classroom is entirely justifiable in order to marginalize racist elements and show solidarity with black children who are at the receiving end of racist jibes. In Northern Ireland's already segregated schools where counter religionists are not usually present to be offended, and where patterns of ethnic differentiation are more porous and have less ideological underpinning, I suspect such a strategy of control is not justified.

Perhaps rather than demanding that young Protestants abandon overnight their popular cultural 'tradition', it might be more appropriate for educationalists to provide a learning context within which young Protestants have the opportunity to explore and question their own culture of tradition. History teaches us that Protestant experience in Ireland is more complex than most Loyalists acknowledge. For instance, few young Loyalists realise that both the creation of the idea of an Irish nation and indeed of revolutionary republicanism were largely 'Protestant' inventions. In contemporary Ulster history must be redeemed. As we have seen, the young are already implicitly engaged in an exploration of the limits and contradictions of their parental culture through their subcultural activity. Can critical youth-work practice assist them in making this exploration a more reflexive process?

Within the school this will require, as the SCSP argued, a more imaginative approach to the secondary curriculum. It will require much greater attention to Ulster history as well as the general British history currently taught. This will entail launching history projects exploring Protestant history – and its repressed radical currents, particularly the heritage of Presbyterian radicalism. It will require an engagement with Loyalist mythologies of history. The tercentenary celebrations of the Siege of Derry in 1989 and the Battle of the Boyne of 1990 provide a vibrant popular cultural context within which to critically interrogate the Loyalist historical memory. Such projects require inspired drama work. One suspects that youth theatre in Ulster has already achieved more in fomenting critical interrogation of ethnic and gender identities and exclusions amongst Northern Ireland's young people than all the school-based cultural studies programmes combined. Rock music as a vehicle for youthful self-expression and as a vehicle for communication both across and within the sectarian divide must be encouraged within youth clubs. As we have seen, the rock genre, particularly punk, did manage in the past to provide a non-sectarian habitus for Ulster youth. The youth service can play its part by providing venues for rock gigs and resources for popular music workshops which might (as reggae or indeed Irish traditional music projects have done) serve as a vehicle for communal and ethnic self-expression and examination. A stage-managed collision between rock music and the world of the marching band is long overdue. Video production and photographic documentation must be utilized to allow young people to record and map the lives of their communities and the material problems they confront.

All of this will require a serious commitment to providing for the political education of Northern Ireland's young people. In my experience the teenage young are intensely interested in political questions and, if encouraged, surprisingly open to examine critically their own ideological standpoints. The tragedy remains that they are rarely given the opportunity to do this. Young Loyalists, in particular, recognize how politically and culturally inarticulate their community has been in the past under Unionist hegemony. It is the youth service which is perhaps best placed to provide a secure and informal milieu for young people to discuss political issues and question their own, their peers' and perhaps their teachers' attitudes.

Simply bringing young Protestants and Catholics together in ritualized encounters where each party is expected to abandon for the duration their deeply-held convictions seems to achieve little of lasting importance. Both groups return to the stockade and to their prejudices. Perhaps, rather than attempting to manufacture in the educational closet an artificial rapprochement between young Protestants and Catholics (whether through the curriculum or through a token, if well-meaning, exchange and liaison programme across the divide), we might encourage young working-class Protestants to critically examine their own culture of tradition. In a sense as we have seen our young people are already engaged in this task – on the streets. In truth, there can be no real 'mutual understanding' without an adequate self-understanding of one's own culture and its limits and contradictions.

Above all, those who chastise street-wise young Loyalists for their bigotry must ask themselves how within this cultural formation a more progressive form of ethnicity might emerge. We might ask under what political conditions could the Protestants of Ulster escape the historical cul-de-sac that their dependence on British imperialism has led them into? This, of course, is not primarily an educational issue. But it stares every educationalist concerned with the problem of sectarianism straight in the face. For if, as we have argued, sectarianism is primarily an expression of the persistence of objective social and economic divisions still underwritten by British imperialism, then it is unlikely to be seriously tackled within the existing political order. We await the avenging angel of history.

Notes

1 Youth Culture and Ethnic Identity

1. The CCCS authors clearly locate youth subcultural rituals within a more extensive repertoire of working-class 'strategies and responses' as regards the rule of capital:

    negotiation, resistance, struggle: the relations between a subordinate and a dominant culture, wherever they fall within this spectrum, are always intensely active, always oppositional, in a structural sense (even if this opposition is latent, or experienced simply as the normal state of affairs) (Hall and Jefferson, 1976).

2. As Dick Hebdige noted in a discussion of the appropriation of black musical style within white subcultures:

    We can watch played out on the loaded surfaces of the British working-class youth cultures a phantom history of race relations since the war (Hebdige, 1979).

3. Indeed if they *were* to speak in such terms and proclaim as the prime object of their political loyalty a real or imagined sovereign state of 'Ulster', we would find their political attitudes and behaviour rather easier to understand. But, by and large, except for those on the margins of the Protestant political community in the North (associated with 'the political wing' of the Ulster Defence Association) they do not.

4. This intriguing term has been introduced into the vocabulary of political anthropology by Benedict Anderson (Anderson, 1983).

5. For a useful survey of the conflicting analyses of the Irish Question within the Left see Martin (1981) and Pringle (1978).

6. The case for the two-nation theory has been most forcefully put by the British and Irish Communist Organization (1975) though it has its academic supporters (see Boal, 1978).

7. Douglas Hyde, a leading figure in the Irish Language Movement, and first President of the Irish Free State. Padraig Pearse, poet, scholar and revolutionary nationalist who died in the Easter rising 1916.

8. For the best historical account of Orangeism see Gibbon (1975).
9. For a detailed historical account of the class tensions within Loyalist see Patterson (1983).
10. As Ron Wiener notes, locating these sociological changes in the restructuring of the Northern Ireland economy from the 1950s:

> It was the influx of new industry, the setting up of the growth areas, the continuing deterioration of living conditions in the inner city areas and the onset of redevelopment which was to change this (Wiener, 1978).

11. Sarah Nelson (1984) in her perceptive study of contemporary Loyalism reports the sense of intellectual and cultural inferiority that working-class Loyalists express with regard to Republicans.

2   Sons and Daughters of the Gael: Youth in Irish Social Thought

1. I am indebted to Luke Gibbons for bringing the writings of Rev. Devane to my attention.
2. In mid-1960s Dublin the Church tried to close down a number of the newer rock clubs which had emerged in the city as they had in Belfast. This move provoked a protest march of rock enthusiasts through the city in 1966 and from then rock music became identified with the youthful crusade against clericism and conservative nationalism.
3. For a discussion of the influence of the Community Studies tradition within Irish social science see Bell (1981).
4. The tide has turned once again in Ireland as regards emigration. It is reckoned that some 200,000 persons left the Republic of Ireland to settle abroad between 1981 and 1988, the majority of these to England, but considerable numbers to the US, where it is reckoned there are currently up to perhaps 80,000 Irish illegal immigrants working in the country, most of them under thirty.
5. For a discussion of the incidence of involvement of juveniles in civil disturbance see Cairns (1987).
6. Quoted in Taylor and Nelson (1978).
7. These figures are taken from the study: *Young People and Youth Services in Northern Ireland* (New University of Ulster, 1978).
8. For details see Cairns (1987).
9. As Macauley and Troy (1983) reported in their statistical analysis of child psychiatric referrals in Northern Ireland's main assessment clinic, the number of children referred was at its lowest in 1972 – the year in which, by any criterion, political violence in Northern Ireland was undoubtedly at one of its highest levels.
10. Quoted in Cairns (1987).
11. For example, the results of studies in which large samples of Belfast school children were asked to complete behaviour-rating scales

were compared with identical tests, conducted by the English researcher Michael Rutter among samples of English pupils from the Isle of Wight and London. Not surprisingly, the Belfast children showed higher levels of anti-social and neurotic behaviour on these scales than those from the Isle of Wight. On the other hand they scored less on these scales than children from Inner London. In other words, in relative terms, Belfast children 'compare favourably' with children from similar British areas of urban deprivation.

12. The term 'Habitus' has been introduced into the vocabulary of contemporary sociology by the French social theorist Pierre Bourdieu (1977). It attempts to facilitate our understanding of the linkage between, on the one hand, the objective determinations of human practice (social and economic structures) and, on the other hand, the experiential world of social subjects who collectively act within the material world. Bourdieu defines the Habitus as 'an acquired system of generative schemes objectively adjusted to the particular conditions in which it is constituted.'

13. In addition, Derry's size and physical integrity make it particularly attractive to the ethnographer concerned to relate the social phenomenon to be studied – in my case Protestant youth-cultural formations – to the totality of social relations existing in a particular locality.

14. This was brought home to me one day in the most immediate of ways. One evening shortly after beginning the fieldwork, I conducted a particularly tortuous interview with a group of teenage girls in one of the youth clubs. I asked them about their attitudes to the sectarian conflict and towards young Catholics. Later I asked the youth leader why the girls had been so reticent. He reminded me politely that the father of one of the girls had been shot dead by the IRA some weeks earlier.

15. On the other hand some of the researchers were not immune from the threat of violence. One from a Catholic background had to ask himself if he was prepared to interview a group of young Loyalists who it seemed likely had played some part in burning down the home of a close relative.

16. Our research attracted, however, the attention of the Northern Ireland Special Branch as parents of children in our school survey who were in the security forces demanded to know why their children had been 'interrogated' about their political attitudes. In these situations, where confidentiality is regarded as not merely an ethical nicety but a matter of life and death, professional assurances cut little ice!

17. As our survey of Protestant secondary schools indicated, less than one in five of secondary school pupils were involved in marching bands, although almost half the sample indicated their interest and support for a particular local band (for details see Chapter 4).

18. From the outset we had no illusions that such a quantitave survey could provide us with a complete picture of changing attitudes and

practices. For a start the study had no *systematic* longitudinal
dimension which could provide the appropriate statistical basis for
evaluating attitudinal change over a long time. Perhaps more
seriously, the survey questionnaire method, with its necessary fore-
shortening and hypostatization of the young people's responses to
our formal questions in the interests of the 'quantification imperative', is of necessity an insensitive research instrument, blind to the
meaningful nuances of youthful discourse and practice. Moreover,
any set of survey results displayed as a myriad of figures, frequencies
and tabulations spewn out of computer, require *interpretation*. At
best the survey might give us some leads to follow up in the
ethnographic process and it might go some way in allowing us to
estimate the *representivity* of our ethnographic sample.

3   Situating Sectarianism: Territory, Identity and Empire in Ulster

1. This in no way diminishes the analytical significance of *Capital* which
    is after all a work of political economy not general sociology.
2. The legacy of Partition is explored in the Morgan and Purdy
    collection: *Ireland: Divided Nation – Divided Class* (1980).
3. As Paul Gilroy (1982) has argued:

    the British left has been reluctant to approach the Pandora's box
    of racial politics [   ] the simplistic reduction of 'race' to class
    which has guided their practice for so many years has been thrown
    into confusion by intense and visible BLACK struggles. . .

4. In the first instance researchers like Hebdige (1979) began to
    speculate about the relation between white and black subcultural
    movements of the late 1970s. The increasing marginalization of
    youth in Britain seemed to be encouraging a subcultural deconstruc-
    tion of 'Britishness' amongst certain sections of white youth, as
    witnessed for instance in punk's 'symbolic treason' and assault on
    British imperial identity. Punk, argues Hebdige, appropriated stra-
    tegies of cultural resistance from Rastafarianism to construct an
    oppositional 'white ethnicity'. The outbreak of the urban riots in
    1982 which saw white and black youth stand together to confront the
    police, provided a more concrete example of this dynamic between
    marginalization and ethnic assertion.
5. Indeed the CCCS group were to subject the community studies
    tradition to a searching critique; see, for instance, Critcher, Clarke
    and Johnston (1979).
6. Building on the analysis of the English Marxist historians, Thomp-
    son (1963), Johnston (1979) Stedman-Jones (1974), the CCCS
    theorists attempted to link the spheres of production and consump-
    tion, of labour process and residential life, wage form and commun-
    ity existence, in their understanding of the making and remaking of
    the English working class.

7. In for instance Hebdige's (Hall and Jefferson, 1976) early ethnography.

8. As Springhall (1977) documents both Scouting and the Boys Brigade established themselves early in Ulster and had wide popularity amongst the Protestant middle classes.

9. Quoted in Doak (1978). In the following account of riot and civil strife in Derry I am indebted to Conor Doak who has made his M.A. (1978) thesis on the same subject available to me. This painstakingly-researched dissertation proved to be an invaluable source for one who lacks the patience of the historian as regards original documentation.

10. Although by the end of the century the proportion of Catholics in the total population of Belfast had declined somewhat.

11. Madame Bovet, a French visitor to Derry in 1889, was to describe the pillar caustically as, 'another instance of the British madness of putting its heroes like parrots on a perch' (quoted in Mullin, 1986).

12. For a detailed and somewhat harrowing account of the sectarian strife in nineteenth and early twentieth century Belfast see Boyd (1987).

13. There was a limited literary search in the years after 1888 to identify the cultural characteristics of the Ulster Protestant, viz: John Harrison, *The Scot in Ulster* (1888), F. Frankfort Moore, *The Truth About Ulster* (1914), J. Heron, *The Ulster Scot* (1900). And the latter could declare:

> The truth is that the Ulster Scot, reared on the Shorter Catechism, is a type of character distinct from other types; not perhaps as imaginative or versatile as the Irish Celt, nor as vivacious as the Frenchman, nor as stolid as the German, but with rugged strength and firmness of moral fibre, thoroughly self-reliant and independent, determined to stand on his own feet rather than to lean upon others, with patience and dogged perseverance, not showy or demonstrative, but reserved and self contained in his religion as in other things. . .

However these not unperceptive sketches of the personality of the Ulster Protestant fall far short of a literary representation of an emergent nation and, indeed, have little relation to the eugenically inspired, racial stereotypes of the Irish employed in England in that period.

14. This figure is based on the recorded decline of politically registered Protestants on the city side and their parallel increase on the East Bank of Derry.

4 Sketches of the Marching Season

1. It is not without irony that many of these Loyalist paramilitary songs derive their tunes from long-established Republican ballads.

2. The tradition of Loyalist wall painting in Derry goes back to the late 1920s when Bobby Jackson adorned an end wall in the Fountain with a picture of William on a black charger crossing the Boyne (a mural which is still preserved today in the redeveloped estate by the Jackson family). For an interesting account of the mural tradition and its role within popular political discourse see Rolston (1987).

3. Within the Orange fraternity are to be found other more elite orders such as the Royal Black Perceptory and the Purple Arch Chapter. The Apprentice Boys of Derry is an entirely separate organization and is a federation of separate clubs organized throughout Ulster and in parts of Scotland. Its membership overlaps to some extent with that of the Orange Order, but is more working class in its composition and of late more militant in its politics. The Orange Order has an affiliation with the Unionist Party. The Apprentice Boys has no official political affiliation but has a strong DUP lobby within its ranks and has as members all the leading lights of that party including Ian Paisley.

4. Most of the bands pay weekly dues towards the costs of uniforms and instruments and elect one amongst them to take charge of their funds.

5. A number of bandsmen in both the 'Sons' and the 'Boys' were members of the local Rangers Supporters Club and travelled regularly to Glasgow to see the team play.

6. Most of the younger bands purchase their instruments and uniforms (tailor-made by a specialist firm in Belfast) by means of Credit Company loans. Someone, usually the older leader, has to sign for these. This can be a high risk venture given the short life of many of the 'Blood and Thunder' bands.

7. Access to these small area statistics enables a researcher to build up a useful sketch of the social structure of specific neighbourhoods.

8. Sue Jenvey (1972) has described the emergence of the Tartans in Belfast.

9. The documentary *Real Lives: At the Edge of the Union*.

5 Youth and Ghettoization in Northern Ireland

1. Derry throughout the nineteenth century had a strong Liberal political tradition. Within the Presbyterian population, the largest Protestant denomination in the city, this had acted as a partial foil to the spread of Orangeism. However by the end of the 1880s, with the extension of the franchise increasing the size of the Catholic vote in Derry, and with the growing national strength of Parnell's nationalists, Presbyterian liberalism (in terms of electoral support for Liberal candidates in parliamentary election) quickly evaporated, signalling, in Murphy's words 'acceptance of tory/episcopalian hegemony in social and cultural matters' (1981).

2. *Youth in Derry* (The New University of Ulster, Adult Education, 1971).

3. Although the closure of the BSR plant, which had had a workforce of 1,500 at the peak of its expansion, traumatically demonstrated to all in Derry the inconstancy of multinational investment in Northern Ireland.

4. Interestingly in Belfast the skinhead style seems to have been 'claimed' as subcultural property by Loyalist youth. Indeed a number of Protestant kids I spoke to admitted that whereas they could easily distinguish between 'Jaffas' and 'Fenians' (Protestants and Catholics) in Derry, they were at a loss to do so when confronted with the Belfast skinhead, who one kid described as 'wild Fenian looking'!

5. Though by historical accident because of the flight of Protestant families to the East Bank, a number of Maintained (state) schools are now fairly mixed, as Catholic parents have opted to send their children to these previously exclusively-Protestant schools.

6. The National Front does not stand in elections in Northern Ireland and, in Derry at least, I was not able to locate any members of the organization. However, their paper was sold at Loyalist parades by Front supporters from elsewhere in Northern Ireland and a number of the young people I interviewed had read it.

7. This point is actively pursued by Frank Wright in his seminal study of Ulster Loyalism (1973).

8. Cf. Russell (1973).

6 Economic Marginalization and Blocked Inheritance

1. For further details see, *Londonderry Area Plan: Review 1981–86*, 'Economic Analysis', (Londonderry Divisional Planning Office, Department of the Environment, 1984).

2. Despite the popular myths that abound about the reversal of conjugal roles in the Derry family because of endemic male unemployment, there is little evidence that the widespread participation of Derry women in waged employment has led to any significant erosion of patriarchy within the working-class family in the region – any more than it has done elsewhere.

3. A useful summary of youth occupational data can be found in Osborne and Cormack's work for the FEA (*Research paper 11*, 1987), and in the report *Youth Unemployment and Training*, prepared by the NI Economic Council, March 1982.

4. It should be noted that the 1981 Census is a somewhat unreliable source of data for Londonderry, as it is for a number of other regions in Northern Ireland. Many nationalists for political reasons did not return their census forms. In addition the shooting dead by the IRA of a census enumerator curtailed collection of completed forms, rendering the usually efficient administration of the census deficient.

5. Figures from Statistical Bulletin of the Department of Education for Northern Ireland, 1981.

6. For an interesting study of Protestant and Catholic responses to unemployment see Howe (1987).
7. Protestant Derry has managed to produce only one community entrepreneur of any stature – the maverick political figure Glenn Barr. Barr played a key role in the organization of the Loyalists' Workers' Strike in 1974 and was regarded as the chief political strategist in the Ulster Defence Association. He became strongly identified with attempts to promote the goal of an independent Ulster. Protestants by and large remained resistant to this radical step and Barr retired from active Loyalist politics, becoming involved instead in various community development schemes. He was eventually appointed as manager of the East Bank YTP scheme, a scheme much praised in that, somewhat against the odds, it managed to recruit both Catholic and Protestant young people as trainees, which makes it fairly unique in Northern Ireland terms.
8. For details, see *Belfast Household Survey*, Northern Ireland Housing Executive, 1979.

Postscript on practice

1. Thus an otherwise incisive text like Frank Wright's *Northern Ireland: A Comparative Analysis* (1987) falls back on ontological speculation on the origins of violence when confronted with the demands of political analysis and strategy.
2. Of course with the advances of the populist Right in England and the ongoing crisis within the British Labour Party as it embraces a 'post-Fordist' programme, the scope for a radical reformist strategy in Britain has been being drastically reduced – as the GLCists discovered to their cost.
3. For an account of the early years of Northern Ireland's education system see Akenson (1973).
4. Quoted in David Jenkins et. al., *Chocolate, Cream, Soldiers*, Final Evaluation Report on the Schools Cultural Studies Project (New University of Ulster, 1984).
5. In Jenkins op. cit.
6. In Jenkins op. cit.

Bibliography

Akenson, D., (1973) *Education and Enmity: The Control of Schooling in Northern Ireland 1920–50* (Newton Abbot: David & Charles).

Anderson, B., (1983) *Imagined Communities* (London: Verso).

Arensberg, C., and Kimball, S. (1968) *Family and Community in Ireland* (Cambridge: Harvard University Press).

Barth, F. (ed.) (1969) *Ethnic Groups and Boundaries* (Lada: Allan & Unwin).

Bell, D., (1981) 'The Community Studies Tradition and Irish Social Science', *International Journal of Sociology and Social Policy*, vol. 1, no. 2.

Bell, D., (1984) *Innocents with Dirty Hands: British Social Democracy and Northern Ireland* mimeo (Dublin: NIHE).

Boal, F., (1978) 'Two Nations in Ireland', *Antipode*, vol. 12, no. 1.

Bourdieu, P. (1977) *Outline of a Theory of Practice* (Cambridge: Cambridge University Press).

——, and Passeron, J.-C. (1977) *Reproduction in Education, Society and Culture* (London: Sage).

Boyd, A., (1987) *Holy War in Belfast* (Belfast: Pretani Press).

British and Irish Communist Organization (BICO), (1975) *The Two Irish Nations* (Dublin: Athol Press).

Brody, H., (1974) *Inishkillane; Change and Decline in the West of Ireland* (Harmondsworth: Penguin).

Burton, F., (1978) *The Politics of Legitimacy; Struggles in a Belfast Community* (London: RKP).

Byrne, D., (1978) 'The De-industrialization of Northern Ireland', *Antipode*, vol. 12, no. 1.

Cairns, E., (1987) *Caught in the Cross Fire: Children and the Northern Ireland Conflict* (Belfast: Appletree Press).

Cashmore, E., (1979) *Rastaman; the Rastafarian Movement in England* (London: Allen and Unwin).

Clarke, J., (1976) 'The Skinheads and the Magical Recovery of Community' in Hall, S. and Jefferson, T. et al. *Resistance Through Rituals; Youth Subcultures in Post War Britain* (London: Hutchinson).

Clarke, J., Hall, S., Jefferson, T. and Roberts, B., (1976a) 'Subcultures, Cultures and Class' in Hall, S. and Jefferson, T. (eds) *Resistance Through Rituals; Youth Subcultures in Post-War Britain* (London: Hutchinson).

Clarke, J., Critcher, C. and Johnston, R., (1979) *Working-Class Culture: Studies in History and Theory* (London: Hutchinson).

Cockburn, C., (1979) *Local State: Management of Cities and People* (Lada: Plato).

Clifford, J., (1987) 'Beyond The Salvage Paradigm' in Foster, H. (ed), *Discussions in Contemporary Culture* (Seattle: Bay Press).

Cohen, A., (1985) *The Symbolic Construction of Community* (London: Tavistock).

Cohen, P., (1972) 'Subcultural Conflict and Working-class Community', *Working Papers in Cultural Studies*, No. 2, Spring.

———, (1984) 'Against the New Vocationalism' in Bates, I. et al. *Schooling for the Dole; the New Vocationalism* (London: Macmillan).

———, (1988) 'Perversions of Inheritance: Studies in the Making of Multi-racist Britain' in Cohen, P. and Bains, H. *Multi-Racist Britain* (London: Macmillan).

Corrigan, P. and Leonard, P., (1980) *Social Work Practice under Capitalism* (London: Macmillan).

Curran, F., (1986) *Derry: Countdown to Disaster* (Dublin: Gill and Macmillan).

Curtis, L. (1971) *Apes and Angels: the Irish Man in Victorian Caricature* (Newton Abbot: David & Charles).

Curtis, L., (1984) *Nothing but the Same Old Story; the Roots of Anti-Irish Racism* (London: Information on Ireland).

Darby, J. and Morris, G., (1974) *Intimidation in Housing* (Belfast. HMSO).

Darby, J. and Murray, D., (1980) *The Vocational Aspirations and Expectations of School Leavers in Londonderry and Strabane* Research Paper 6, Fair Employment Agency (Belfast: FEA).

Department of Education for Northern Ireland, (1981) Statistical Bulletin (Belfast: HMSO).

Department of the Environment (NI), (1980) *Londonderry Area Plan Review 1981–96: Employment* (Belfast: DOE).

Department of Finance (NI), (1985) *Policy Planning Research Unit Monitor 2/85*, Religion, (Belfast: HMSO).

Devane, R., (1942) *Challenge from Youth* (Dublin: The Richview Press).

Doak, C. (1978) *Rioting and Civil Strife in the City of Londonderry during the Nineteenth and Early Twentieth Centuries*, MA thesis (Belfast: Queen's University).

Duffy, T., (1985) 'Urban Living Conditions and Public Health in Derry 1815–1885', Templemore, *Journal of the North-West Archeological and Historical Society*, vol. 1. (Derry).

Eysenck, H., (1953) *The Uses and Abuses of Psychology* (Harmondsworth: Penguin).

Fair Employment Agency (NI), (1987a) *Religion, Occupations and Employment 1971–81*, Research Paper no. 11 (Belfast: FEA).

———, (1987b) *Report of an Investigation into Derry City Council* (Belfast: FEA).

———, (1988) Eleventh Annual Report (Belfast: FEA).

Farrell, M., (1976) *Northern Ireland – the Orange State* (London: Pluto).

———, (1983) *Arming the Protestants; the Formation of the Ulster Special Constabulary and the Royal Ulster Constabulary 1920–27* (London: Pluto).

Forde, W., (1967) 'The Aimless Rebellion', *Christus Rex*, vol. XXI, no. 1.

Frazer, M., (1973) *Children and Conflict* (London: Secker and Warburg).

Gellner, E., (1983) *Nations and Nationalism* (Oxford: Basil Blackwell).

Gibbon, P., (1975) *The Origins of Ulster Unionism* (Manchester: Manchester University Press).

Gilroy, P., (1982) 'Steppin' out of Babylon – Race, Class and Autonomy' in Centre for Contemporary Cultural Studies, *The Empire Strikes Back* (London: Hutchinson).

Hall, S. and Jefferson, T., (1976) *Resistance Through Rituals; Youth Subcultures in Post-war Britain* (London: Hutchinson).

———, et al., (1978) *Policing the Crisis* (London: Macmillan).

Hare, N., (1973) 'The Future of Black Youth' in Gotlieb, D. (ed), *Youth in Contemporary Society* (London: Sage).

Hebdige, D., (1976) 'Reggae, Rastas and Rudies' in Hall, S. and Jefferson, T., *Resistance Through Rituals; Youth Subcultures in Post War Britain* (London: Hutchinson).

———, (1979) *Subculture: the Meaning of Style* (London: Methuen).

Hepburn, T. (1978) *The Conflict of Nationality in Modern Ireland: Documents of Modern History* (London: Edward Arnold).

———, (1983) 'Work, Class and Religion in Belfast 1871–1911', *Irish Journal of Economic and Social History*, vol. X, 33–50.

Heskin, K., (1980) 'Children and Young People in Northern Ireland: A Research Review', in Harbinson, J. and Harbinson, J., (eds), *A Society under Stress; Children and Young People in Northern Ireland* (London: Open Books).

Howe, L., (1987) *Doing the Double: Wages, Jobs and Benefit in Belfast* paper presented to ESRC Conference, Economic and Social Research in Northern Ireland, Queens University Belfast in January.

Humphries, S., (1981) *Hooligans and Rebels; an Oral History of Working Class Childhood and Youth 1889–1939* (Oxford: Basil Blackwell).

Institute of Contemporary Arts, (1981) *No Country for Old Men* (London: ICA).

Jenkins, D. (1984) *Chocolate, Cream, Soldiers*, Final Evaluation Report on Schools Cultural Studies Project, New Univ. of Ulster.

Jenkins, R., (1983) *Lads, Citizens and Ordinary Kids; Working-class Youth Life-styles in Belfast* (London: RKP).

Jenvey, S., (1972) 'Sons and Haters: Ulster Youth in Conflict', *New Society*, 20 July.

Johnston, R. (1979) 'Three Problematics', in Critcher, C. *et al.*, *Working Class Culture* (Lasa: Hutchinson).

Kelly, W., (1978) *Firm and Deep: A History of the Belfast Battalion of the Boy's Brigade* Boys Brigade (Belfast).

London–Edinburgh Weekend Return Group, (1979) In and Against the State (London: Black Rose Press).

Lyons, H. (1973) 'The Psychological Effects Of The Civil Disturbances On Children', *Northern Teacher*, Winter.

Macauley, M. and Troy, M., (1983) 'The Impact of Urban Conflict and Violence on Children Referred to a Child Guidance Clinic' in Harbinson, J. (ed), *Children of the Troubles: Children in Northern Ireland* (Belfast: Stranmillis College Learning Resources Unit).

McCann, E., (1974) *War in an Irish Town* (Harmondsworth: Penguin).

——, (1987) 'The Derry City Story', New Year Special (Hot Press) Dublin.

Martin, J., (1981) 'The Conflict in Northern Ireland: Marxist Interpretations' *Capital and Class* 18, London.

Marx, K., (1970) *Capital* Vol. 1 (London: Lawrence & Wishart).

Millar, D., (1978) *Queen's Rebels; Ulster Loyalism in Historical Perspective* (Dublin: Gill and Macmillan).

Moore, R., (1984) 'Schooling and the World of Work' in Bates, I. et al., *Schooling for the Dole; the New Vocationalism* (London: Macmillan).

Morgan, A. and Purdy, B. (eds), (1980) *Ireland: Divided Nation – Divided Class* (London: Ink Links).

Morrisey, M. (ed), (1984) *The Other Crisis: Unemployment in Northern Ireland* (Belfast: Ulster Polytechnic).

Mullin, T., (1986) *Derry – Londonderry; Ulster's Historic City* (Coleraine: Coleraine Bookshop).

Murphy, D., (1981) *Derry, Donegal and Modern Ulster 1790–1921* (Derry: Aileach).

Nelson, S., (1984) *Ulster's Uncertain Defenders* (Belfast: Appletree).

Niva, M., (1984), 'Youth Service Provision, Social Order and the Question of ????', in McRobbie, A. and Niva, m. (eds), *Gender and Generation* (Lava: Macmillan).

Northern Ireland Economic Council, (1982) *Youth Unemployment and Training* (Belfast: HMSO).

Northern Ireland Housing Executive, (1979) *Belfast Household Survey* (Belfast: NIHE).

Northern Ireland Youth Council, (1942) *Annual Report* (Belfast: HMSO).

Northern Ireland Youth and Sports Council, (1971) *Report for Period 1968–71* (Belfast: HMSO).

O'Dowd, L., Rolston, B. and Tomlinson, M., (1980) *Northern Ireland: Between Civil Rights and Civil War* (London: CSE Books).

Patterson, H., (1980) *Class Conflict and Sectarianism* (Belfast: Blackstaff).

Pearson, G., (1983) *Hooligan; a History of Respectable Fears* (London: Macmillan).

Policy Planning and Research Unit (NI Department of Finance), *YTP Cohort Study* (1984) First Stage Report, (1985) Second Stage Report, (1986) Third Stage Report, (Belfast: DOF).

Pringle, D., (1978) 'The Northern Ireland Conflict: A Framework For Discussion', *Antipode*, vol. 12, no. 1.

Rees, T., (1980) *Study of Schemes of Direct Job Creation in NI*, (Commission of European Communities, Brussels).

Rolston, B., (1987) 'Politics, Painting and Popular Culture: the Political Wall Murals of Northern Ireland', *Media, Culture and Society* vol. 9, 5–28.

Rottman, D. and O'Connell, P., (1982) 'The Changing Social Structure of Ireland' in Litton, F. (ed), *Unequal Achievement: the Irish Experience 1957–1982* (Dublin: IPA).

Rowthorn, R., (1981) 'Northern Ireland: an Economy in Crisis', *Cambridge Journal of Economics* vol. 5, no. 1, 1–31.

Russell, J., (1973) 'Violence and the Ulster Schoolboy', *New Society* 26th July.

Rutter, M. et al., (1975) Attainment and Adjustment in Two Geographical Areas, *British Journal of Psychiatry*, 493–509, 126.

Semmel, B., (1960) *Imperialism and Social Reform* (London: Routledge).

Smith, A., (1984) 'Ethnic Persistence and National Transformation', *British Journal of Sociology*, vol. XXXV, no. 3.

Springhall, J., (1977) *Youth, Empire and Society* (London: Croom Helm).

Stedman-Jones, G., (1974) 'Working Class Culture and Working Class Politics in London 1870–1900', *Journal of Social History*, vol. 7, no. 4.

Swift, R., (1987) 'The Outcast Irish in the British Victorian City: Problems and Perspectives', *Irish Historical Studies XXV*, no. 99.

Tajfel, H., (1974) 'Social Identity and Intergroup Behaviour', *Social Science Information*, 13, 65–93.

Taylor, L. and Nelson, S., (1978) *Young People and Civil Conflict in Northern Ireland* (Belfast: DHSS).

Thompson, E., (1968) *The Making of the English Working Class* (Harmondsworth: Pelican).

Thompson, L., (1985) *The Political Mythology of Apartheid* (New Haven: Yale University Press).

Tomlinson, M., (1980) 'Housing, the State and the Politics of Segregation' in O'Doed, L., et al. *Northern Ireland Between Civil Rights and Civil War* (London: CSE Books).

Weinreich, P., (1985) 'The Operationalization of Identity Theory in Racial and Ethnic Relations' in Rex, J. and Mason, D. (eds), *Theories of Race and Ethnic Relations* (Cambrige: Cambridge University Press).

Wiener, R., (1978) *The Rape and Plunder of the Shankill; Community Action the Belfast Experience* (Belfast: Farset Press).

Willis, P., (1984) 'Youth Unemployment: A New Social State', *New Society*, 29th March.

Wright, F., (1973) 'Protestant Ideology and Politics in Ulster', *European Journal of Sociology*, vol. 14, no. 2, 213–280.

——, (1987) *Northern Ireland: a Comparative Analysis* (Dublin: Gill and Macmillan).

Index

229

More youth questions — and some answers

Whether you're a teacher, youth worker, social worker, employer or parent, you'll know that young people and their needs have never been more important.

YOUTH IN SOCIETY, the National Youth Bureau's interprofessional magazine for everyone concerned with and about young people, puts issues like juvenile crime, leisure and community involvement into perspective.

Every month, experienced practitioners offer insights into their own approach to work with young people and suggest ways in which you can apply their techniques and learn from their successes and mistakes.

And the Bureau's information team provides details of the latest books and resources, courses and conferences — essential information for everyone responding to the needs of youth in society.

YOUTH SERVICE SCENE, the Bureau's monthly newspaper, contains the latest news, information and resources for youth workers and others concerned with youth affairs and social education.

Whether you work full-time or part-time, in the statutory or the voluntary sector, *Scene* keeps you in touch with what's happening nationally and in other areas, and up to date with the latest theory and practice.

We'll gladly send you sample copies and subscription order forms if you contact us at

National Youth Bureau, 17-23 Albion Street, Leicester LE1 6GD. Telephone 0533.471200.

65 BLEECKER STREET NYC 10012 212·475·4000